THE HEINLE
PICTURE
DICTIONARY

English/Español

THOMSON ™

HEINLE

Australia ◇ Canada ◇ Mexico ◇ Singapore ◇ United Kingdom ◇ United States

THOMSON
HEINLE

The Heinle Picture Dictionary
English/Español

Publisher, Global ELT: *Christopher Wenger*
Publisher, Adult & Academic: *James W. Brown*
Senior Acquisitions Editor, Adult & Academic: *Sherrise Roehr*
Acquisitions Editor (International Bilingual Editions):
 Mary Sutton-Paul
Director of Product Development: *Anita Raducanu*
Senior Development Editor: *Jill Korey O'Sullivan*
Developmental Editor: *Rebecca Klevberg*
Editorial Assistants: *Katherine Reilly, John Hicks, and*
 Christine Galvin
International Marketing Manager: *Eric Bredenberg*
Director of Marketing: *Amy Mabley*
Senior Marketing Manager, Adult ESL: *Donna Lee Kennedy*

Production Manager: *Sally Cogliano*
ELT Academic and Training Director: *Francisco Lozano*
Senior Production Editor: *Maryellen E. Killeen*
Senior Print Buyer: *Mary Beth Hennebury*
Photo Researcher: *Melissa Goodrum*
Photo Editor and Permissions Manager: *Sheri Blaney*
Indexer: *Alexandra Nicherson*
Translation: *Ana María Batis García*
 Instituto de Educación de Aguascalientes
 Universidad Autónoma de Aguascalientes
Project Management, Design, and Composition:
 Proof Positive/Farrowlyne Associates, Inc.
Cover Design: *Proof Positive/Farrowlyne Associates, Inc.*
Cover Image: *© 2004 Roy Wiemann c/o the ispot.com*
Printer: *Transcontinental*

Printed in Canada
 2 3 4 5 6 — 07 06 05

For more information contact Thomson Heinle, 25 Thomson Place, Boston, MA 02210 USA, or you can visit our Internet site at http://elt.thomson.com

Credits appear on page 294, which constitutes a continuation of the copyright page.

For permission to use material from this text or product, submit a request online at http://www.thomsonrights.com

Any additional questions about permissions can be submitted by email to thomsonrights@thomson.com

English/Español Edition ISBN: 1-4130-0549-7

Contents

Acknowledgments

The publisher would like to thank the following reviewers, consultants, and participants in focus groups:

Marie Adele Ryan
Alumni
São Paulo, Brazil

Susan Alexandre
Trimble Technical High School
Ft. Worth, TX

Lizbeth Ascencio
Dona Ana Branch
  Community College
Las Cruces, NM

Pam S. Autrey
Central Gwinnett High School
Lawrenceville, GA

JoEllen Barnett
K.E. Taylor Elementary School
Lawrenceville, GA

Linda Boice
Elk Grove Unified School District
Sacramento, CA

Chan Bostwick
Los Angeles Unified School District
Los Angeles, CA

Diana Brady-Herndon
Napa Valley Adult School
Napa, CA

Mona Brantley
Des Moines Area
  Community College
Ankeny, Iowa

Petra Callin
Child Services Center,
  Portland Public Schools
Portland, OR

David Chávez
Horizonte Instruction and
  Training Center
Salt Lake City, UT

Kathy Connelly
Ed Shands Adult School
Oakland, CA

María de Lourdes Colín Escalona
Toluca, Mexico

Sam Cucciniello
Belmont High School
Los Angeles, CA

Jennifer Daniels
Mesa County Valley School
  District 51
Grand Junction, CO

Jeff Diuglio
Boston University CELOP /
  Harvard IELP
Auburndale, MA

Dana Dusbiber
Luther Burbank High School
Sacramento, CA

Michal Eskayo
St. Augustine College
Chicago, IL

Sara Farley
Wichita High School East
Wichita, KS

Kathleen Flynn
Glendale Community College
Glendale, CA

Utzuinic Garcés
Mexico City, Mexico

Nancy Garcia
Riverbank High School
Riverbank, CA

Gerónima Garza
Cypress-Fairbanks
  Independent School District
Houston, TX

Sally Gearhart
Santa Rosa Junior College
Santa Rosa, CA

Julie Gomez-Baker
Mesa Unified School District
Mesa, AZ

Virginia Guleff
Miramar College
Escondido, CA

Katalin Gyurindak
Mt. San Antonio College
Walnut, CA

Orin Hargraves
Westminster, MD

Iordana Iordanova
Triton College
River Grove, IL

Ocean Jones
Merced High School
Merced, CA

Gemma Kang
Wonderland
Seoul, Korea

Vicki Kaplan
Adams 12 Schools
Thornton, CO

Dale R. Keith
Miami-Dade County
  Public Schools
Miami, FL

Alyson Kleiber
Stamford Public Schools
Stamford, CT

Jean Lewis
Clark County School District
Las Vegas, NV

Virginia Lezhnev
Center for Language
  Education and Development
Washington, DC

Fife MacDuff
União Cultural
São Paulo, Brazil

Mabel Magarinos
Orange County Public Schools
Orlando, FL

Elizabeth Minicz
William Rainey Harper College
Palatine, IL

Dianne Mortensen
John J Pershing Intermediate
  School
Brooklyn, NY

Kathryn Nelson
Wichita High School North
Wichita, KS

Andrea O'Brien
Lawrence Adult Learning Center
Lawrence, MA

Denis O'Leary
Rio del Valle Jr. High School
Oxnard, CA

Dianne Ogden
Snow College
Ephraim, UT

Paula Pacheco Costa Reis
Casa Thomas Jefferson
Brasília, Brazil

Bari N. Ramirez
L.V. Stockard Middle School
Dallas, TX

Nelda Rangel
Brownsville ISD Adult Ed
Brownsville, TX

David L. Red
Fairfax County Public Schools
Falls Church, VA

Eric Rosenbaum
BEGIN Managed Programs
New York, NY

Federico Salas
North Harris College—
  Community Education
Houston, TX

Claudia Sasía Pinzón
Instituto México de Puebla AC
Puebla, Mexico

Linda Sasser
Alhambra School District
San Gabriel, CA

Laurie Shapero
Miami Dade Community College
Miami, FL

Rayna Shaunfield
College of the Mainland
Texas City, TX

Carmen Siebert-Martinez
Laredo Community College
Laredo, TX

Luciana J. Soares de Souza
Britannia Juniors
Rio de Janeiro, Brazil

Susanne Stackhouse
Language Etc.
Washington, DC

Chris Lawrence Starr
Level Creek Elementary
Sewanee, GA

Betty Stone
SCALE—Somerville Center for
  Adult Learning Experience
Somerville, MA

Charlotte Sturdy
Boston, MA

Rebecca Suarez
University of Texas
El Paso, TX

Kathy Sucher
Santa Monica College
Santa Monica, CA

Marcilia da Penha Taveira
Casa Thomas Jefferson
Brasília, Brazil

The Teachers of the Harvard
  Bridge Program
Harvard Bridge to Learning
  Program
Cambridge, MA

William Vang
Sacramento City Unified
  School District
Sacramento, CA

James R. Voelkel
Dibner Institute for the History of
  Science and Technology
Cambridge, MA

Wendell Webster
Houston READ Commission
Houston, TX

Colleen Weldele
Palomar College
San Marcos, CA

Al Profesor

Acerca de The Heinle Picture Dictionary

The Heinle Picture Dictionary es una fuente invaluable de vocabulario para estudiantes que estudian inglés. Presenta el vocabulario más esencial para los estudiantes de nivel inicial o intermedio en un formato único. A diferencia de los diccionarios convencionales que ilustran las palabras que se quieren traducir de una manera aislada, *The Heinle Picture Dictionary* transmite el significado de las palabras con ilustraciones de contextos significativos basados en el mundo real. Además ofrece a los estudiantes una multitud de oportunidades para ver, usar, escuchar y practicar estas palabras en contexto.

El diccionario está organizado en 16 unidades temáticas. Dentro de la unidad, cada lección de dos páginas se enfoca en un tópico relacionado al tema principal de la unidad. Por ejemplo, en la unidad de *Casa*, hay lecciones que se refieren a diferentes tipos de casas, a cuartos específicos de una casa, a cómo encontrar una casa, a los problemas de mantenimiento, a las tareas domésticas, etc.

El punto central de cada lección es la lista de palabras y la ilustración o ilustraciones correspondientes y/o la fotografía o fotografías que ilustran las palabras. Las listas de palabras están organizadas para facilitar su búsqueda, de acuerdo al orden en el que están ilustradas en el diseño de cada página. Las palabras en singular de cada lista están precedidas de un artículo indefinido (o de un artículo definido, en los casos especiales en los que éste es más común o apropiado). Se incluyen los artículos con el fin de ayudar a los estudiantes a entender cuándo y cómo deben de usarse con las palabras del diccionario.

Cada lección incluye *Words in Context*, *Words in Action* y *Word Partnerships*. *Words in Context* consiste en una lectura corta que demuestra una selección de las palabras de la lista. *Words in Action* consiste en un par de actividades para ayudar a los estudiantes a colocar las palabras de un modo significativo. *Word Partnerships* es una selección de locuciones de palabras que pone a los estudiantes en contacto con parejas de palabras en inglés, que se utilizan con mucha frecuencia, y que se encuentran en las listas.

Basado en investigación científica

The Heinle Picture Dictionary se elaboró tomando en cuenta la investigación científica. Esta investigación apoya la idea de que el vocabulario se aprende más eficazmente a través de la exposición repetida y variada (Anderson, 1999), así como también a través de un método estratégico (Taylor, Graves, Van den Broek, 2000). *The Heinle Picture Dictionary* proporciona a los estudiantes no solamente ilustraciones claras para facilitar el significado de palabras, sino también numerosas oportunidades para conocer y usar el nuevo vocabulario. El resultado es un método para aprender vocabulario que refuerza la comprensión del significado de las palabras y ayuda en la adquisición de nuevos vocablos.

The Heinle Picture Dictionary se adapta a una variedad de situaciones y propósitos, lo cual lo hace sumamente útil, tanto para su uso en el salón de clase como para el estudio independiente. *The Heinle Picture Dictionary* puede utilizarse no sólo como libro de consulta para palabras aisladas de vocabulario, sino también como apoyo para el aprendizaje de la lengua. Asimismo es realmente provechoso hacer uso de la extensa variedad de recursos que están disponibles en este libro, la cual constituye el fin medular del programa de *The Heinle Picture Dictionary*.

Word Lists

La siguiente lista incluye algunas ideas que pueden usarse en clase, a fin de facilitar la práctica del vocabulario:

- **Lluvia de ideas para hacer acopio de ellas.** Con los libros cerrados, pida a los estudiantes que hagan una lluvia de ideas sobre las palabras que piensan que pueden estar en la lección que está por iniciar. Luego pídales que verifiquen cuántas de ellas adivinaron.
- **Verifique lo que los estudiantes ya saben.** Pida a los estudiantes que repasen las listas de palabras e identifiquen las imágenes de acuerdo a sus números.
- **Presente el vocabulario.** Presente a los estudiantes cada una de las palabras. Pídales que lo/la escuchen a usted o que escuchen la grabación y que repitan. Ayúdelos con la pronunciación y verifique la comprensión.
- **Examine a sus estudiantes.** Pida a sus estudiantes que señalen las imágenes que correspondan a las palabras que usted diga. O dígales que señalen las imágenes que correspondan a palabras que formen parte de una oración o de un párrafo que usted lea en voz alta.
- **Haga que sus estudiantes se examinen unos a otros.** El estudiante A cubre la lista de palabras y el estudiante B le pide al estudiante A que señale la ilustración correcta. O pida a los estudiantes que trabajen en pares para definir el significado de palabras de la lista y que utilicen sus propias palabras.
- **Juegue Bingo.** Pida a los estudiantes que escojan cinco palabras de la lista y que las escriban en un papel. Diga las palabras en voz alta al azar. Cuando un estudiante tenga una palabra en su lista, la marca. El primer estudiante que marque todas las palabras de su lista, gana.
- **Clasifique.** Pida a los estudiantes que clasifiquen el vocabulario en una gráfica o en un diagrama. Los modelos de muchas gráficas y diagramas están disponibles en el *Activity Bank CD-ROM* o pueden ser elaborados por los estudiantes.
- **Haga un dictado.** Haga a sus estudiantes exámenes de ortografía, dícteles las *Words in Context* o dícteles oraciones que contengan el vocabulario. Esto también puede hacerse en una actividad en pares en la que un estudiante dé las palabras u oraciones a otro.
- **Haga que sus estudiantes formulen oraciones o párrafos.** Pida a sus estudiantes que produzcan oraciones o párrafos en los que usen el vocabulario de la lista.
- **Pida más vocabulario.** Pida a sus estudiantes vocabulario adicional relacionado con el tema de la lección.
- **Fomente el intercambio de ideas.** Hable sobre el tema de la lección, utilice el nuevo vocabulario.
- **Dé tareas de la vida real.** Haga que sus estudiantes usen el vocabulario en tareas de la vida real, tales como hacer planos de un edificio o de una casa, dar indicaciones de cómo llegar a un lugar, dar instrucciones, llenar formatos, etc.

Words in Context

Words in Context presenta a los estudiantes las palabras de las listas en el contexto de una lectura sobre el tema de la lección. Además de introducir el vocabulario de la lección en un contexto, estas lecturas ofrecen diversas posibilidades pedagógicas. Ofrecen información interesante que se puede utilizar para estimular la conversación en el salón de clase. Las lecturas también pueden usarse para dictados en el aula o como modelos de redacción.

Words in Action

La sección de *Words in Action* proporciona a los estudiantes actividades para desarrollar diferentes habilidades, con el fin de practicar y reafirmar el vocabulario. Estas actividades son especialmente útiles como una aplicación de lo visto, después de que los estudiantes se sienten a gusto con el nuevo vocabulario.

Word Partnerships

La sección de *Word Partnerships* ofrece a los estudiantes agrupaciones de palabras comunes y de uso frecuente con las palabras de la lista. Puede ser útil mostrar ilustraciones o llevar al aula ejemplos de la vida real de locuciones con sustantivos y adjetivos, o "actuar" locuciones con verbos ante el grupo. Muchas de las actividades para las listas de palabras sugeridas anteriormente pueden también funcionar con las *Word Partnerships*.

Enseñanza de la gramática con *The Heinle Picture Dictionary*

Las escenas de *The Heinle Picture Dictionary* pueden usarse como una herramienta eficaz para la práctica de tiempos gramaticales. A continuación se sugiere un método para usar el diccionario en la enseñanza de la gramática.

Diga a sus estudiantes que observen la escena en una de las lecciones. Identifique un tiempo. Por ejemplo, si usted está enseñando el presente continuo, pida a sus estudiantes que imaginen que todo lo que se ve en la escena está sucediendo en ese momento.

1. Identifique el contexto. Normalmente puede ser un relato, una conversación en clase, o una tarea. Evite corregir a los estudiantes en este momento.

2. Revele el objetivo. Que los estudiantes sepan el tema gramatical en el que se van a enfocar.

3. Presente la estructura en una gráfica sencilla. Recuerde tener presente el contexto.

4. Pida a los estudiantes que describan la ilustración y que usen el tiempo que se está practicando. Como un reto adicional, puede pedir a los estudiantes que se hagan preguntas acerca de lo que ven.

5. Promueva la práctica tanto oral como escrita.

6. Evalúe el uso y comprensión de la estructura por parte de los estudiantes.

7. Ofrezca una aplicación que permita que los estudiantes usen la estructura de una manera más independiente y menos guiada.

La misma escena puede usarse una y otra vez para la enseñanza de diferentes tiempos. En la siguiente ocasión que se utilice para enseñar o repasar un tiempo gramatical, los estudiantes ya estarán familiarizados con el vocabulario, de tal manera que les será más fácil concentrarse en la gramática.

Materiales Complementarios

The Lesson Planner. El *Lesson Planner* a colores proporciona planes de clase completos en tres niveles para cada lección del diccionario. Los niveles están codificados como sigue:

★ = Beginning Low

★★ = Beginning

★★★ = Beginning High/Intermediate Low

Los grupos frecuentemente difieren en el nivel exacto, así que por favor considere estos niveles sólo como sugerencias.

Principalmente se dan para indicar el grado de dificultad, que va en aumento en las lecciones.

Los planes de clase llevan al instructor a través de cada etapa de la lección, de la preparación, introducción, y presentación a la práctica y aplicación. El *Lesson Planner* incluye el *Activity Bank CD-ROM*, el cual tiene actividades adicionales para cada unidad. Estas hojas de trabajo pueden ser utilizadas y personalizadas por el instructor.

Cada uno de los planes de clase proporcionados en *The Heinle Picture Dictionary* para cada lección está diseñado para usarse en el período de una clase. Este planeador es diferente a la guía tradicional para el profesor, ya que no sólo da sugerencias sobre qué hacer con los materiales del estudiante, sino que también le ayuda a organizar su experiencia completa de clase con un método probado y productivo. Los planes de clase dirigidos hacia el logro de objetivos, proponen una variedad de tareas y actividades que culminan en la etapa de aplicación y con frecuencia en un proyecto opcional.

En la medida en que usted incorpore sus planes de clase en su práctica docente, descubrirá cómo este método asegura la enseñanza efectiva y el aprendizaje exitoso de la lengua. El formato del plan de clase consiste en lo siguiente:

- **Preparación y Repaso**—A los estudiantes se les dan tareas y actividades que activarán sus conocimientos previos y los prepararán para la lección.

- **Introducción**—A los estudiantes se les da el objetivo de la lección. Este es un paso esencial, ya que los estudiantes deben conocer qué es lo que van a estar aprendiendo y por qué lo van a aprender.

- **Presentación**—Los profesores presentan nuevo material, verifican la comprensión de los estudiantes y los preparan para la práctica.

- **Práctica**—Los estudiantes practican una actividad indicada por el profesor.

- **Evaluación**—El profesor verifica la habilidad de los estudiantes al hacer la práctica previa como un indicador de que ya están preparados para llevar a cabo la aplicación.

- **Aplicación**—Los estudiantes demuestran su habilidad para cumplir con el objetivo de una lección de una manera más independiente y menos guiada por el profesor.

The Heinle Picture Dictionary Workbooks. Hay dos *Heinle Picture Dictionary Workbooks*, cada uno con su propio programa complementario de audio. Hay uno para principiantes y otro para estudiantes intermedios. Los cuadernos de trabajo a colores están correlacionados, página por página al diccionario. Tienen gran variedad de actividades que incluyen actividades para escuchar, con el fin de apoyar el aprendizaje de los estudiantes.

The Heinle Picture Dictionary Interactive CD-ROM. Este CD-ROM interactivo proporciona una abundancia de actividades interactivas para reafirmar el vocabulario aprendido en *The Heinle Picture Dictionary*.

The Heinle Picture Dictionary Audio CDs. Incluyen las lecturas y las listas de palabras.

Esperamos que *The Heinle Picture Dictionary* se convierta para sus estudiantes en un recurso para el aprendizaje atractivo y significativo de la lengua. Por favor comuníquese con nosotros para darnos comentarios y sugerencias en www.heinle.com.

El presente

THE HEINLE PICTURE DICTIONARY

constituye una obra de consulta sencilla y actualizada que proporciona lo siguiente:

Dieciséis unidades temáticas con cuatro mil entradas ilustradas a todo color, breves lecturas, locuciones de uso frecuente, y actividades de aprendizaje.

"Words in Context" proporciona un ejemplo de las voces en su uso habitual por medio de una breve lectura al nivel del estudiante principiante.

"Word Partnerships" acelera la adquisición de vocabulario nuevo a través del conocimiento de las locuciones de uso más frecuente.

"Words in Action" facilita la comprensión de las voces por medio de ejercicios de pensamiento crítico.

SAMPLE LESSON PLANS

Fruits and Nuts

from *The Heinle Picture Dictionary Lesson Planner for Unit 7, page 82*

from *The Heinle Picture Dictionary Lesson Planner for Unit 7, page 83*

- Consciente de que el maestro cuenta con poco tiempo para desarrollar sus múltiples tareas el **Lesson Planner** (Dosificador) contiene 300 lecciones para apoyarlo en el uso del **The Heinle Picture Dictionary** en clase.

  Todas las lecciones se han diseñado a tres niveles de aprendizaje. Estas se señalan de la siguiente manera:

  ★ = Beginning Low

  ★★ = Beginning

  ★★★ = Beginning High/ Intermediate Low

- El **Activity Bank CD-ROM** (que acompaña el **Lesson Planner**) contiene actividades reproducibles que el maestro puede modificar de acuerdo a sus necesidades tanto para uso dentro del salón de clases o para asignar como tareas individuales.

- **The Heinle Picture Dictionary Workbooks,** niveles principiante e intermedio, apoyan el estudio de vocabulario y pronunciación. Un programa de audio acompaña cada cuaderno de trabajo.

- **The Heinle Picture Dictionary Interactive CD-ROM** es una eficaz herramienta para practicar el vocabulario mediante actividades, juegos y el uso de gráficos.

Numbers
Números

0 zero
cero

1 one
uno

2 two
dos

3 three
tres

4 four
cuatro

Words in Context

Some cultures have special birthdays. In Mexico, a girl's **fifteenth** birthday is special. She has a party called the *quinceaños*. In Japan, **twenty** is the beginning of adulthood. In Japan, people celebrate their **twentieth** birthday on January 15, the Day of Adults. In Thailand and Korea, the **sixtieth** birthday is the most important one.

9 nine
nueve

8 eight
ocho

7 seven
siete

6 six
seis

5 five
cinco

10 ten
diez

11 eleven
once

12 twelve
doce

13 thirteen
trece

30 thirty *treinta*	**70** seventy *setenta*	**1,000** one thousand *mil*
40 forty *cuarenta*	**80** eighty *ochenta*	**10,000** ten thousand *diez mil*
50 fifty *cincuenta*	**90** ninety *noventa*	**100,000** one hundred thousand *cien mil*
60 sixty *sesenta*	**100** one hundred *cien*	**1,000,000** one million *un millón*

14 fourteen
catorce

15 fifteen
quince

16 sixteen
dieciséis

17 seventeen
diecisiete

18 eighteen
dieciocho

19 nineteen
diecinueve

20 twenty
veinte

21 twenty-one   veintiuno

Word Partnerships

an odd	number
an even	
a lucky	number

21st	twenty-first	21° vigésimo primero
20th	twentieth	20° vigésimo
19th	nineteenth	19° decimonoveno
18th	eighteenth	18° decimoctavo
17th	seventeenth	17° decimoséptimo
16th	sixteenth	16° decimosexto
15th	fifteenth	15° decimoquinto
14th	fourteenth	14° decimocuarto
13th	thirteenth	13° decimotercero
12th	twelfth	12° duodécimo
11th	eleventh	11° undécimo
10th	tenth	10° décimo
9th	ninth	9° noveno
8th	eighth	8° octavo
7th	seventh	7° séptimo
6th	sixth	6° sexto
5th	fifth	5° quinto
4th	fourth	4° cuarto
3rd	third	3° tercero
2nd	second	2° segundo
1st	first	1° primero

Fractions
Fracciones

$1/4$ = one-quarter / a quarter
= un cuarto

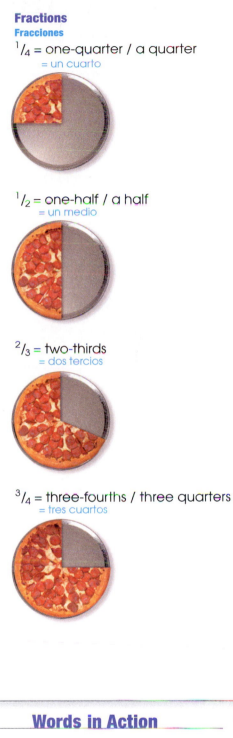

$1/2$ = one-half / a half
= un medio

$2/3$ = two-thirds
= dos tercios

$3/4$ = three-fourths / three quarters
= tres cuartos

Words in Action

1. Work in a group. Practice reading the following:
   - 25 minutes / 62 students / 98 pages
   - 12th birthday / 16th floor / 21st of May
2. Work with a partner. Ask and answer these questions:
   - What's your street address?
   - What's your phone number?

3

Time
Tiempo

Periods of time
Periodos de tiempo

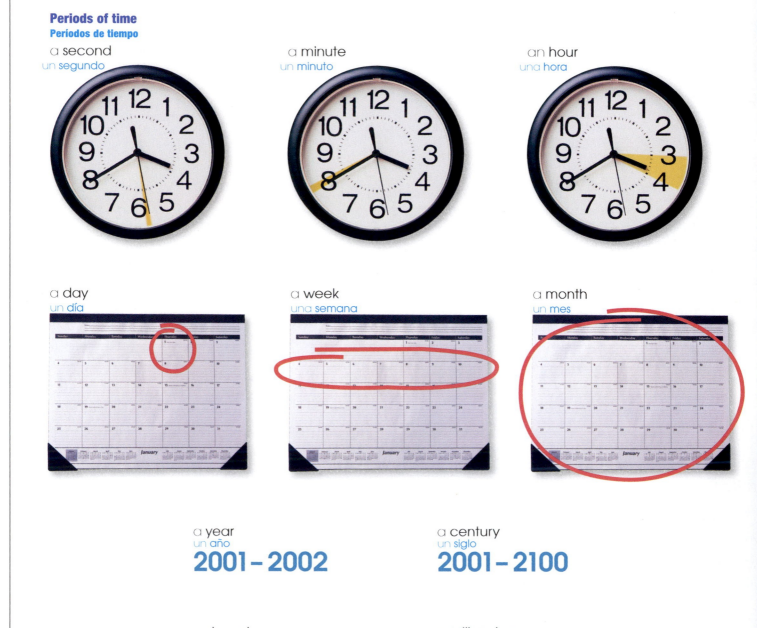

a second
un segundo

a minute
un minuto

an hour
una hora

a day
un día

a week
una semana

a month
un mes

a year
un año
2001 – 2002

a century
un siglo
2001 – 2100

a decade
una década
2001 – 2010

a millennium
un milenio
2001 – 3000

Times of day
Horas del día

sunrise / dawn

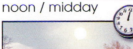

salida del sol / amanecer

morning

mañana

noon / midday

mediodía

afternoon

tarde

evening

anochecer / tarde

sunset / dusk

puesta del sol / crepúsculo

night

noche

midnight

medianoche

Clock times
Horas del reloj

 six o'clock
seis en punto

 six-oh-five /
five past six /
five after six
seis cinco / seis y cinco

 six fifteen /
(a) quarter past six /
(a) quarter after six
seis quince / seis y quince /
seis y cuarto

six twenty-five /
twenty-five past six /
twenty-five after six
seis veinticinco / seis y
veinticinco

six-thirty /
half past six
seis treinta / seis y treinta /
seis y media

six thirty-five /
twenty-five to seven /
twenty-five of seven
seis treinta y cinco /
veinticinco para las siete /
siete menos veinticinco

six forty-five /
(a) quarter to seven /
(a) quarter of seven
seis cuarenta y cinco / seis y
cuarenta y cinco / siete
menos cuarto

 six fifty-five /
five to seven /
five of seven
seis cincuenta y cinco / seis y
cincuenta y cinco / cinco
para las siete

Word Partnerships

at	ten o'clock
	night
in	the morning
	the evening
every	day
once a	week
	month
this	week
last	month
next	year
two hours	ago
five months	

Words in Action

1. What time do you usually get up? Have breakfast? Leave home in the morning? Have lunch? Go to bed?

2. What is your favorite time of day? Why? Discuss with a partner.

Calendar
Calendario

1 date
fecha

2 yesterday
ayer

3 today
hoy

4 tomorrow
mañana

Days of the week
Días de la semana

5 Monday
lunes

6 Tuesday
martes

7 Wednesday
miércoles

8 Thursday
jueves

9 Friday
viernes

10 Saturday
sábado

11 Sunday
domingo

Words in Context

The Month Poem

Thirty days has **September,**
April, June, and **November.**
All the rest have thirty-one
Except **February.**
February has twenty-eight most of the time,
But one year in four it has twenty-nine.

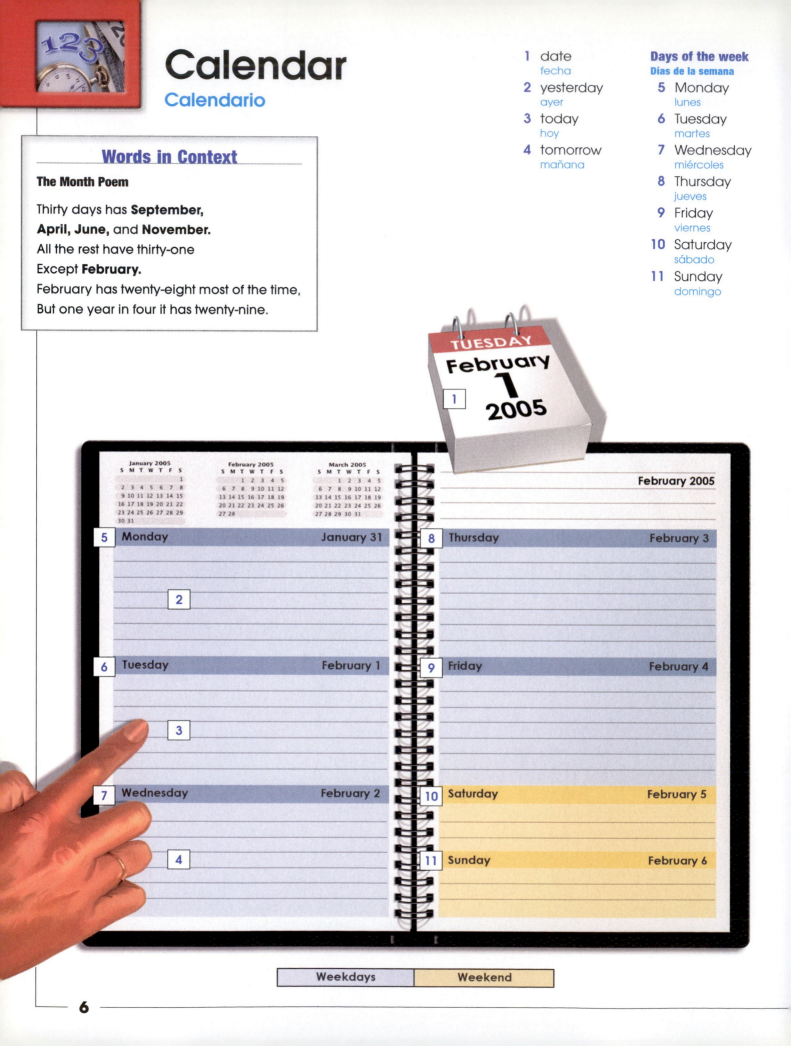

TUESDAY

February **1** 2005

January 2005
S	M	T	W	T	F	S
						1
2	3	4	5	6	7	8
9	10	11	12	13	14	15
16	17	18	19	20	21	22
23	24	25	26	27	28	29
30	31					

February 2005
S	M	T	W	T	F	S
		1	2	3	4	5
6	7	8	9	10	11	12
13	14	15	16	17	18	19
20	21	22	23	24	25	26
27	28					

March 2005
S	M	T	W	T	F	S
		1	2	3	4	5
6	7	8	9	10	11	12
13	14	15	16	17	18	19
20	21	22	23	24	25	26
27	28	29	30	31		

February 2005

5 Monday — January 31

2

6 Tuesday — February 1

3

7 Wednesday — February 2

4

8 Thursday — February 3

9 Friday — February 4

10 Saturday — February 5

11 Sunday — February 6

Weekdays | Weekend

6

Seasons
Estaciones

12 spring
primavera

13 summer
verano

14 fall / autumn
otoño

15 winter
invierno

Months of the year
Meses del año

16 January
enero

17 February
febrero

18 March
marzo

19 April
abril

20 May
mayo

21 June
junio

22 July
julio

23 August
agosto

24 September
septiembre

25 October
octubre

26 November
noviembre

27 December
diciembre

Word Partnerships

in	March
	April
	(the) summer
	(the) fall
on	Monday
	Tuesday
	March 10
	April 5

12 **13** **14** **15**

2005

16 January

S	M	T	W	T	F	S
						1
2	3	4	5	6	7	8
9	10	11	12	13	14	15
16	17	18	19	20	21	22
23	24	25	26	27	28	29
30	31					

17 February

S	M	T	W	T	F	S
		1	2	3	4	5
6	7	8	9	10	11	12
13	14	15	16	17	18	19
20	21	22	23	24	25	26
27	28					

18 March

S	M	T	W	T	F	S
		1	2	3	4	5
6	7	8	9	10	11	12
13	14	15	16	17	18	19
20	21	22	23	24	25	26
27	28	29	30	31		

19 April

S	M	T	W	T	F	S
					1	2
3	4	5	6	7	8	9
10	11	12	13	14	15	16
17	18	19	20	21	22	23
24	25	26	27	28	29	30

20 May

S	M	T	W	T	F	S
1	2	3	4	5	6	7
8	9	10	11	12	13	14
15	16	17	18	19	20	21
22	23	24	25	26	27	28
29	30	31				

21 June

S	M	T	W	T	F	S
			1	2	3	4
5	6	7	8	9	10	11
12	13	14	15	16	17	18
19	20	21	22	23	24	25
26	27	28	29	30		

22 July

S	M	T	W	T	F	S
					1	2
3	4	5	6	7	8	9
10	11	12	13	14	15	16
17	18	19	20	21	22	23
24	25	26	27	28	29	30
31						

23 August

S	M	T	W	T	F	S
	1	2	3	4	5	6
7	8	9	10	11	12	13
14	15	16	17	18	19	20
21	22	23	24	25	26	27
28	29	30	31			

24 September

S	M	T	W	T	F	S
				1	2	3
4	5	6	7	8	9	10
11	12	13	14	15	16	17
18	19	20	21	22	23	24
25	26	27	28	29	30	

25 October

S	M	T	W	T	F	S
						1
2	3	4	5	6	7	8
9	10	11	12	13	14	15
16	17	18	19	20	21	22
23	24	25	26	27	28	29
30	31					

26 November

S	M	T	W	T	F	S
		1	2	3	4	5
6	7	8	9	10	11	12
13	14	15	16	17	18	19
20	21	22	23	24	25	26
27	28	29	30			

27 December

S	M	T	W	T	F	S
				1	2	3
4	5	6	7	8	9	10
11	12	13	14	15	16	17
18	19	20	21	22	23	24
25	26	27	28	29	30	31

Words in Action

1. What's your favorite season? Month? Day? Why? Discuss with a partner.

2. What are three dates that are important to you? These can be birthdays, anniversaries, or holidays. Discuss with a partner.

Money and Shopping

Dinero y Compras

Coins
Monedas

1 a penny / one cent / 1¢
un penique / un centavo / 1¢

2 a nickel / five cents / 5¢
un níquel / cinco centavos / 5¢

3 a dime / ten cents / 10¢
una moneda de diez centavos / 10¢

4 a quarter / twenty-five cents / 25¢
una moneda de veinticinco centavos / 25¢

5 a half dollar / fifty cents / 50¢
medio dólar / cincuenta centavos / 50¢

Bills
Billetes

6 one dollar / a one-dollar bill / $1
un dólar / un billete de un dólar / $1

7 five dollars / a five-dollar bill / $5
cinco dólares / un billete de cinco dólares / $5

8 ten dollars / a ten-dollar bill / $10
diez dólares / un billete de diez dólares / $10

9 twenty dollars / a twenty-dollar bill / $20
veinte dólares / un billete de veinte dólares / $20

10 fifty dollars / a fifty-dollar bill / $50
cincuenta dólares / un billete de cincuenta dólares / $50

11 one hundred dollars / a one hundred-dollar bill / $100
cien dólares / un billete de cien dólares / $100

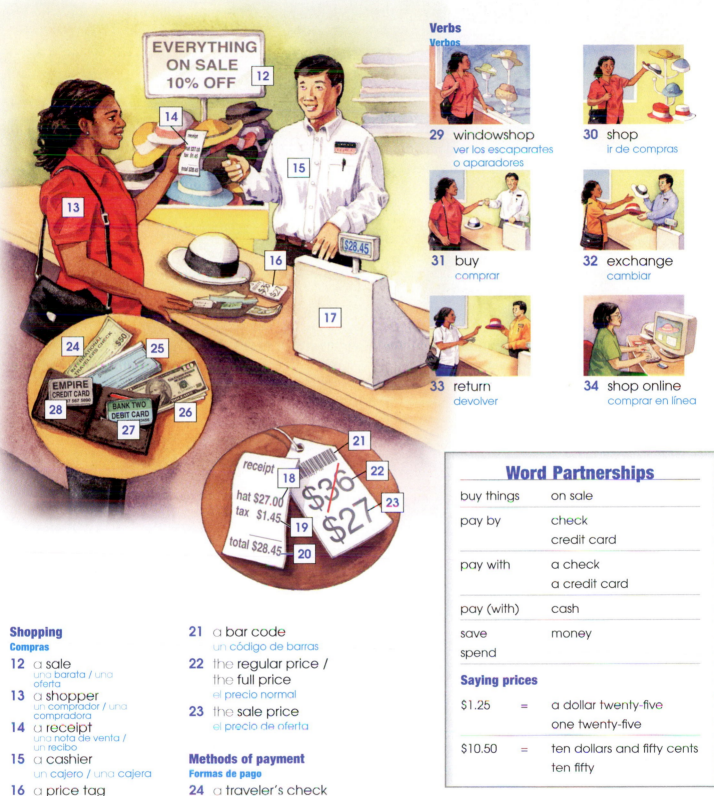

29 windowshop
ver los escaparates
o aparadores

30 shop
ir de compras

31 buy
comprar

32 exchange
cambiar

33 return
devolver

34 shop online
comprar en línea

EVERYTHING ON SALE 10% OFF

$28.45

receipt
hat $27.00
tax $1.45
total $28.45

Shopping
Compras

12 a sale
una barata / una oferta

13 a shopper
un comprador / una compradora

14 a receipt
una nota de venta / un recibo

15 a cashier
un cajero / una cajera

16 a price tag
una etiqueta de precio

17 a cash register
una caja registradora

18 the price
el precio

19 the sales tax
el impuesto sobre ventas

20 the total
el total

21 a bar code
un código de barras

22 the regular price /
the full price
el precio normal

23 the sale price
el precio de oferta

Methods of payment
Formas de pago

24 a traveler's check
un cheque de viajero

25 a (personal) check
un cheque (personal)

26 cash
efectivo

27 a debit card
una tarjeta de débito

28 a credit card
una tarjeta de crédito

Word Partnerships

buy things	on sale
pay by	check
	credit card
pay with	a check
	a credit card
pay (with)	cash
save	money
spend	

Saying prices

$1.25	=	a dollar twenty-five
		one twenty-five
$10.50	=	ten dollars and fifty cents
		ten fifty

Words in Action

1. What do you pay for with a credit card? What do you pay for with a check? What do you pay for with cash? Discuss with a partner.

2. Do you have any bills in your pocket? Which ones? Do you have any coins? Which ones?

Colors
Colores

Words in Context

Colors can make us feel different ways. **Yellow** can make us happy. **Orange** can make us feel full of energy. **Black** can make us feel sad. **Blue** can make us feel calm.

Primary colors
Colores primarios

red
rojo / roja

yellow
amarillo / amarilla

blue
azul

1 red rojo / roja	**7** lime green verde limón	**13** gold dorado / dorada	**19** orange naranja / anaranjado / anaranjada
2 maroon marrón	**8** teal azul verdoso	**14** purple morado / morada	**20** white blanco / blanca
3 coral coralino / coralina	**9** blue azul	**15** violet violeta	**21** cream / ivory crema / marfil
4 pink rosa	**10** turquoise turquesa	**16** brown café	**22** black negro / negra
5 green verde	**11** navy (blue) azul marino	**17** beige / tan beige / tostado	**23** gray gris
6 olive green verde olivo	**12** yellow amarillo / amarilla	**18** taupe gris oscuro	**24** silver plateado / plateada

Word Partnerships

light	pink	
dark	purple	
pale	gray	
	blue	
	green	
a	bright	color
	cheerful	
	rich	
	dull	

Words in Action

1. Look around the room. How many colors can you find? Make a list.

2. Work with a partner. Describe the color of one of your classmates' clothes. Your partner will guess the classmate.
   - Student A: *Someone is wearing green and blue.*
   - Student B: *It's Marcia!*

In, On, Under
En, Sobre, Abajo

Words in Context

Look around you. Can you answer these questions?

- What's **in front of** you?
- What's **behind** you?
- What do you see **above** you?
- Is there someone or something **close to** you? Who or what?

Word Partnerships

right	under
	next to
just	behind
	in front of
	to the left of
	above

1 This cat is **on top of** the shelves.
   Este gato está en la parte superior de los anaqueles.

2 This cat is **far from** the other cats.
   Este gato está lejos de los otros gatos.

3 This cat is **on** a box.
   Este gato está sobre una caja.

4 This cat is **between** two boxes.
   Este gato está entre dos cajas.

5 These kittens are **in / inside** a box.
   Estos gatitos están en / dentro de una caja.

6 This kitten is **outside (of)** the box.
   Este gatito está fuera de la caja.

7 This cat is jumping **off** the shelves.
   Este gato está brincando hacia fuera de los anaqueles.

8 This cat is **on the left of / to the left of** cat number 9.
   Este gato está a la izquierda del gato número 9.

9 This cat is **on the right of / to the right of** cat number 8.
   Este gato está a la derecha del gato número 8.

10 This cat is **above / over** cat number 13.
    Este gato está arriba / encima del gato número 13.

11 This cat is **next to / beside** the shelves.
    Este gato está junto a / al lado de los anaqueles.

12 This cat has a ribbon **around** its neck.
    Este gato tiene un listón alrededor del cuello.

13 This kitten is **below / under** cat number 10.
    Este gatito está debajo / abajo del gato número 10.

14 This kitten is **behind** the shelves.
    Este gatito está detrás de los anaqueles.

15 This kitten is **near / close to** the shelves.
    Este gatito está cerca / junto a los anaqueles.

16 This kitten is **underneath** the shelves.
    Este gatito está debajo de los anaqueles.

17 This cat is **in front of** the shelves.
    Este gato está enfrente de los anaqueles.

Words in Action

1. Cover the list of words. Ask a partner questions like this:
    ■ *Where is cat number 10?*

2. Describe where things are in your classroom. Write ten sentences using ten different prepositions.

Opposites
Opuestos

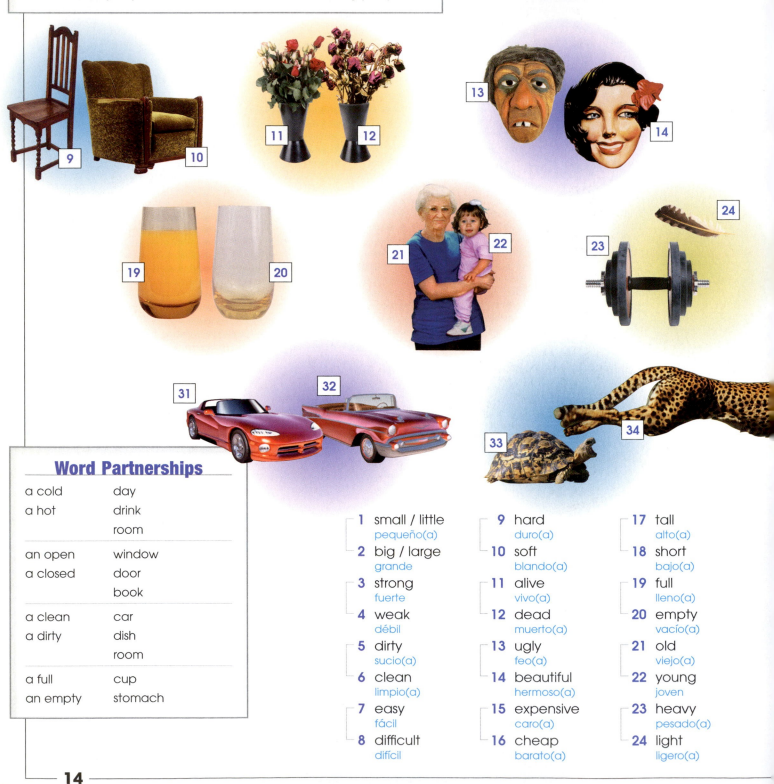

Word Partnerships

a cold	day
a hot	drink
	room
an open	window
a closed	door
	book
a clean	car
a dirty	dish
	room
a full	cup
an empty	stomach

1 small / little
pequeño(a)

2 big / large
grande

3 strong
fuerte

4 weak
débil

5 dirty
sucio(a)

6 clean
limpio(a)

7 easy
fácil

8 difficult
difícil

9 hard
duro(a)

10 soft
blando(a)

11 alive
vivo(a)

12 dead
muerto(a)

13 ugly
feo(a)

14 beautiful
hermoso(a)

15 expensive
caro(a)

16 cheap
barato(a)

17 tall
alto(a)

18 short
bajo(a)

19 full
lleno(a)

20 empty
vacío(a)

21 old
viejo(a)

22 young
joven

23 heavy
pesado(a)

24 light
ligero(a)

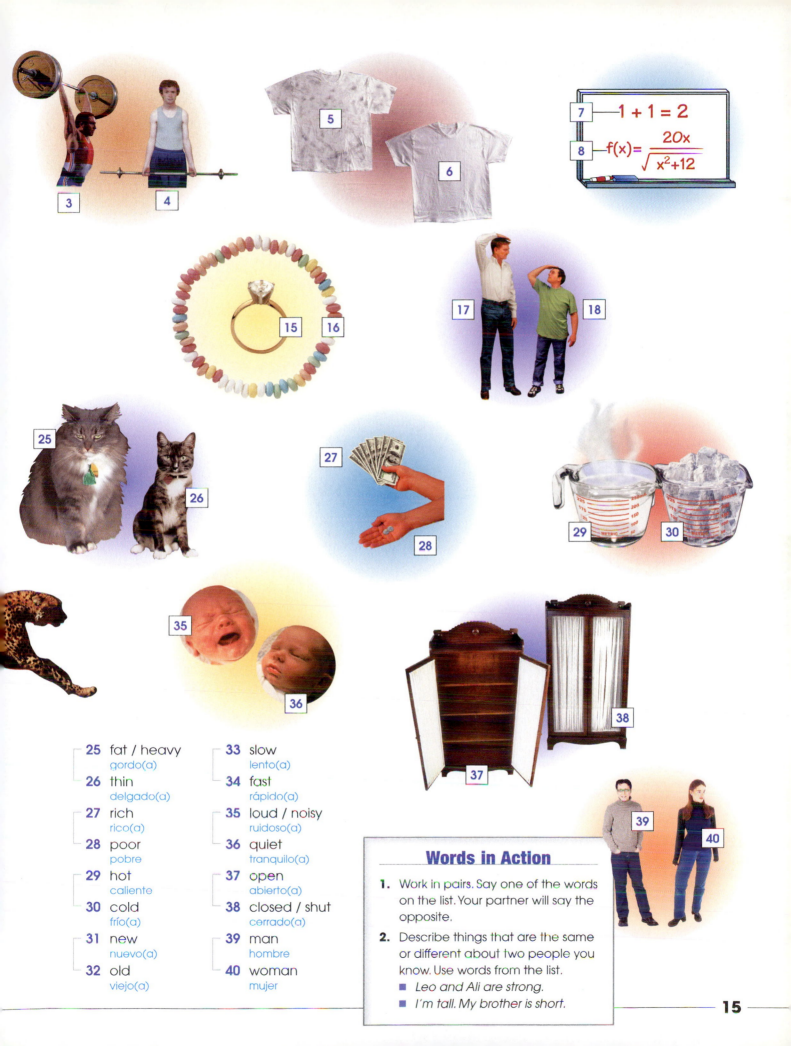

1 + 1 = 2

$$f(x) = \frac{20x}{\sqrt{x^2+12}}$$

25 fat / heavy gordo(a)	**33** slow lento(a)
26 thin delgado(a)	**34** fast rápido(a)
27 rich rico(a)	**35** loud / noisy ruidoso(a)
28 poor pobre	**36** quiet tranquilo(a)
29 hot caliente	**37** open abierto(a)
30 cold frío(a)	**38** closed / shut cerrado(a)
31 new nuevo(a)	**39** man hombre
32 old viejo(a)	**40** woman mujer

Words in Action

1. Work in pairs. Say one of the words on the list. Your partner will say the opposite.

2. Describe things that are the same or different about two people you know. Use words from the list.
   - *Leo and Ali are strong.*
   - *I'm tall. My brother is short.*

The Telephone

El Teléfono

Words in Context

Do you want to make a **long-distance phone call** in the U.S.? **Pick up** the **receiver** and **dial** 1 + the **area code** + the **phone number.** Do you need **directory assistance**? You can dial **411.** Remember, there are four **time zones** in the U.S. When it is 9:00 P.M. in Los Angeles, it's midnight in New York!

1 a pay phone
un teléfono público

2 a receiver
un auricular

3 a calling card /
a phone card
una tarjeta telefónica

4 a coin
una moneda

5 911 / emergency assistance
asistencia de emergencia

6 411 / information / directory assistance
información / asistencia de directorio

7 a coin return
una devolución de monedas

8 a telephone book / a phone book
una guía telefónica / un directorio telefónico

9 a local call
una llamada local

10 a long-distance call
una llamada de larga distancia

11 an international call
una llamada internacional

12 time zones
husos horarios

13 a caller
un llamador / una llamadora / una persona que llama

14 a phone jack
un conector telefónico

15 a cord
un cable

16 a headset
un juego de audífonos / auriculares

17 an operator
un operador / una operadora

18 an answering machine
una contestadora

19 a cordless phone
un teléfono inalámbrico

20 a cell phone / a mobile phone
un teléfono celular

21 an antenna
una antena

22 an area code
un código de área

23 a telephone number / a phone number
un número telefónico / un número de teléfono

24 **pick up** the phone
tomar el auricular

25 **dial** a number
marcar un número

26 **hear** the phone ring
escuchar el timbre del teléfono

27 **answer** the phone
contestar el teléfono

28 **have** a conversation
tener una conversación

29 **hang up** the phone
colgar el teléfono

Word Partnerships

make	an international call
	a long-distance call
	a local call
call	directory assistance
	911
look up	a phone number
telephone	company
	service
	bill

Words in Action

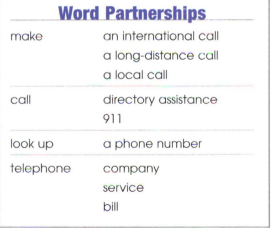

1. What is your area code and phone number?

2. How often do you make local, long-distance, and international calls? . Who do you call? Why? Discuss with a partner.

Classroom
Salón de Clases

31 cheat on a test
hacer trampa en un examen

32 fail a test
reprobar un examen

Words in Context

What does the ideal **classroom** look like? Some experts think that a classroom should look friendly. It should have comfortable **seats** and **desks**. It should have a large **bookshelf** with many **books**. It should also have bright **posters** and **bulletin boards** to show **students'** work.

1

AaBbCcDdEeFfGgHhIiKkLlMmNnOoPpQqRrSsTtUuVvWwXxYyZz

6

Homework for Friday:
Read page 78.
Answer the questions.

5

2 **3** **4**

7

9

10

11

8

23

READ

19 **20**

21 **22**

Learn English Book 1

25

24

26

Word Partnerships

go to	the board
write on	
erase	
a high school	student
a college	
an international	
a graduate	
a hard / difficult	test / exam
an easy	
a midterm	
a final	

33 study for a test
estudiar para un examen

34 take a test
hacer un examen

35 pass a test
pasar un examen

1 the alphabet
el alfabeto

2 a teacher
un maestro / una maestra

3 chalk
gis / tiza

4 a (blackboard) eraser
un borrador (para pizarrón)

5 a homework assignment
una tarea

6 a (black)board
un pizarrón

7 a bulletin board
un tablón de anuncios

8 a flag
una bandera

9 a globe
un globo terráqueo

10 a bookshelf
un librero

11 a book
un libro

12 a map
un mapa

13 a clock
un reloj

14 a (white)board
un pintarrón

15 a marker
un marcador

16 an overhead projector
un retroproyector

17 a table
una mesa

18 a workbook
un cuaderno de trabajo / un libro de trabajo

19 a pen
una pluma

20 a pencil
un lápiz

21 a desk
un escritorio

22 an eraser
un borrador

23 a poster
un cartel

24 a cassette player / a tape recorder
una grabadora

25 a student
un estudiante / una estudiante

26 a chair / a seat
una silla / un asiento

27 a notebook
un cuaderno

28 a grade
una calificación

29 a test / an exam
un examen

30 a textbook
un libro de texto

Words in Action

1. Work with a group. Make a list of everything in your classroom. Which group has the longest list?

2. Cover the word list. Find one word in the picture that starts with each of the following letters: a, b, c, d, e, f, g, h.

Listen, Read, Write
Escuche, Lea, Escriba

Words in Context

People learn languages in different ways. Some students like to **listen** to the language. Others like to **write** lists of words. Others like to **read** a lot or **talk** with a group and **discuss** their ideas. What about you? How do you learn languages best?

I THINK THAT . . .

I study English.

1 raise your hand
levante su mano

2 hand in your paper
entregue sus trabajos

3 collect the papers
recoja los trabajos

4 copy the sentence
copie la oración / el enunciado

5 exchange papers
intercambie trabajos

6 write your name
escriba su nombre

7 read
lea

8 look up a word
(in the dictionary)
busque una palabra
(en el diccionario)

9 close your book
cierre su libro

10 open your book
abra su libro

11 discuss your ideas
intercambie sus ideas

12 listen
escuche

13 spell your name
deletree su nombre

14 take a break
tome un descanso / receso

15 sit down
siéntese

16 go to the board
pase al pizarrón

17 erase the board
borre el pizarrón

22 **Match** the items.
relacione
1. 3 ⤬ four
   4 ⤬ three

23 **Cross out** the wrong answers.
tache
1. 2 + 2 = ̶3̶   4   ̶5̶

24 **Check** the correct answer.
marque
1. 2 + 2 = ___ 3   ✓ 4

25 **Correct** the mistake.
corrija
1. 2 + 2 = ̶3̶ 4

26 **Fill in** the blank.
llene
1. 2 + 2 = 4

27 **Underline** the correct answer.
subraye
1. 2 + 2 =   3   <u>4</u>   5

28 **Circle** the correct answer.
encierre en un círculo
1. 2 + 2 =   3   ④   5

29 **Darken** the correct oval.
obscurezca
1. 2 + 2 =   ◯ 3   ● 4

Word Partnerships

read	silently
	aloud / out loud
	to your partner
discuss	with a partner
	with a group
listen	to me
	carefully
	to your partner
	and repeat

---

18 hand out papers
   reparta los trabajos
19 stand up
   póngase de pie / párese
20 talk with a group
   hable en un grupo
21 share a book
   comparta un libro
22 match
   relacione
23 cross out
   tache

24 check
   marque
25 correct
   corrija
26 fill in
   llene
27 underline
   subraye
28 circle
   encierre en un círculo
29 darken
   obscurezca

Words in Action

1. Take turns giving and following classroom instructions. For example, one person says: *Stand up.* The other person stands up.

2. Which activities do you often do in class? Make a list.

School

La Escuela

Words in Context

In the U.S., a **principal** manages the school. **Guidance counselors** help students plan their **schedules.** Students take home **report cards** a few times a year, and parents must sign them. Many students participate in **extracurricular activities** such as **drama clubs** or **sports.**

EXTRACURRICULAR ACTIVITIES
SPORTS
SOCCER
BASEBALL
DRAMA CLUB

JOIN THE SPANISH CLUB

CAREER AND COLLEGE PLANNING

PRINCIPAL

SCHOOL BUS

Word Partnerships

elementary	school
middle	
high	
join	a team
	a club

George Washington High School
1st Semester Grade Report

To the Parents of: **James A**

HR	SUBJECT	TEACHER	1	EXAM	2	EXAM
1	Biology	Stephens	B-	B	C+	C
2	English 2	Geofferies	A	A	A	A
3	Intro Journal	Bennett	A	A	A	A-
4	Seminar	Hurst	CR		CR	
5	Algebra 2	Jakobs	E	D	D+	C

1st Semester	Monday	Tue
8:00–9:25	ogy	Bio
9:25–10:20	Orchestra	His
10:20–10:40	Study Hall	Br
10:40–11:00	Break	Stud
11:00–11:55	Spanish I	Spa
11:55–12:30	Lunch	Lu
12:30–1:25	English II	Eng
1:25–2:20	Algebra	Alg

1	a coach un entrenador	7	a (school) library una biblioteca (escolar)	14	a locker una gaveta	21	sports deportes
2	a team un equipo	8	a school nurse un enfermo / una enfermera escolar	15	a backpack una mochila	22	Spanish club club de español
3	a language lab un laboratorio de idiomas	9	a teachers' lounge un salón de maestros	16	a principal un director / una directora	23	drama club club de teatro
4	a gym un gimnasio	10	a restroom / a bathroom un baño	17	a guidance counselor un asesor / una asesora	24	a report card una boleta de calificaciones
5	bleachers graderías	11	a water fountain un bebedero	18	an auditorium un auditorio	25	a (student) schedule un horario (de estudiante)
6	a cafeteria una cafetería	12	a school bus un autobús escolar	19	a graduation una graduación	26	a permission slip un formato de permiso
		13	a loudspeaker un altavoz	20	a classroom un salón de clases	27	an absence note un justificante

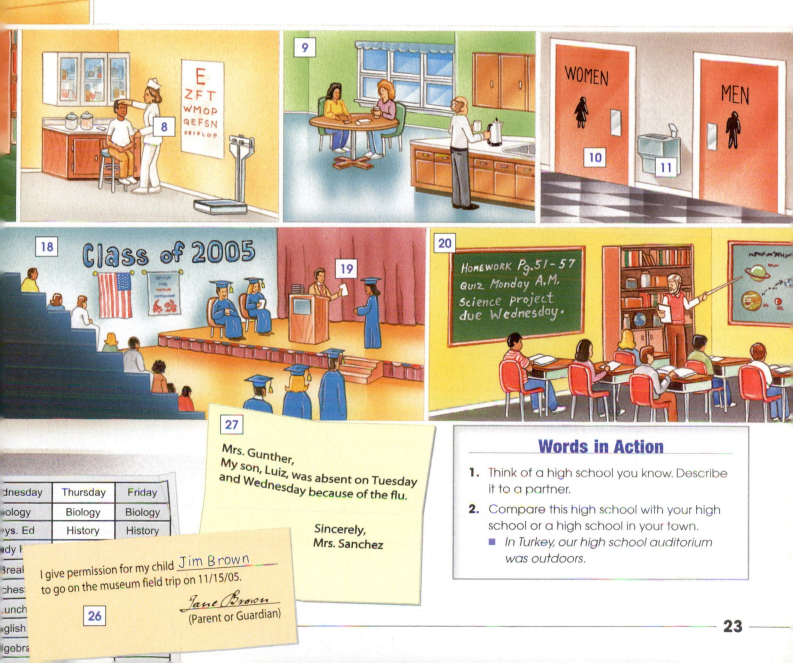

27

Mrs. Gunther,
My son, Luiz, was absent on Tuesday and Wednesday because of the flu.

Sincerely,
Mrs. Sanchez

I give permission for my child Jim Brown to go on the museum field trip on 11/15/05.

Jane Brown
26 (Parent or Guardian)

dnesday	Thursday	Friday
ology	Biology	Biology
ys. Ed	History	History
dy H		
Breal		
chest		
unch		
glish		
gebra		

Words in Action

1. Think of a high school you know. Describe it to a partner.

2. Compare this high school with your high school or a high school in your town.
   - *In Turkey, our high school auditorium was outdoors.*

Computers
Computadoras

Words in Context

Computers keep getting smaller and faster. Scientists built the first computer in the 1940s. It was the size of a large room. In the 1970s, stores began to sell **desktop computers.** Then, in the 1990s, small **laptops** appeared. Now tiny **handheld computers** are popular.

Verbs
Verbos

30 be online
estar en línea

31 enter your password
escribir su contraseña

32 select text
seleccionar texto

33 click
dar / hacer clic

34 scan
escanear

35 print (out)
imprimir

2005 Monthly Reports

Expense Report

Monthly Report

Word Partnerships

connect to	the (Inter)net
surf	

open	an e-mail (message)
send	
delete	

open	a window
close	

Internet symbols

@	at
.	dot
/	(forward) slash
:	colon

1 a CD-ROM
un CD-ROM

2 a disk
un disquete

3 a window
una ventana

4 a toolbar
una barra de herramientas

5 a folder
una carpeta

6 a cursor
un cursor

7 a file
un archivo

8 a (drop down) menu
un menú

9 icons
íconos

10 a scroll bar
una barra de desplazamiento

11 a cable
un cable

12 a power strip
una tira de contactos

13 a projector
un proyector

14 a scanner
un escáner

15 a printer
una impresora

16 a PDA / a handheld (computer)
una PDA / una computadora de mano

17 a desktop (computer)
una computadora de escritorio

18 a key
una tecla

19 a monitor
un monitor

20 a screen
una pantalla

21 a keyboard
un teclado

22 an e-mail (message)
un (mensaje de) correo electrónico

23 a laptop (computer) / a notebook (computer)
una computadora portátil

24 a trackpad / a touchpad
una almohadilla de contacto

25 software / a (computer) program
software / un programa para computadora

26 a mouse pad
una almohadilla para ratón

27 a mouse
un ratón

28 a CD-ROM drive
una unidad de CD-ROM

29 the (Inter)net / the (World Wide) Web
el / la internet / la red mundial

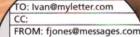

TO: Ivan@myletter.com
CC:
FROM: fjones@messages.com
SUBJECT: HI!!

Hi Ivan,
Thanks for your e-mail.
I'll give you a call tonight.
Fred

Words in Action

1. Draw a computer. Without looking at the word list, label each part of the computer.

2. Practice reading aloud these addresses:
   - president@whitehouse.gov
   - http://hpd.heinle.com

25

Family
La Familia

1
2

3
4
5
6

11
12
13
14
15

23

24

19
20

25
18

26

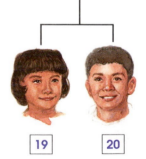

27 be married
casarse

28 be divorced
divorciarse

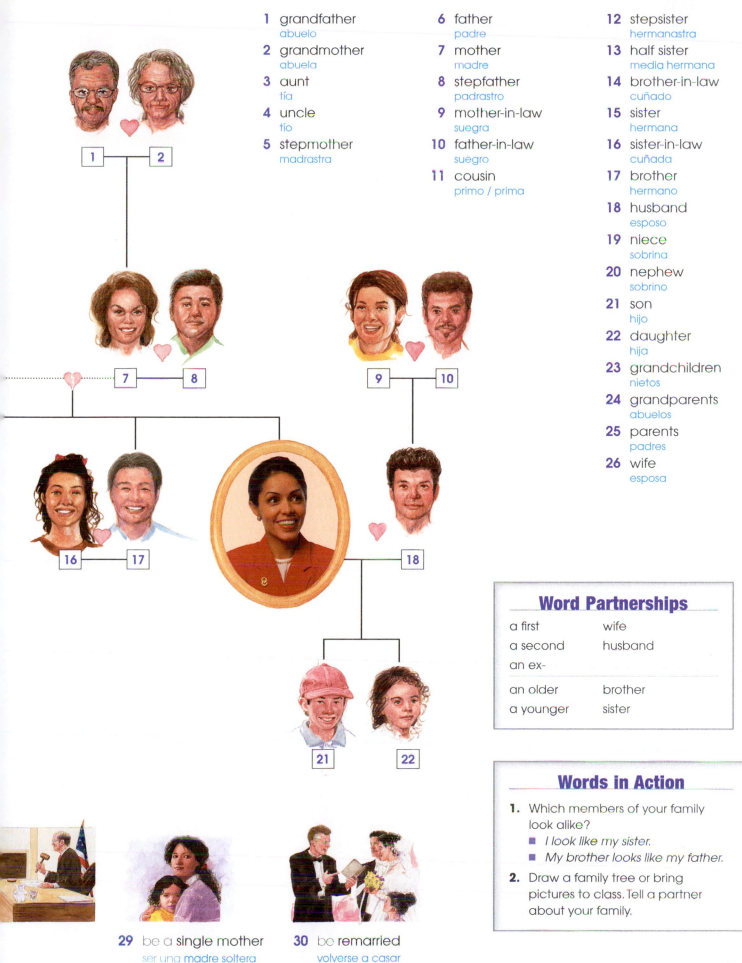

1 grandfather
   abuelo

2 grandmother
   abuela

3 aunt
   tía

4 uncle
   tío

5 stepmother
   madrastra

6 father
   padre

7 mother
   madre

8 stepfather
   padrastro

9 mother-in-law
   suegra

10 father-in-law
   suegro

11 cousin
   primo / prima

12 stepsister
   hermanastra

13 half sister
   media hermana

14 brother-in-law
   cuñado

15 sister
   hermana

16 sister-in-law
   cuñada

17 brother
   hermano

18 husband
   esposo

19 niece
   sobrina

20 nephew
   sobrino

21 son
   hijo

22 daughter
   hija

23 grandchildren
   nietos

24 grandparents
   abuelos

25 parents
   padres

26 wife
   esposa

Word Partnerships

a first	wife
a second	husband
an ex-	
an older	brother
a younger	sister

Words in Action

1. Which members of your family look alike?
   - *I look like my sister.*
   - *My brother looks like my father.*

2. Draw a family tree or bring pictures to class. Tell a partner about your family.

29 be a **single** mother
   ser una **madre soltera**

30 be **remarried**
   volverse a casar

Raising a Child
Criar a un Niño

28

1 **love** him
amarlo

2 **nurse** him
amamantarlo

3 **rock** him
mecerlo

4 **hold** him
abrazarlo

5 **feed** him
alimentarlo

6 **carry** him
llevarlo

7 **bathe** him
bañarlo

8 **change** his diapers
cambiarle los pañales

9 **play with** him
jugar con él

10 **pick** him **up**
alzarlo

11 **dress** him
vestirlo

12 **comfort** him
consolarlo

13 **discipline** him
disciplinarlo

14 **protect** him
protegerlo

15 **encourage** him
estimularlo

16 **help** him
ayudarlo

17 **praise** him
premiarlo

18 **drop** him **off**
dejarlo

19 **pick** him **up**
recogerlo

20 **read** to him
leerle

21 **put** him **to bed**
llevarlo a la cama

Word Partnerships		
grow (up)	fast	
	quickly	
read	a book	
	a story	

Verbs
Verbos

22 **crawl**
gatear

23 **cry**
llorar

24 **behave**
portarse bien

25 **misbehave**
portarse mal

26 **grow**
crecer

27 **grow up**
crecer

Words in Action

1. Write a list of "Rules for Parents." Share your rules with the class.
   - *Parents must always protect their children.*

2. Talk with a group. What are the ten most important things to do for a child? Make a list. Put the most important things first.

Life Events
Eventos en la Vida

Words in Context

The Life of Princess Diana

1980
Diana **falls in love** with Prince Charles.

1982
Diana **has a baby,** Prince William.

1996
Charles and Diana get divorced.

1961
Princess Diana **is born.**

1981
Diana and Charles **get married.**

1984
Diana has another baby, Prince Henry.

1997
Diana **dies** in a car accident.

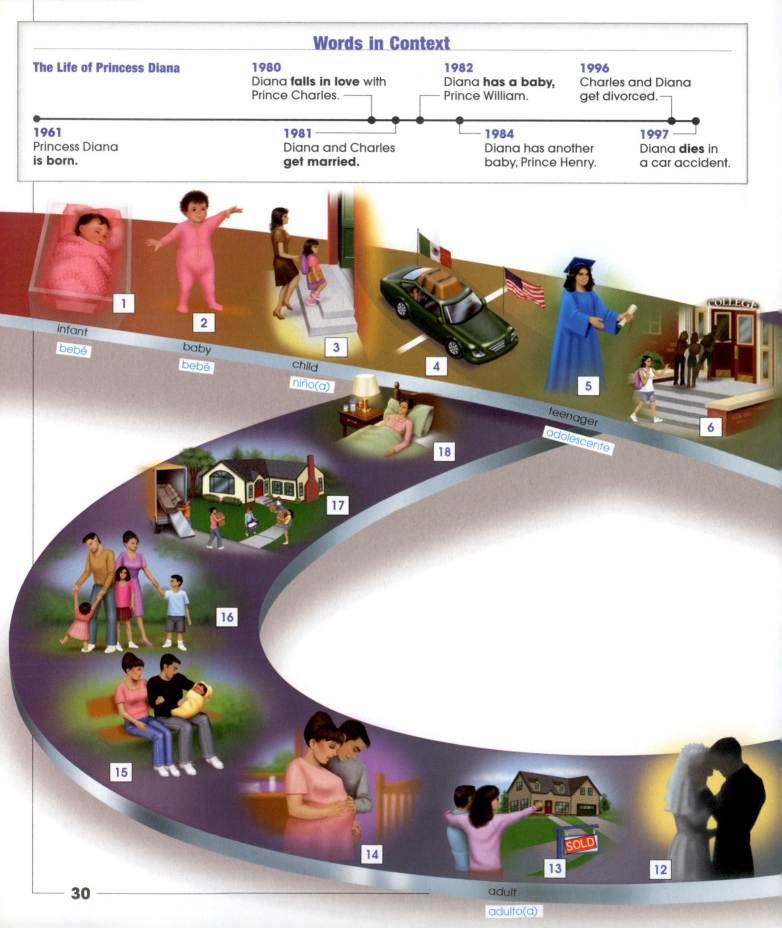

1

2

3

4

5

6

infant
bebé

baby
bebé

child
niño(a)

teenager
adolescente

18

17

16

15

14

13

12

adult
adulto(a)

1 be born
   nacer

2 learn to walk
   aprender a caminar

3 start school
   empezar la escuela

4 immigrate
   inmigrar

5 graduate from high school
   graduarse de preparatoria

6 go to college
   ir a la universidad

7 rent an apartment
   rentar un apartamento

8 get a job
   conseguir un trabajo

9 date
   hacer una cita

10 fall in love
   enamorarse

11 get engaged
   comprometerse

12 get married
   casarse

13 buy a house
   comprar una casa

14 be pregnant
   estar embarazada

15 have a baby
   tener un bebé

16 raise a family
   criar a una familia

17 move
   mudarse

18 get sick
   enfermarse

19 take a vacation
   tomar unas vacaciones

20 celebrate a birthday
   celebrar un cumpleaños

21 become a grandparent
   ser abuelo / abuela

22 retire
   retirarse / jubilarse

23 travel
   viajar

24 die / pass away
   morir

HAPPY RETIREMENT

senior (citizen)
persona de la tercera edad

FIRST DATE

Word Partnerships

celebrate	a holiday
	an anniversary
	an engagement
raise	children
	a son
	a daughter

Words in Action

1. Write a time line of your own life. Use "The Life of Princess Diana" as a model.

2. What do you think are the three most important events in a life?

Face and Hair
La Cara y el Pelo

Words in Context

The way people wear their hair changes often. One year, **long hair** is the fashion for women. The next year, it is **short hair.** Sometimes **curly hair** is popular. But then soon everyone wants **straight hair.** Men's fashions change too. Sometimes **sideburns** are long and sometimes they are short. **Beards** and **mustaches** come and go.

1

2

3

4

5

6

7

8

9

10

11

12

13

14

15

16

Word Partnerships

a friendly	face
a happy	
a pretty	
thin	hair
thick	
reading	glasses
prescription	

1	red hair	16	a beard
	pelo / cabello rojo		una barba
2	brown hair	17	straight hair
	pelo / cabello castaño		pelo / cabello lacio
3	black hair	18	curly hair
	pelo / cabello negro		pelo / cabello chino / rizado
4	blond hair	19	wavy hair
	pelo / cabello rubio		pelo / cabello ondulado
5	gray hair	20	pierced ears
	pelo / cabello gris (canoso)		orejas perforadas
6	freckles	21	braids
	pecas		trenzas
7	a scar	22	a bun
	una cicatriz		un chongo
8	a mustache	23	bangs
	un bigote		flequillos
9	a dimple	24	a ponytail
	un hoyuelo		una cola de caballo
10	a wrinkle	25	cornrows
	una arruga		trencitas
11	short hair	26	pigtails
	pelo / cabello corto		coletas
12	shoulder-length hair	27	a mole
	pelo hasta los hombros		un lunar
13	long hair	28	glasses
	pelo / cabello largo		lentes
14	bald		
	calvo / calva		
15	sideburns		
	patillas		

Daily Activities
Actividades Diarias

Words in Context

José and I have two children and we both work. Our lives are busy. I usually **wake up** early. I **go** to work at 6:00 A.M. I'm a clerk at a market. José wakes the kids up and **takes** them to school. I go home at noon and **have** lunch. Then José goes to work. I **do** the housework and **make** dinner. The children **go** to bed before José returns at 10:00 P.M. The next day we **get up** and do it all again!

1. **wake up**
   despertar
2. **get up**
   levantarse
3. **brush** your teeth
   cepillarse los dientes
4. **take** a shower
   bañarse / tomar una ducha
5. **comb** your hair
   peinarse el pelo
6. **shave**
   rasurarse
7. **put on** makeup
   maquillarse
8. **get dressed**
   vestirse
9. **eat** breakfast /
   have breakfast
   desayunarse
10. **take** your child to school
    llevar a su hijo / hija
    a la escuela
11. **go** to work
    ir a trabajar
12. **take** a coffee break
    tomar un receso / un descanso
13. **eat** lunch / **have** lunch
    almorzar
14. **go** home
    ir a casa
15. **take** a nap
    dormir una siesta
16. **exercise** / **work out**
    hacer ejercicio
17. **do** homework
    hacer la tarea
18. **make** dinner
    preparar la cena

19. **eat** dinner / **have** dinner
    cenar
20. **take** a walk
    dar un paseo
21. **do** housework
    hacer el oficio
22. **take** a bath
    tomar un baño / bañarse
23. **go** to bed
    irse a la cama / acostarse
24. **sleep**
    dormir
25. **watch** television
    ver televisión

Words in Action

1. Take turns asking and answering questions about the picture.
   - Student A: *What does the family do in the morning?*
   - Student B: *They wake up, get dressed, and eat breakfast.*

2. Tell your partner about your typical morning.
   - *I wake up at 9:00. First I brush my teeth and then I take a shower.*

Walk, Jump, Run
Caminar, Saltar, Correr

Words in Context

I live in Los Angeles. What a busy place it is! I often **run** because I am always late. I have to **get on** the bus at 8:00 in order to arrive at work by 9:00. There is a lot of traffic. It is probably faster to **walk.** But I study English while I **ride** the bus. I am learning a lot!

1

2

3

4

9

8

6

7

5

15

16

21

22

23

24

25

26

1 fly
volar

2 leave
irse

3 enter / go in
entrar

4 march
marchar

5 get out (of)
salir de

6 get in
entrar

7 fall
caer / caerse

8 slip
resbalar / resbalarse

9 jog
trotar

10 cross
cruzar

11 run
correr

12 get on
subirse

13 walk
caminar

14 get off
salir / bajar de

15 stand up
pararse

16 sit (down)
sentarse

17 follow
seguir

18 lead
guiar / dirigir

19 go down
bajar / bajarse

20 go up
subir / subirse

21 crawl
gatear / arrastrarse

22 kneel
arrodillarse

23 squat
ponerse en cuclillas

24 jump
brincar

25 push
empujar

26 ride
montar

27 pull
jalar

Word Partnerships

fall	off
jump	down
	over
get in	a car
get out of	a taxi
get on	a train
get off	a bus
ride	a bicycle / a bike
	a motorcycle
	a horse
cross	the street

Words in Action

1. What five things do you do every day? Use words from the list.

2. Take turns acting out some of the verbs on the list. The other students will guess what you are doing.

Feelings
Sentimientos

Words in Context

People cry when they feel **sad** or **homesick**. Sometimes they also cry when they are **happy, angry,** or **scared.** People laugh when they are happy. Sometimes they also laugh when they are **nervous** about something.

1 proud
  orgulloso(a)
2 happy
  feliz
3 angry
  enojado(a)
4 interested
  interesado(a)
5 calm
  tranquilo(a)

6 nervous
  nervioso(a)
7 embarrassed
  avergonzado(a)
8 in love
  enamorado(a)
9 full
  lleno(a) /
  satisfecho(a)
10 hungry
  hambriento(a)

11	thirsty sediento(a)	16	homesick nostálgico(a)	20	excited emocionado(a)	24	comfortable cómodo(a)
12	frustrated frustrado(a)	17	lonely solitario(a) / solo(a)	21	sad triste	25	uncomfortable incómodo(a)
13	bored aburrido(a)	18	confused confundido(a)	22	surprised sorprendido(a)		
14	sick / ill enfermo(a)	19	afraid / scared asustado(a)	23	tired cansado(a)		
15	worried preocupado(a)						

Word Partnerships

angry	about
confused	
embarrassed	
happy	
afraid	of
proud	
tired	
frustrated	by
confused	

Words in Action

1. How do you feel right now? Use one or more words from the list.

2. Find a picture of a person in a magazine or newspaper. How do you think the person feels?

   - *She is not smiling. She looks bored or angry. Maybe she is in pain.*

39

Wave, Greet, Smile
Saludar, Sonreír

Words in Context

Ways to **greet** people differ from country to country. In the U.S., people often **shake hands** when they first meet. In Japan, people frequently **bow** to each other. In Chile, women often **hug** and **kiss** each other.

1

8

7

I'm sorry. 9

You look great today! 10

16

15

18

17

19

20

1 argue *discutir*	**9** apologize *disculparse*	**17** hug *abrazar*
2 greet *saludar*	**10** compliment *felicitar / piropear*	**18** smile *sonreír*
3 visit *visitar*	**11** agree *estar de acuerdo*	**19** help *ayudar*
4 shake hands *estrechar las manos*	**12** disagree *estar en desacuerdo*	**20** wave *saludar*
5 touch *tocar*	**13** comfort *alentar / consolar*	**21** kiss *besar*
6 have a conversation *tener una conversación*	**14** bow *inclinarse*	**22** dance *bailar*
7 give a gift *dar un regalo*	**15** introduce *presentar*	**23** invite *invitar*
8 write a letter *escribir una carta*	**16** call *llamar*	**24** congratulate *felicitar*

Word Partnerships

agree	with
dance	
argue	
apologize	to
bow	
wave	

Words in Action

1. How do men and women in your culture greet someone new? How do they greet good friends? Family members?

2. Write five sentences about your best friend. Use words from the list.

Documents
Documentos

Words in Context

There are **documents** for almost every important event in life. When you are born, you get a **birth certificate.** When you graduate from school, you get a **diploma.** You get a **driver's license** when you are ready to drive. You apply for a **passport** before you travel to another country. And you get a **marriage certificate** when you get married.

Personal Information *(please print)*

1 **Name** Hong 2 John 3 E 4
LAST FIRST MIDDLE INITIAL

5 **Sex** ☒ Male ☐ Female

6 **Date of birth** 6 / 21 / 1960
MONTH DAY YEAR

7 **Place of birth** Los Angeles, CA

8 **Soc. Sec. No.** 135-XX-2887

9 **Telephone No.** 415 / 555 - 8765
AREA CODE

10 **E-mail** jhong@bower.com

Address

11 452 Austin St.
STREET
San Jose CA 95112
12 CITY 13 STATE 14 ZIP

15 *John E Hong*
SIGNATURE

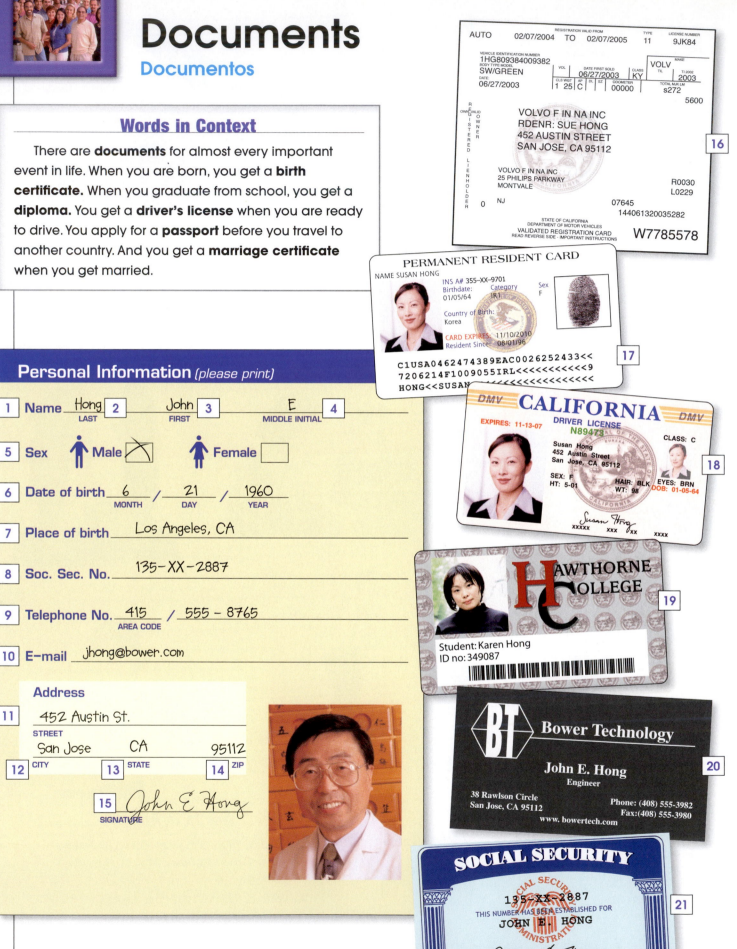

16

AUTO 02/07/2004 TO 02/07/2005 TYPE 11 LICENSE NUMBER 9JK84
VEHICLE IDENTIFICATION NUMBER
1HG809384009382
BODY TYPE MODEL VOL DATE FIRST SOLD CLASS VOLV MAKE
SW/GREEN 06/27/2003 KY TI 2002 2003
DATE: CLS WGT AP DL SZ ODOMETER TOTAL MJK LM
06/27/2003 1 25 C 00000 s272
5600
VOLVO F IN NA INC
RDENR: SUE HONG
452 AUSTIN STREET
SAN JOSE, CA 95112
VOLVO F IN NA INC
25 PHILIPS PARKWAY R0030
MONTVALE L0229
0 NJ 07645
144061320035282
STATE OF CALIFORNIA
DEPARTMENT OF MOTOR VEHICLES
VALIDATED REGISTRATION CARD W7785578
READ REVERSE SIDE - IMPORTANT INSTRUCTIONS

17

PERMANENT RESIDENT CARD
NAME SUSAN HONG
INS A# 355-XX-9701
Birthdate: Category Sex
01/05/64 IR1 F
Country of Birth:
Korea
CARD EXPIRES: 11/10/2010
Resident Since: 08/01/96
C1USA0462474389EAC0026252433<<
7206214F1009055IRL<<<<<<<<<<<9
HONG<<SUSAN

18

DMV **CALIFORNIA** DMV
EXPIRES: 11-13-07 DRIVER LICENSE
N89473 CLASS: C
Susan Hong
452 Austin Street
San Jose, CA 95112
SEX: F HAIR: BLK EYES: BRN
HT: 5-01 WT: 98 DOB: 01-05-64
Susan Hong
XXXXX XXX XX XXXX

19

HAWTHORNE **C**OLLEGE
Student: Karen Hong
ID no: 349087

20

BT Bower Technology
John E. Hong
Engineer
38 Rawlson Circle Phone: (408) 555-3982
San Jose, CA 95112 Fax:(408) 555-3980
www.bowertech.com

21

SOCIAL SECURITY
135-XX-2887
THIS NUMBER HAS BEEN ESTABLISHED FOR
JOHN E HONG
John E. Hong
SIGNATURE

A (registration) form
Un formulario de registro

1. **name**
   nombre
2. **last name / surname / family name**
   apellido
3. **first name**
   nombre de pila
4. **middle initial**
   inicial del segundo nombre
5. **sex / gender**
   sexo
6. **date of birth**
   fecha de nacimiento
7. **place of birth**
   lugar de nacimiento
8. **Social Security number**
   número de Seguro Social
9. **telephone number**
   número telefónico / de teléfono
10. **e-mail address**
    correo electrónico
11. **street address**
    domicilio
12. **city**
    ciudad
13. **state**
    estado
14. **zip code**
    código postal
15. **signature**
    firma

Documents
Documentos

16. **a vehicle registration card**
    una tarjeta de registro de vehículo
17. **a Resident Alien card / a green card**
    una tarjeta de residente / una tarjeta verde
18. **a driver's license**
    una licencia de manejar
19. **a student ID**
    una identificación de estudiante
20. **a business card**
    una tarjeta de presentación
21. **a Social Security card**
    una tarjeta del Seguro Social
22. **a passport**
    un pasaporte
23. **a visa**
    una visa
24. **a birth certificate**
    un acta de nacimiento
25. **a marriage certificate**
    un acta de matrimonio
26. **a Certificate of Naturalization**
    una carta de naturalización
27. **a college degree**
    un grado universitario
28. **a high school diploma**
    un certificado de escuela secundaria

24

State of California
UNITED STATES OF AMERICA

CERTIFICATE OF BIRTH
FROM THE RECORDS OF BIRTHS IN THE CITY OF
LOS ANGELES, CA U.S.A.

Record # 479

1	Full Name of Child	Karen Hong
2	Date of Birth	March 2, 1988
3	Gender and Plurality	

25

Certificate of **Marriage**

This Certifies That

John E. Hong

Born 6/21/60   Place of birth   Los Angeles, CA

and

Susan Hong

Born 1/5/64   Place of birth   Korea

26

THE UNITED STATES OF AMERICA

ORIGINAL
TO BE GIVEN TO
THE PERSON NATURALIZED

No. A98-45H-937

Petition No   575

Personal description of holder as of date of naturalization. Date of birth   01/05/64   sex   F   complexion   Fair   color of eyes   Brown   color of hair   Black   height   5   feet   1   in.   weight   98   pounds   visible distinctive marks   None   Marital status   Single   former nationality   Korean

I certify that the description above given is true, and that the photograph affixed hereto is a likeness of me.

Susan Hong
(complete and true signature of holder)

355-XX-9701

Be it known that at a term of the   District   Los Angeles County   California   held pursuant to law on   5/2/85   Susan Hong   then residing at   4501 Broward Ln

22

PASSPORT

United St...
of Amer...

23

Visas
January/Valid   February/Valid

JAPAN IMMIGRATION
3 NOV. 2002
Status: Temporary Visitor
Duration: 90 days

27

Paulson University

by authority of the Board of Regents and on recommendation of the Faculty

hereby confers upon

28

John Kennedy High School

Word Partnerships

apply for	a passport
get	a marriage license
have	a green card
sign	your name
print	
say	
fill in / fill out	a form
an application	form
an order	

7

Words in Action

1. Which documents do you have? Make a list.
2. Role-play. Student A is registering for a class. Student B is asking for personal information.
   - Student A: *Hi, I'd like to register for a class.*
   - Student B: *Sure. What's your last name?*

In Witness Thereof the... this Signatures of the Officers of the same are hereunto affixed this eleventh day of June, 1999.

Herschal McLeod
Principal of High School

Ray A...
Chairman of the Board
Wally Marshall

Nationalities
Nacionalidades

Words in Context

Women from many different countries have been in space. In 1963 Valentina Tereshkova, a **Russian** woman, was the first woman in space. Sally Ride was the first **American** woman in space. Chiaki Mukai was the first **Japanese** woman in space. A **French** woman, a **Canadian** woman, and an **English** woman have also been in space.

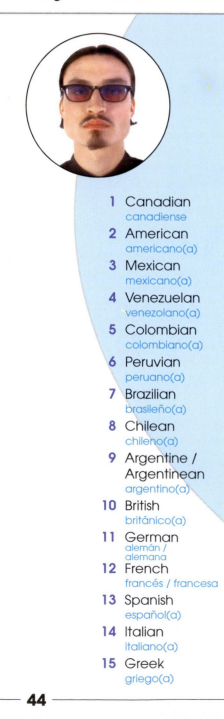

1 Canadian
  canadiense
2 American
  americano(a)
3 Mexican
  mexicano(a)
4 Venezuelan
  venezolano(a)
5 Colombian
  colombiano(a)
6 Peruvian
  peruano(a)
7 Brazilian
  brasileño(a)
8 Chilean
  chileno(a)
9 Argentine /
  Argentinean
  argentino(a)
10 British
   británico(a)
11 German
   alemán /
   alemana
12 French
   francés / francesa
13 Spanish
   español(a)
14 Italian
   italiano(a)
15 Greek
   griego(a)

16 Turkish
   turco(a)
17 Iranian
   iraní
18 Egyptian
   egipcio(a)
19 Saudi Arabian
   árabe
20 Nigerian
   nigeriano(a)
21 Russian
   ruso(a)
22 Indian
   indio(a)
23 Chinese
   chino(a)
24 Korean
   coreano(a)
25 Japanese
   japonés /
   japonesa
26 Thai
   tailandés /
   tailandesa
27 Vietnamese
   vietnamita
28 Filipino
   filipino(a)
29 Malaysian
   malasio(a)
30 Australian
   australiano(a)

Map labels: 1 CANADA · 2 UNITED STATES · 3 MEXICO · 4 VENEZUELA · 5 COLOMBIA · 6 PERU · 7 BRAZIL · 8 CHILE · 9 ARGENTINA

10 UNITED KINGDOM

11 GERMANY

12 FRANCE

13 SPAIN

14 ITALY

15 GREECE

16 TURKEY

17 IRAN

18 EGYPT

19 SAUDI ARABIA

20 NIGERIA

21 RUSSIA

22 INDIA

23 CHINA

24 REPUBLIC OF KOREA

25 JAPAN

26 THAILAND

27 VIETNAM

28 PHILIPPINES

29 MALAYSIA

30 AUSTRALIA

Words in Action

1. With a partner, practice matching countries and nationalities. One person will say a country. The other will say the nationality. Take turns.
- Student A: *Brazil*
- Student B: *Brazilian*

2. Do you have classmates or friends from other countries? Make a list of their nationalities.

Places Around Town
Lugares en el Pueblo

Words in Context

I come from Concon, a small town in Chile. There's a **church**, a **gas station**, a **school**, and a soccer **stadium**. There is no **mall**, no **hospital**, no **library**, and no **movie theater**. Concon is beautiful. There are **parks** in the town and beaches nearby. Sometimes I get homesick for my little town.

1 a factory
una fábrica

2 a stadium
un estadio

3 a mall
un centro comercial

4 a motel
un motel

5 a mosque
una mezquita

6 a school
una escuela

7 a synagogue
una sinagoga

8 a hospital
un hospital

9 a college
una universidad

10 a police station
una estación de policía

11 a theater
un teatro

12 a movie theater
una sala de cine

13 a church
una iglesia

14 a post office
una oficina de correo

15 an office building
un edificio de oficinas

16 a fire station
una estación de bomberos

17 a city hall / a town hall
un palacio municipal

18 a library
una biblioteca

19 a courthouse
un palacio de justicia

20 a gas station
una estación de gasolina /
una gasolinera

21 a parking garage
un estacionamiento

22 a high-rise (building)
un edificio de muchos pisos

23 a car dealership
un lote de compra-venta de autos

24 a sidewalk
una acera

25 a corner
una esquina

26 an intersection
un cruce

27 a street
una calle

28 a park
un parque

Word Partnerships

a narrow	street
a wide	
a dead-end	
a quiet	
a busy	

an elementary	school
a middle	
a high	
a public	
a private	

H

MEMORIAL HOSPITAL

8

7

CITY CINEMA

NOW PLAYING
Dragon Love 2

DRAGON LOVE 2

12

13

20

19

18

Waterville
Library

24

25

26

27

GAS
99

28

Words in Action

1. One person describes the location of a building in the picture. The other person guesses what the building is.
   - Student A: *It's between the city hall and the courthouse.*
   - Student B: *The library!*

2. Which of the places on the list are in your town (or in the town closest to your home)?

Shops and Stores

Tiendas

Words in Context

Americans shop a lot before holidays. Before Thanksgiving, **supermarkets** sell a lot of food. Just before Christmas, **department stores** and **toy stores** are crowded. Around Valentine's Day, **florists** and **jewelry stores** are very busy.

1 an electronics store
una tienda de electrónica

2 a clothing store
una tienda de ropa

3 a shoe store
una zapatería

4 a gift shop
una tienda de regalos

5 a jewelry store
una joyería

6 a sporting goods store
una tienda de artículos deportivos

7 a toy store
una juguetería

8 a furniture store
una mueblería

9 a bookstore
una librería

10 a music store
una tienda de música

11 a hair salon /
a beauty salon
un salón / una sala de belleza

12 a barbershop
una peluquería

13 a health club / a gym
un gimnasio

14 a thrift shop /
a second-hand store
una tienda de artículos de segunda mano

15 a copy shop
un centro de copiado

16 a nail salon
un salón / una sala de manicure

17 a (dry) cleaner
una tintorería

18 a video store
una tienda de video

19 a flower stand
una florería

20 a coffee shop
un café

21 a pet store
una tienda de mascotas

22 a bakery
una pastelería

23 a laundromat
una lavandería

24 a fast food restaurant
un restaurante de comida rápida

25 a department store
una tienda de departamentos

26 a drugstore /
a pharmacy
una farmacia

27 a supermarket
un supermercado

28 an ice cream stand
un puesto de helados

29 a photo kiosk
un kiosko / quiosco de fotografía

30 a flea market
un tianguis

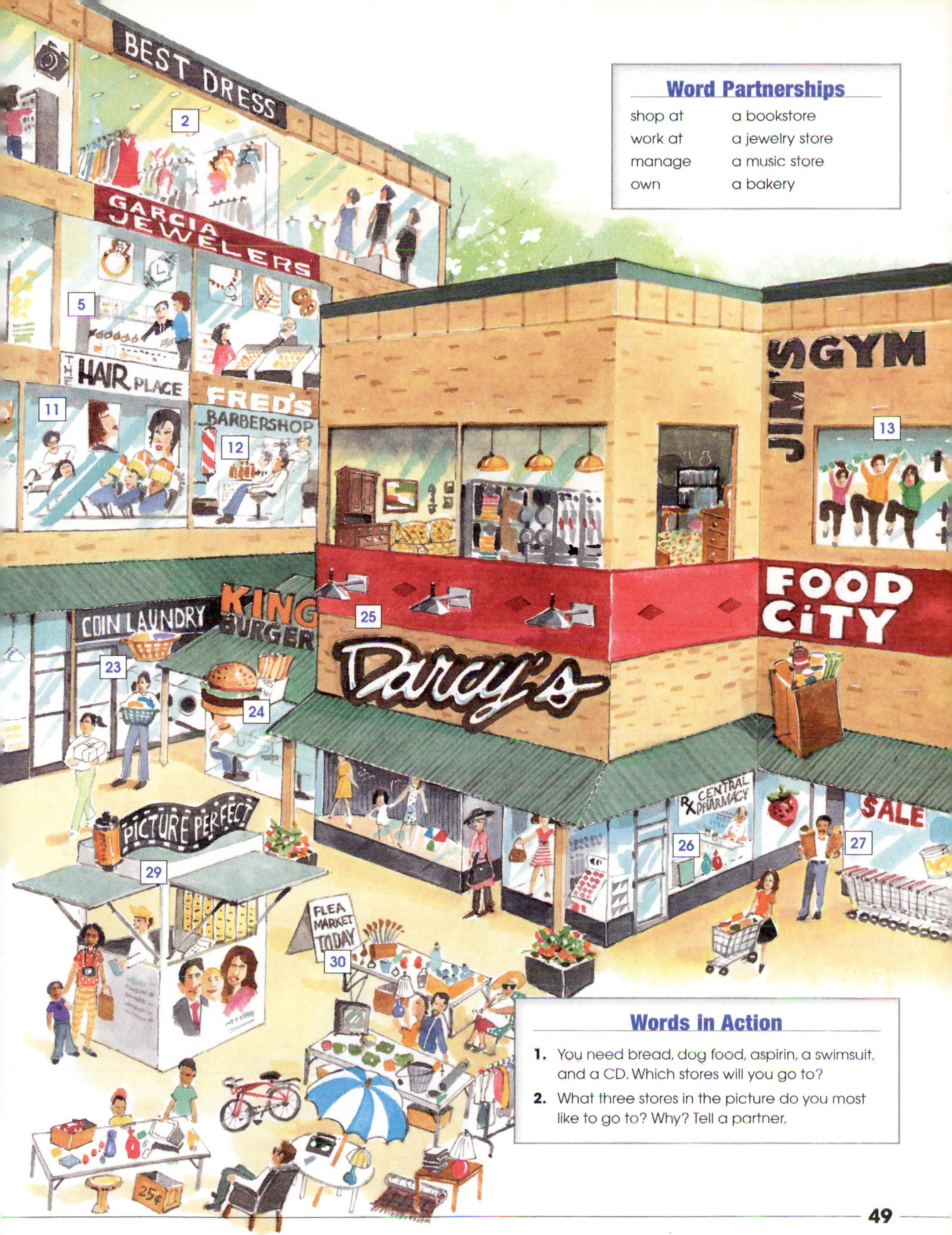

BEST DRESS
2
GARCIA JEWELERS
5
THE HAIR PLACE
11
FRED'S BARBERSHOP
12
JIM'S GYM
13
COIN LAUNDRY
23
KING BURGER
24
25
Darcy's
FOOD CITY
CENTRAL PHARMACY
26
SALE
27
PICTURE PERFECT
29
FLEA MARKET TODAY
30
25¢

Word Partnerships

shop at	a bookstore
work at	a jewelry store
manage	a music store
own	a bakery

Words in Action

1. You need bread, dog food, aspirin, a swimsuit, and a CD. Which stores will you go to?
2. What three stores in the picture do you most like to go to? Why? Tell a partner.

Bank

Banco

| 1 |
| 2 |
| 3 |
| 4 |
| 5 |
| 6 |
| 7 |
| 8 |
| 9 |

2.5%

LOAN OFFICER

BANK MANAGER

| 10 |

Central Bank
5001 BAY ST. BROOKLYN, NY 11235

CHECKING
Monthly Statement   Account 00001546093
Statement Period: 04/22/05 through 05/21/05

| 11 |

Page 1 of 1
Enclosures: 0

| 12 |

n Brown
Parker St.
oklyn, NY 11235

g Balance:	$552.32	Deposits/Cre
alance:	$552.32	Interest Paid
Balance:	$552.32	Checks/Debi

Deposits

cription

GINNING BALANCE
05/21   ENDING BALANCE

John Brown
63 Parker Street
Brooklyn, NY 11235

712
12-3/456

Pay to the
order of

| 13 | Date _____ $ _____

_____ Dollars

CENTRAL BANK

For _____
⑆123456789⑆ 001122333⑆ 9876

IF YOU HAVE ANY QUESTIONS
VISIT ANY BRANCH OFFICE
TO REPORT A LOST OR STOLE

.2.32
.32

 **20** ATM

21

 CALbank ATM

22
5815 5661 2345 6789
John Brown

1 a safe-deposit box /
a safety-deposit box
una caja de seguridad

2 a security guard
un / una guardia de seguridad

3 a vault
una bóveda

4 a teller
un cajero / una cajera

5 a teller window
una ventanilla de cajero

6 cash / money
efectivo

7 a customer
un / una cliente

8 a bank manager
un / una gerente de banco

9 a loan officer
un funcionario / una funcionaria de préstamos

10 a (monthly) statement
un estado de cuenta mensual

11 a checking account number
un número de cuenta bancaria

12 a checkbook
una chequera

13 a check
un cheque

14 a (savings account) passbook
una libreta (de cuenta de ahorros)

15 interest
interés

16 a deposit
un depósito

17 a withdrawal
un retiro

18 a balance
un saldo

19 a money order
un giro postal

20 an ATM
un cajero automático / un distribuidor automático de billetes de banco

21 a drive-up window
una ventanilla de servicio a automovilistas

22 an ATM card /
a bankcard
una tarjeta electrónica / una tarjeta bancaria

Verbs
Verbos

23 wait in line
hacer fila / cola

24 insert your ATM card
inserte su tarjeta electrónica

25 enter your PIN
teclee / marque su número de identificación personal

26 withdraw cash
retire el dinero en efectivo

27 make a deposit
haga un depósito

28 remove your card
retire su tarjeta

SAVINGS ACCOUNT

	% INTEREST	+DEPOSITS	– WITHDRAWALS	BALANCE
en account		$500.00		$500.00
xtbooks			$75.00	$425.00
terest	$3.21			$428.21
thday gift from Mom		$25.00		$453.21
terest	$3.68			$456.99

14 **15** **16** **17** **18**

19
UNITED STATES POSTAL SERVICE
POSTAL MONEY ORDER
SERIAL NUMBER
03313978165
YEAR. MONTH. DAY 2004-09-25
POST OFFICE 017720
U.S. DOLLARS AND CENTS
$1,500.00¢
PAY TO Chow Realty
ADDRESS 425 W. 62nd Alameda Blvd.
AMOUNT ONE THOUSAND FIVE HUNDRED DOLLARS & 00¢
NEGOTIABLE ONLY IN THE U.S. AND POSSESSIONS
FROM John Brann
63 Parker St
Brooklyn NY
CLERK 004
:000008003: 03313978165

Words in Action

1. When was the last time you went to the bank? What did you do there? What part of the bank did you go to? Who did you speak to?

2. Work with a partner. One person says the steps to using an ATM. The other acts out the steps.

Post Office
Oficina de Correo

Words in Context

Do you want the **mail** you **send** to arrive safely and on time? Be sure to use a **zip code** on every **letter** and **package**. Also be sure to use a **return address**. A **postal clerk** can **weigh** your mail so you will know how much **postage** to put on it.

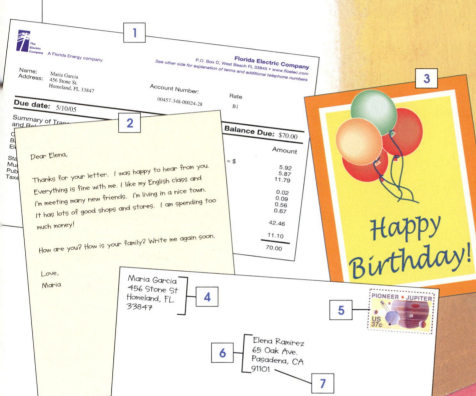

1	a bill	7	a zip code	12	a stamp machine	18	a postmark
	un giro postal		un código postal		una máquina de estampillas / timbres		un sello postal
2	a letter	8	an envelope	13	a post office box /	19	overnight mail /
	una carta		un sobre		a P.O. Box		next-day mail
3	a greeting card	9	a mailbox		un apartado postal		correo expreso
	una tarjeta de felicitación		un buzón	14	a catalog	20	a (postal) clerk
4	a (return) address	10	a mail carrier /		un catálogo		un empleado / una empleada de correo
	una dirección de remitente		a letter carrier	15	a (postal) scale		
5	a stamp		un mensajero / una mensajera		una báscula postal		
	una estampilla / un timbre postal	11	a mail truck	16	a postcard		
6	a (mailing) address		un camión de correo		una tarjeta postal		
	una dirección de correo			17	a package		
					un paquete		

52

Tomorrow.

Verbs
Verbos

21 address
dirigir

22 weigh
pesar

23 put a stamp on
estampillar

24 mail / send
enviar

Word Partnerships

a business	letter
a personal	
a love	
a first class	stamp
a book of	stamps
a sheet of	
a roll of	
a postage-paid	envelope
a self-addressed stamped	

Words in Action

1. What kinds of mail do you send? What kinds do you get? What is your favorite kind of mail to receive? What is your least favorite? Discuss with a group.

2. Describe your last visit to the post office. What did you do? Who did you talk to? What did you see? Tell your partner.

Library
Biblioteca

Words in Context

Libraries can change people's lives. In 1953, **author** Frank McCourt arrived in New York City from Ireland. One day a man told Frank to go to a library. So Frank did. He got a **library card, checked out** a **book,** and fell in love with reading. All of the reading he did at the library helped Frank McCourt become a successful **writer.** Now people can read his **autobiography** in 30 different languages!

Verbs
Verbos

26 look for a book
buscar un libro

27 check out books
sacar libros

Reading Room

1

3

4

2

Reference Desk

Title **War and Peace**
Author **Tolstoy** 6

5

12

11

13

14

15

16

19

Chinese Cooking 22

18

Observer
FIRE BURNS FOREST

17

WAR & PEACE

20

21

Leo Tolstoy

28 read
leer

29 return books
devolver libros

1 the **periodical** section
la sección de publicaciones periódicas

2 a **magazine**
una revista

3 a **microfilm** machine
una máquina de microfilmes

4 the **reading room**
la sala de lectura

5 the **reference desk**
el escritorio de consultas / la central de consultas

6 an **online catalog** / a computerized catalog
un catálogo electrónico

7 the **fiction** section
la sección de novela

8 the **nonfiction** section
la sección de libros fuera de la novela

9 a **dictionary**
un diccionario

10 an **encyclopedia**
una enciclopedia

11 a **librarian**
un bibliotecario / una bibliotecaria

12 a **library card**
una tarjeta de biblioteca

13 a **hardcover** (book)
un libro de pasta dura

14 a **paperback** (book)
un libro de bolsillo

15 an **atlas**
un atlas

16 the **circulation desk** / the **checkout desk**
el escritorio de registro

17 a **newspaper**
un periódico

18 a **headline**
un titular / un encabezado

19 a **title**
un título

20 a **novel**
una novela

21 an **author** / a **writer**
un autor / una autora, un escritor / una escritora

22 a **cookbook**
un libro de cocina

23 a **biography**
una biografía

24 an **autobiography**
una autobiografía

25 a **picture book**
un libro ilustrado

Fiction **7**

Nonfiction **8**

Reference

9

10

Children's Section

25

Gandhi's Life By Jane Smith **23**

My Life by Abraham Lincoln **24**

Word Partnerships

a library	book
a good	book
a boring	writer
a detective	novel
a romance	
a science-fiction	
a historical	

Words in Action

1. Imagine you will spend an afternoon in this library. What will you do?

2. Discuss the following questions with a group:
- What is your favorite book?
- What is your favorite magazine?
- What is your favorite newspaper?

Daycare Center

Guardería

Words in Context

Parents should look for the following things at a **daycare center:**

- Are the children busy and happy?
- Do the **childcare workers** take good care of the children?
- Is there a special room for **newborns**?
- Are the **high chairs, potty chairs,** and **changing tables** clean?

Word Partnerships

a cute a newborn	baby
baby	food
a clean a dirty	diaper
change	a diaper
play with put away share	toys

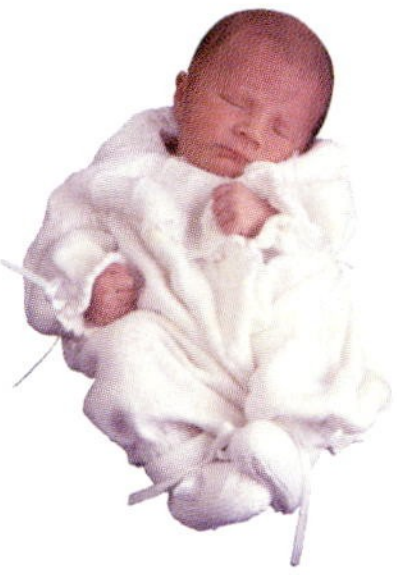

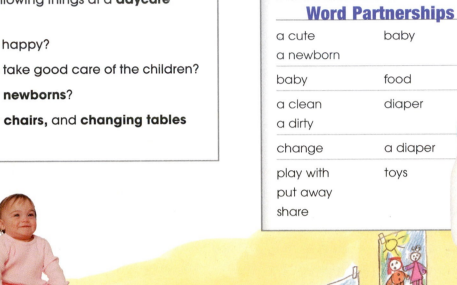

31 a newborn
un recién nacido / una recién nacida

32 an infant / a baby
un / una bebé

33 a toddler
un niño pequeño / una niña pequeña

34 a preschooler
un niño / una niña preescolar

1 a nipple
una mamila

2 a bottle
un biberón

3 a crib
una cuna

4 a playpen
un corral / un corralito

5 a rest mat
una colchoneta

6 a baby swing
un columpio para bebé

7 a teething ring
un aro para dentición /
una mordedera

8 a parent
un padre / una madre

9 a baby carrier
una bolsa de canguro / una
cangurera

10 a rattle
una sonaja

11 a stroller
una carriola

12 a cubby
un casillero

13 a girl
una niña

14 a boy
un niño

15 toys
juguetes

16 a bib
un babero

17 a childcare worker
un niñero / una niñera

18 a high chair
una silla alta

19 formula
fórmula

20 a potty chair
un baño entrenador

21 a diaper pail
un bote para pañales

22 (baby) powder
talco (para bebé)

23 (baby) lotion
loción (para bebé)

24 (baby) wipes
toallitas húmedas (para
bebé)

25 a pacifier
un chupón

26 a changing table
una mesa / cómoda
cambiadora

27 a (disposable)
diaper
un pañal desechable

28 training pants
un (calzón) entrenador

29 a (cloth) diaper
un pañal (de tela)

30 a diaper pin
un alfiler de seguridad /
un seguro para pañal

Words in Action

1. Which are the 10 most important items for a newborn? Discuss and make a list with a group.

2. Imagine you have a one-year-old baby. You are taking a trip on an airplane. Which items will you take?

City Square

El Centro

HOTEL
Central Square Hotel

TAXI

Freeman Art Gallery

METRO BANK

ATM

HANDICAPPED PARKING

STOP

STOP

1 a hotel un hotel	**6** a (traffic) cop un oficial (de tránsito)	**11** a (fire) hydrant un hidrante	**16** a sidewalk una banqueta
2 a bank un banco	**7** a fountain una fuente	**12** a street vendor un vendedor ambulante	**17** a pedestrian un peatón / una peatona
3 an art gallery una galería de arte	**8** a café un café	**13** a travel agency una agencia de viajes	**18** a crosswalk un cruce / crucero para peatones
4 a streetlight un arbotante / un poste de luz	**9** a billboard un anuncio espectacular / una valla publicitaria	**14** a handicapped parking space un espacio de estacionamiento para discapacitados	**19** a sign un señalamiento de tránsito
5 a traffic accident un accidente de tránsito	**10** a monument un monumento	**15** a curb una acera	**20** a (parking) meter un estacionómetro / parquímetro

Keep Our
City Clean! **9**

24

Vincent
Van
Gogh
EXHIBITION

Cafe Rio

8

13
World
Travel

10

12

23

i

21

7

11

20

22

25
NEWS

21 a tourist
information booth
un módulo / una caseta
de información
22 a street musician
un músico ambulante
23 a statue
una estatua
24 a museum
un museo
25 a newsstand
un puesto de periódico

Word Partnerships

an art	museum
a science	
a natural history	
a street	sign
a neon	
a sidewalk	café
an outdoor	

Words in Action

1. Imagine you are a tourist in this city square. Where will you go? What will you do?

2. Think about the town or city you live in or near. Make a list of all the things you can find there.

Crime and Justice
Crimen y Justicia

Words in Context

Iceland has very little **crime.** There are only four **prisons,** and many of the **prisoners** are part-time! There are usually only one or two **murders** a year, and crimes like **armed robbery** are extremely rare. There are sometimes **muggings** in the capital city of Reykjavík, but Iceland is still one of the safest countries in the world.

1 auto theft
  robo de automóviles

2 bribery
  soborno

3 burglary
  robo con allanamiento de morada

4 theft
  robo

5 drug dealing
  tráfico de estupefacientes / drogas

6 drunk driving
  conducir en estado de ebriedad

7 arson
  incendio premeditado

8 graffiti
  grafito

9 mugging
  asalto / robo con violencia

10 murder
   asesinato

11 shoplifting
   robo de tiendas

12 vandalism
   vandalismo

13 gang violence
   pandillerismo

14 armed robbery
   asalto a mano armada

15 an arrest
   un arresto

16 a victim
   una víctima

17 a witness
   un / una testigo

18 a criminal
   un / una criminal

19 handcuffs
   esposas

20 a police officer
   un / una oficial de policía

21 a trial
   un juicio

22 a jury
   un jurado

23 a judge
   un juez / una jueza

24 a lawyer /
   an attorney
   un abogado / una abogada

25 a courtroom
   una corte

26 a jail / a prison
   una prisión / un reclusorio

27 a prisoner
   un prisionero / una prisionera

Word Partnerships

a fair	trial
a speedy	
commit	a crime
witness	
report	
go to	prison
spend time in	
get out of	

Words in Action

1. Talk with a group. Which crimes are most common in your community?

2. Put the crimes in a list from the least serious crime to the most serious crime. Discuss your list with a partner.

Types of Homes
Tipos de Casas

Words in Context

Do you live in a **house,** an **apartment,** or a **condo?**
There are many other kinds of homes, too. For example,
some people in the Sahara Desert live in **tents.** Some
people in the U.S. live in **mobile homes.** And some
people near the North Pole live in **igloos.**

Word Partnerships

live in	a house
	an apartment
	a dorm
live on	a houseboat
	a ranch

62

1 a house
una casa

2 a tent
una tienda de campaña

3 a cottage
una casa de campo

4 a (log) cabin
una cabaña

5 a chalet
un chalet

6 a duplex / a two-family house
una casa duplex

7 a mobile home
una casa móvil

8 a farmhouse
una granja

9 an apartment
un apartamento

10 a condominium / a condo
un condominio

11 a villa
una villa

12 a townhouse
una casa adosada

13 a houseboat
una casa flotante

14 a palace
un palacio

15 an igloo
un iglú

16 a ranch
un rancho

17 a retirement home
un asilo para mayores / para ancianos

18 a dormitory / a dorm
una residencia universitaria /
un internado

19 a castle
un castillo

20 the city / an urban area
la ciudad / una zona urbana

21 the suburbs
los suburbios

22 a small town
un pueblo pequeño

23 the country / a rural area
el campo / un área rural

14

18

19

Words in Action

1. What kinds of homes have you lived in or stayed in? Tell your class.

2. You can stay in three of these homes. Which three will you choose? Why?

Finding a Place to Live
Encontrar un Lugar para Vivir

Words in Context

Are you **looking for** an apartment? It isn't always easy. Read the classified ads in newspapers and talk to your friends. **Make** appointments to see a lot of apartments. Before you **sign** a lease, talk to the landlord. **Ask** questions like these:

- How much is the security deposit?
- When is the rent due?
- When can I **move in**?

Renting an Apartment
Rentar un Apartamento / Departamento

1. **look for** an apartment
   buscar un apartamento / departamento
2. **make** an appointment (with the landlord)
   hacer una cita (con el propietario / la propietaria, el dueño / la dueña)
3. **meet** the landlord
   conocer al dueño / a la dueña
4. **see** the apartment
   ver el apartamento / departamento
5. **ask** questions
   hacer preguntas
6. **sign** the lease
   firmar el contrato de arrendamiento
7. **pay** a security deposit
   pagar un depósito
8. **get** the key
   conseguir la llave
9. **pack**
   empacar
10. **load** a van or truck
    cargar una camioneta o camión
11. **unpack**
    desempacar
12. **arrange** the furniture
    acomodar los muebles
13. **decorate** the apartment
    decorar el apartamento / departamento
14. **pay** the rent
    pagar la renta
15. **meet** the neighbors
    conocer a los vecinos

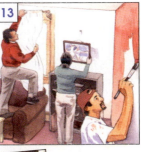

Buying a House
Comprar una Casa

16 **call** a realtor
llamar al corredor / a la corredora
de bienes raíces

17 **look at** houses
ver casas

18 **make** a decision
tomar una decisión

19 **make** an offer
hacer una oferta

20 **negotiate** the price
negociar el precio

21 **inspect** the house
revisar la casa

22 **apply for** a loan
solicitar un préstamo

23 **make** a down payment
pagar un enganche

24 **sign** the loan documents
firmar los documentos del préstamo

25 **move in**
mudarse

26 **make** the (house) payment
hacer el pago (de la casa)

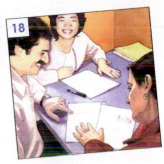

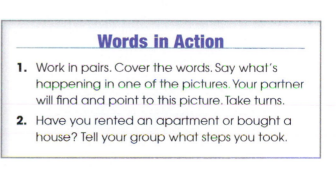

Word Partnerships

look for	an apartment	in the classified ads
		online
		with a realtor
pay	the rent	early
		late
		on time

Words in Action

1. Work in pairs. Cover the words. Say what's happening in one of the pictures. Your partner will find and point to this picture. Take turns.

2. Have you rented an apartment or bought a house? Tell your group what steps you took.

Apartment Building

Edificio de Apartamentos

Words in Context

I'm the **superintendent** of an **apartment building** in Los Angeles. We have 30 **unfurnished apartments.** Most of these are **studios.** We have a **laundry room** in the **basement.** There's no **doorman,** but I watch everyone who comes in the **lobby.** I take good care of my building.

1

2

3

4

5

6

7

8

9

10

11

12

13

14

15

16

17

18

19

20

1 a storage space
un espacio para almacenamiento /
para guardar cosas

2 a dumpster
un depósito de basura

3 a superintendent /
a super
un / una intendente

4 stairs
escaleras

5 a furnace
una estufa

6 a water heater
un calentador de agua

7 a basement
un sótano

8 a parking space
un espacio para
estacionamiento

9 a studio
(apartment)
un (apartamento)
estudio

10 a tenant
un inquilino /
una inquilina

11 a roommate
un compañero / una compañera de
cuarto / apartamento

12 a hallway
un pasillo

13 a one-bedroom
apartment
un apartamento de una
recámara

14 an air conditioner
un aparato de aire
acondicionado

15 a workout room /
a gym
un gimnasio

16 a balcony
un balcón

17 a courtyard
un patio

18 a laundry room
un cuarto de lavandería

19 a fire escape
una escalera de
emergencia

20 an unfurnished
apartment
un apartamento no
amueblado

21 a furnished
apartment
un apartamento
amueblado

22 a lobby
un vestíbulo

23 an elevator
un ascensor / elevador

24 a revolving door
una puerta giratoria

25 a doorman
un portero / una portera

26 a peephole
una mirilla

27 a door chain
un seguro de cadena

28 a dead-bolt (lock)
una chapa de seguridad

29 a doorknob
una perilla

30 an intercom
un intercomunicador

31 a key
una llave

Word Partnerships

| the ground | floor |
| the first |
| the second |
| the third |
| the fourth |

Words in Action

1. Role-play with a partner. One of you is the super of this building. The other is looking for an apartment.
   - *Student A: Is there a laundry room?*
   - *Student B: Yes. It's in the basement.*
2. Describe an apartment building you know.

House and Garden

La Casa y el Jardín

Words in Context

Different cultures have different kinds of **houses.**
North American houses often have **yards** with **lawns.**
People cook on their **grills** and relax on a **patio,**
porch, or **deck.** Some Arab and Mexican houses have
courtyards. Even **windows** are different from place to
place. In France, windows open like **doors.** In Greece
and North Africa, windows are painted blue.

1

2

3

4

7

8

9

10

11

21

22

23

24

25

26

27

28

29

1	a chimney / una chimenea	**11**	a shutter / una contraventana	**21**	a garden / un jardín
2	an attic / un ático	**12**	a door / una puerta	**22**	a patio / un patio
3	a skylight / un tragaluz	**13**	a doorbell / un timbre	**23**	a gate / una puerta
4	a roof / un techo	**14**	a porch / un porche	**24**	a fence / una cerca / una valla
5	a deck / una terraza	**15**	steps / escalones	**25**	hedge clippers / tijeras de podar
6	a grill / a barbecue / un asador	**16**	a garage / una cochera / un garaje	**26**	a wheelbarrow / una carretilla
7	a hammock / una hamaca	**17**	a rake / un rastrillo	**27**	a (garden) hose / una manguera (de jardín)
8	a lawn / grass / césped	**18**	a driveway / camino particular para coches / autos / un antegaraje	**28**	a walk(way) / un camino de entrada
9	a lawn mower / cortadora / podadora de césped	**19**	a garbage can / a trash can / un bote de basura	**29**	a sprinkler / un aspersor
10	a window / una ventana	**20**	a yard / un patio		

Word Partnerships

a flower	garden
a vegetable	

a chain-link	fence
a picket	
a barbed wire	

a front	door
a screen	
a garage	

Words in Action

1. Cover the word list. Name as many parts of the house as you can. Start at the top of the house and work your way down.

2. Draw your dream house. Label all the parts. Show your dream house to a partner. How are they similar? How are they different?

Kitchen and Dining Area
Área de Cocina y Comedor

Words in Context

Before 1900, few **kitchens** had electricity. People used **candles** for light. There were no **refrigerators**, no **ovens**, no **dishwashers**, and no **blenders**. There were no faucets, either. To wash **dishes**, people had to get water from outdoors and heat it over a fire.

1 a microwave (oven)
un horno de microondas

2 a cabinet
un gabinete

3 dishes
platos

4 a shelf
un entrepaño

5 a counter(top)
un mostrador

6 a stove
una estufa

7 a (tea) kettle
una tetera

8 an oven
un horno

9 a potholder
un protector

10 a coffeemaker
una cafetera

11 a spice rack
un especiero

12 a blender
una licuadora

13 a toaster
un tostador

14 a dishwasher
una lavadora de platos /
una lavavajillas

15 a sink
un fregadero

16 a drying rack / a dish rack
un escurreplatos

17 a garbage disposal
una trituradora de basura

18 a dish towel
un secador de platos

19 a freezer
un congelador

20 a refrigerator
un refrigerador

21 a stool
un banco

22 a chair
una silla

23 a plate
un plato

24 a bowl
un tazón

25 a glass
un vaso

26 a placemat
un mantel individual

27 silverware
cubiertos

28 a candle
una vela

29 a teapot
una tetera

30 a mug
un tarro

31 a napkin
una servilleta

32 a table
una mesa

Word Partnerships

a dining room	table
a kitchen	chair
an electric	stove
a gas	
load	the dishwasher
start / turn on	
empty	

Words in Action

1. What do you think are the ten most important things in this kitchen? Why?

2. Work with a group. What things do all of you have in your kitchen? Make a list.

Living Room
La Sala

Words in Context

Some people like lots of furniture in their living rooms—a **sofa**, a **love seat**, a **coffee table**, chairs, a **wall unit**, and several **lamps**. Others like just a rug and a couple of **easy chairs**. In the Middle East, people often sit on **cushions** or low **benches** instead of chairs. And in some Asian countries, people sit on the **floor**.

1 a bench una banca	**9** a (throw) pillow un cojín / un almohadón	**17** a ceiling un techo	**25** a thermostat un termostato
2 a cushion un cojín	**10** a window seat un asiento / una banca al pie de una ventana	**18** a smoke detector un detector de humo	**26** a mantel una repisa de la chimenea
3 an armchair / an easy chair un sillón	**11** a love seat un sofá para dos personas	**19** blinds una persiana	**27** a fireplace una chimenea
4 an end table una mesa lateral	**12** a coffee table una mesa de centro	**20** a curtain una cortina	**28** a fire screen una pantalla de chimenea
5 a lamp una lámpara	**13** an ottoman un otomano	**21** a wall una pared	**29** a house plant una planta de interiores / de sombra
6 a lampshade una pantalla	**14** the floor el piso	**22** a bookcase un librero	**30** a fire una lumbre
7 a wall unit un módulo de pared	**15** a curtain rod un cortinero	**23** a vent un ventilador	**31** a rocking chair una mecedora
8 a sofa / a couch un sofá	**16** a (ceiling) fan un ventilador de techo	**24** a (light) switch un interruptor de luz	**32** an outlet un enchufe

Word Partnerships

a floor	lamp
a table	
a desk	
sit	in an armchair
	in a rocking chair
	on a sofa
	on the floor
	on a cushion

Words in Action

1. How is your living room similar to this one? How is it different? Discuss with a partner.
   - *I have a fireplace like the one in the picture.*
   - *My sofa is bigger than the one in the picture.*

2. Draw your perfect living room. Label all the items in the drawing.

Bedroom and Bathroom
Recámara y Baño

Words in Context

Feng shui is a Chinese art. It suggests ways to make homes healthy and happy. For a calm **bedroom,** your **bed** should not face a door. Your **bedspread** should not touch the floor. In the **bathroom,** the **toilet** should not face the door. You should have many **mirrors.** Mirrors bring happiness.

1 a closet
un closet

2 a blanket
una cobija

3 a carpet
una alfombra

4 a rug
un tapete

5 a drawer
un cajón

6 a dresser
un tocador

7 a mirror
un espejo

8 a (window) shade
una cortinilla

9 an alarm clock
un reloj despertador

10 a night table
un buró / una mesa de noche

11 a pillowcase
una funda

12 a pillow
una almohada

13 a mattress
un colchón

14 a bed
una cama

15 a sheet
una sábana

16 a comforter
un cobertor

17 a bedspread
una colcha

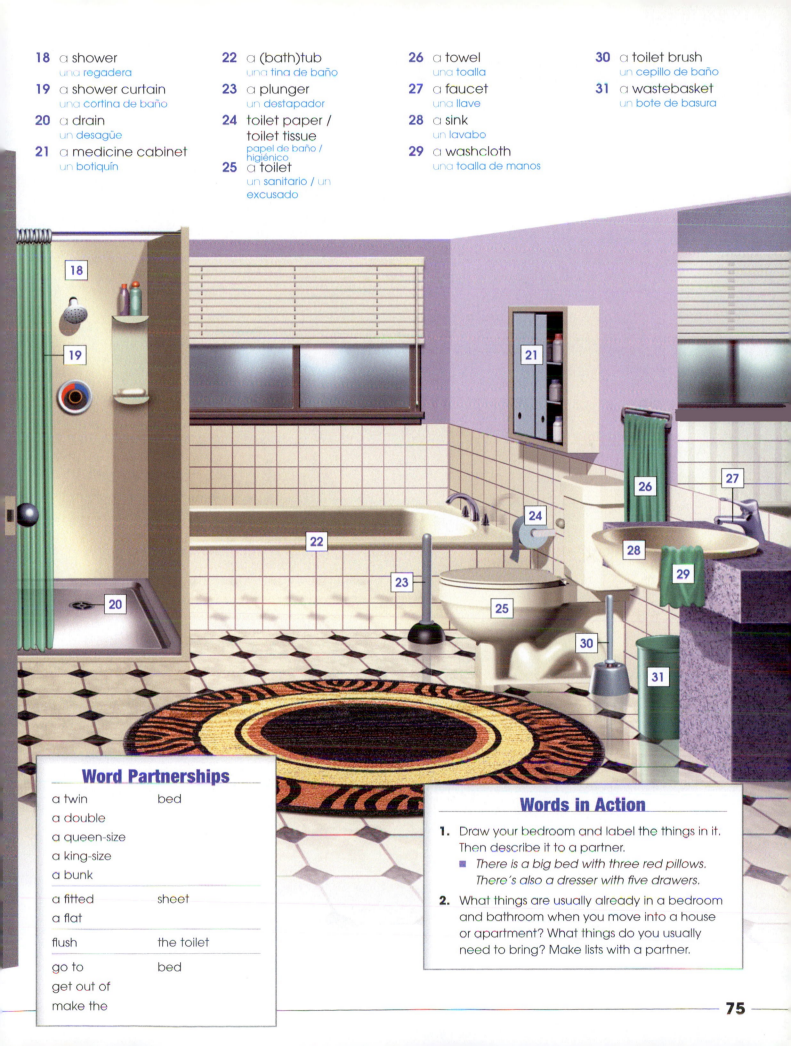

18 a shower
una **regadera**

19 a shower curtain
una **cortina de baño**

20 a drain
un **desagüe**

21 a medicine cabinet
un **botiquín**

22 a (bath)tub
una **tina de baño**

23 a plunger
un **destapador**

24 toilet paper /
toilet tissue
papel de baño /
higiénico

25 a toilet
un **sanitario** / un
excusado

26 a towel
una **toalla**

27 a faucet
una **llave**

28 a sink
un **lavabo**

29 a washcloth
una **toalla de manos**

30 a toilet brush
un **cepillo de baño**

31 a wastebasket
un **bote de basura**

Word Partnerships

a twin	bed
a double	
a queen-size	
a king-size	
a bunk	

| a fitted | sheet |
| a flat | |

| flush | the toilet |

go to	bed
get out of	
make the	

Words in Action

1. Draw your bedroom and label the things in it. Then describe it to a partner.
   - *There is a big bed with three red pillows. There's also a dresser with five drawers.*

2. What things are usually already in a bedroom and bathroom when you move into a house or apartment? What things do you usually need to bring? Make lists with a partner.

Household Problems

Problemas Caseros

23 ants
hormigas

24 mice
ratones

25 rats
ratas

26 termites
comején

27 cockroaches
cucarachas

1 The power **is out**.
No hay corriente.

2 The toilet **is clogged**.
El excusado está obstruido.

3 The roof **leaks**.
El techo tiene una gotera. /
El techo gotea.

4 The wall **is cracked**.
La pared está agrietada.

5 The faucet **drips**.
La llave gotea.

6 The lightbulb **is burned out**.
El foco está fundido.

7 The heater **doesn't work**.
El calentador no funciona.

8 The pipes **are frozen**.
Las tuberías están congeladas.

9 The basement **is flooded**.
El sótano está inundado.

10 The window **is broken**.
La ventana está rota.

11 The lock **is jammed**.
La cerradura está trabada.

12 a **breaker panel**
un panel / un tablero
interruptor

13 a **circuit breaker**
un interruptor de
circuito

14 an **electrician**
un electricista

15 a **plumber**
un plomero

16 a **roofer**
un constructor / un
reparador de techos

17 a **handyman**
un mozo / un
trabajador

18 an **exterminator**
un fumigador

19 a **water meter**
un medidor de agua

20 a **gas meter**
un medidor de gas

21 a **meter reader**
un lector de
medidores

22 a **locksmith**
un cerrajero

Word Partnerships

read	the meter
turn on	
shut off	
flip	the circuit breaker
replace	

Words in Action

1. Discuss these questions: What household problems did you have last year? Who did the repairs?

2. Describe a household problem. Your partner will tell you who to call.
   - Student A: *I can't open the front door. The lock is jammed.*
   - Student B: *Call a locksmith.*

77

Household Chores

Quehaceres Domésticos

Words in Context

In many houses, men and women share **household chores.** For example, in some houses women **do** the cooking, and men **wash** the dishes. Sometimes women **do** the laundry, and men **fold** the clothes. Sometimes women **weed** the garden, and men **rake** the leaves. What chores do you do in your family?

1

2

3

4

5

6

7

13

14

15

16

17

18

19

BILLS TO PAY   BILLS PAID

1 **make** the bed
   tender la cama

2 **change** the sheets
   cambiar las sábanas

3 **do** the laundry
   lavar la ropa

4 **sweep** the floor
   barrer el piso

5 **fold** the clothes
   doblar la ropa

6 **pay** the bills
   pagar las cuentas

7 **vacuum** the carpet
   aspirar la alfombra

8 **dust**
   quitar el polvo

9 **polish** the furniture
   pulir los muebles

10 **clean** the sink
    limpiar el lavabo

11 **scrub** the toilet
    restregar el excusado

12 **mop** the floor
    trapear el piso

13 **empty** the wastebasket
    vaciar el cesto de basura

14 **shake out** the rug
    sacudir un tapete

15 **weed** the garden
    desherbar el jardín / desyerbar el jardín

16 **wash** the car
    lavar el coche / lavar el carro

17 **mow** the lawn /
    mow the grass
    cortar el césped / cortar el pasto

18 **water** the lawn
    regar el césped / regar el pasto

19 **take out** the trash /
    put out the trash
    sacar la basura

20 **rake** the leaves
    recoger las hojas con el rastrillo

21 **do** the dishes /
    wash the dishes
    lavar los platos

22 **cook / do** the cooking
    cocinar

23 **dry** the dishes
    secar los platos

24 **put away** the dishes
    guardar los platos

Word Partnerships

clean	the house
	the bathroom
	your bedroom
polish	the car
	the silver
	the floor

Words in Action

1. Name two household chores you like to do and two you hate to do.

2. Work in a group. Imagine your group is a family—a mother, a father, and teenage children. Divide the household chores on the list among yourselves. Who will do what?

Cleaning Supplies
Utensilios de Limpieza

1 a feather duster
un plumero

2 a dustpan
un recogedor

3 a vacuum cleaner bag
una bolsa para aspiradora

4 vacuum cleaner attachments
accesorios para aspiradora

5 a vacuum (cleaner)
una aspiradora

6 a squeegee
un escurridor para vidrios

7 paper towels
toallas de papel

8 trash bags
bolsas para basura

9 furniture polish
lustramuebles / pulidor para muebles

10 a dust cloth
un sacudidor

11 glass cleaner
limpiador de vidrios

12 dishwasher detergent
detergente para lavavajillas / detergente para lavadora de platos

13 dish soap / dishwashing liquid
jabón para platos / jabón líquido para platos

14 a scouring pad
una fibra limpiadora

15 bug spray / insect spray
insecticida en aerosol

16 a bucket / a pail
una cubeta / un balde

17 a rag
un trapo

18 rubber gloves
guantes de hule

19 cleanser
limpiador

20 a scrub brush
un cepillo para restregar

21 a sponge
una esponja

22 a flyswatter
un matamoscas

23 a stepladder
una escalera de tijera / una escalera de mano

24 a mousetrap
una ratonera

25 a recycling bin
un bote para materiales reciclables

26 a mop
un trapeador

27 a dust mop
un limpión

28 a broom
una escoba

Word Partnerships

heavy-duty	trash bags
20-gallon	
plastic	
a sponge	mop
a string	
a floor	
a push	broom
a kitchen	

Words in Action

1. Name cleaning supplies you use often. What do you use each item for?

2. You need to clean your living room, your bathroom, and your kitchen. Which cleaning items will you use for each room?

Fruits and Nuts

Frutas y Nueces

Words in Context

Grapes are one of the most popular **fruits** in the world. Every day, millions of people enjoy them. Many people also like **apples.** Apples first came from Afghanistan. **Oranges, lemons,** and **limes** are also popular around the world. These fruits came from China.

1
2
3
4
5
11
8
9
10
19
15
16
17
18
23
25
26
27
22
24
30
31
32
33
34

Fruits
Frutas

1 a pear
   una pera
2 a kiwi
   un kiwi
3 an orange
   una naranja
4 a pomegranate
   una granada
5 grapes
   uvas
6 a watermelon
   una sandía
7 a pineapple
   una piña
8 a mango
   un mango
9 a grapefruit
   una toronja
10 an avocado
   un aguacate
11 an apple
   una manzana
12 a cantaloupe
   un melón
13 a coconut
   un coco
14 a lemon
   un limón
15 a plum
   una ciruela
16 an apricot
   un chabacano / un
   albaricoque
17 blueberries
   arándanos
18 a papaya
   una papaya

19 a peach
   un durazno
20 a lime
   una lima agría
21 cherries
   cerezas
22 figs
   higos
23 olives
   aceitunas
24 dates
   dátiles
25 strawberries
   fresas
26 raspberries
   frambuesas
27 raisins
   pasas
28 a tangerine
   una mandarina
29 a banana
   un plátano

Nuts
Nueces

30 pecans
   nueces
   (de pecana)
31 almonds
   almendras
32 pistachios
   pistaches /
   pistachos
33 peanuts
   cacahuates
34 walnuts
   nueces (de nogal)

Word Partnerships

peel	a banana
	an orange
	an apple
crack (open)	a nut
ripe	fruit
juicy	
canned	
dried	
citrus	
tropical	

Words in Action

1. What are your five favorite fruits? Rank them in order. Share your list with your class. Is your list similar to other students' lists?

2. Create a recipe for a delicious fruit drink. Use at least four fruits.

Vegetables
Verduras

Cabbage Slaw Recipe

Cut a head of **cabbage** into thin slices. Then cut a large **cucumber,** a **bell pepper,** a **carrot,** and an **onion** (or three **scallions**) into small pieces. Mix everything together with a little salt. Add a little oil and vinegar and mix everything again.

1	broccoli	10	chickpeas /	18	kidney beans
	brócoli		garbanzo beans		alubias
2	beets		garbanzos	19	a carrot
	remolachas / betabeles	11	a zucchini		una zanahoria
3	asparagus		un calabacín	20	bean sprouts
	espárragos	12	an eggplant		germinado de soya
4	spinach		una berenjena	21	lima beans
	espinaca	13	an artichoke		habas
5	lettuce		una alcachofa	22	a sweet potato
	lechuga	14	celery		camote
6	squash		apio	23	a bell pepper
	calabaza	15	an onion		un pimiento
7	a tomato		una cebolla	24	corn
	un jitomate	16	cauliflower		maíz
8	cabbage		una coliflor	25	a cucumber
	una col	17	a turnip		un pepino
9	pinto beans		un nabo	26	a potato
	frijoles pintos				una papa

Word Partnerships

a head of	cabbage
	cauliflower
	lettuce
an ear of	corn
a spinach	leaf
a lettuce	
fresh	vegetables
frozen	
raw	
organic	

Words in Action

1. Which vegetables do you have in your house right now? Which ones do you eat raw? Which ones have you never eaten?

2. Make two lists: *Vegetables I like* and *Vegetables I don't like*. Compare your lists with a partner.

Meat, Poultry, and Seafood

Carne, Aves y Mariscos

MEAT

Words in Context

Fish and **shellfish** are healthy foods. They contain very little fat. The Koreans and the Japanese eat a lot of **seafood. Clams, oysters, shrimp,** and **tuna** are favorite foods in these countries. However, Americans love **meat.** The average American eats 27 pounds (12.3 kilograms) of **ground beef** a year—mostly in hamburgers.

LAMB

PORK

BEEF

POULTRY

86

SEAFOOD

1 lamb chops
chuletas de cordero

2 leg of lamb
pierna de cordero

3 pork chops
chuletas de cerdo / puerco

4 ham
jamón

5 salami
salami

6 sausages
salchichas

7 pork roast
lomo de puerco

8 ground beef
carne de res molida

9 ribs
costillas

10 steak
bistec

11 roast beef
rosbif

12 liver
hígado

13 veal cutlets
chuletas de ternera

14 lobster
langosta

15 oysters
ostiones / ostras

16 clams
almejas

17 mussels
mejillones

18 crab
cangrejo

19 scallops
vieiras

20 shrimp
camarón

21 filet of sole
filete de lenguado

22 cod
bacalao

23 swordfish
pez espada / dorado

24 salmon
salmón

25 trout
trucha

26 tuna
atún

27 thighs
muslos

28 wings
alas

29 breasts
pechugas

30 turkey
pavo

31 chicken
pollo

32 duck
pato

33 drumsticks / legs
muslos / piernas

SHELLFISH

FISH

Word Partnerships

raw	fish
fresh	
frozen	
grilled	
fatty	meat
lean	
a rare	steak
a medium	
a well-done	

Words in Action

1. Pick your favorite items from the meat, poultry, and seafood sections. Compare your favorites with a partner.

2. Imagine you are having a barbecue. What meat, poultry, and seafood will you buy?

Inside the Refrigerator
En el Refrigerador

Words in Context

Do you want a well-organized **refrigerator**? Here are some suggestions. Keep fruit and vegetables in the drawers. Put **milk, apple juice,** and **orange juice** in the door rack. **Eggs** are safe in the egg container in the door. Always keep raw meat, poultry, and fish on the bottom shelf. **Ice cream** and **frozen vegetables** stay frozen in the freezer.

1 frozen vegetables
   verduras congeladas

2 frozen waffles
   wafles congelados

3 ice cream
   helado

4 ice tray
   charola / molde para hielo

5 soda
   soda / refresco

6 margarine
   margarina

7 mayonnaise
   mayonesa

8 sour cream
   crema agria

9 iced tea
   té helado

10 pickles
   pepinillos

11 tofu
   queso de soya

12 yogurt
   yogurt

13 syrup
   jarabe

14 cream
   crema

15 bottled water
   agua embotellada

16 cake
   pastel

17 jam
   mermelada

18 salad
   ensalada

19 (salad) dressing
   aderezo (para ensalada)

20 bacon
   tocino

21 cold cuts
   carnes frías

22 (cheddar) cheese
   queso (cheddar)

23 butter
   mantequilla

24 (Swiss) cheese
   queso (suizo)

25 eggs
   huevos

26 milk
   leche

27 orange juice
   jugo de naranja

28 apple juice
   jugo de manzana

Word Partnerships

fruit	salad
potato	
pasta	
scrambled	eggs
fried	
hard-boiled	
poached	
mozzarella	cheese
Parmesan	
cottage	

1. Frozen Vegetables
2. Frozen Waffles
3. Real Ice Cream
4.
5. Soda
6. Margarine
7. Mayonnaise
8. Sour Cream
9.
10. Pickles
11. Tofu
12. Yogurt
13. Syrup
14. Cream
15. Spring Water
16.
17. Strawberry Jam
18.
19. Salad Dressing
20. Bacon
21.
22. Cheddar Cheese
23.
24.
25.
26. Milk
27. Orange Juice
28. Apple Juice

Words in Action

1. Think about the foods in the refrigerator. Make three lists: *Very healthy, Less healthy,* and *Not healthy.* Discuss your list with a partner.

2. Plan your dinner tonight using the food in this refrigerator.

Food to Go
Comida para Llevar

Words in Context

Do you eat at the **food court**? Health experts have some advice for you. Don't order a **hot dog** and **french fries.** Order a salad instead. Don't have a **hamburger.** Have **beans** and **rice** instead. And finally, don't order **coffee** or soda. Have water or juice.

1 pizza
pizza

2 lasagna
lasaña

3 spaghetti
espagueti

4 a hamburger
una hamburguesa

5 a bagel
una rosca / una rosquilla

6 fish and chips
pescado con papas fritas

7 french fries
papas a la francesa

8 a hot dog
un hot dog / un perro caliente

9 a baked potato
una papa al horno

10 a sandwich
un sandwich / un emparedado

11 coffee
café

12 tea
té

13 a straw
un popote / una pajilla

14 a muffin
un panquecito / una mantecada

15 a doughnut
una dona

16 ketchup
catsup / salsa de tomate

17 mustard
mostaza

18 chopsticks
palillos

19 rice
   arroz

20 stir-fried vegetables
   verduras salteadas / sofritas

21 chicken teriyaki
   pollo con salsa teriyaki

22 an egg roll
   un rollo primavera

23 sushi
   sushi

24 soy sauce
   salsa de soya

25 a burrito
   un burrito

26 a taco
   un taco

27 salsa
   salsa

28 beans
   frijoles

29 a tortilla
   una tortilla

Words in Action

1. Which take-out foods do you like? Which ones don't you like?

2. Work with a partner. Role-play ordering food at one of the places in the picture.
   - Student A: *Can I help you?*
   - Student B: *Yes, I'd like two egg rolls.*
   - Student A: *Do you want something to drink?*
   - Student B: *Yes. Coffee, please.*

Cooking

Cocinando

Shish Kebab Recipe
Receta de Shish Kebab

1. **Measure** $\frac{1}{4}$ cup of olive oil.
   Mida $\frac{1}{4}$ de taza de aceite de oliva.
2. **Dice** 1 tablespoon of garlic.
   Pique una cucharadita de ajo.
3. **Whisk** the oil and garlic with a little lemon juice.
   Bata el aceite y el ajo con un poco de jugo de limón.
4. **Add** 1 pound of lamb cubes.
   Agregue una libra de carne de cordero en trocitos.
5. **Marinate** overnight in the refrigerator.
   Déjelo marinar toda la noche en el refrigerador.
6. **Grill** the kebabs for 5 minutes on each side.
   Ase a la parrilla los alambres durante 5 minutos por ambos lados.

Breakfast Burrito Recipe
Receta de Burritos para el Desayuno

7. **Scramble** 2 eggs in a bowl.
   Revuelva 2 huevos en un recipiente.
8. **Fry** the eggs.
   Fría los huevos.
9. **Broil** 2 slices of bacon.
   Dore 2 rebanadas de tocino.
10. **Steam** a cup of broccoli.
    Cueza al vapor una taza de brócoli.
11. **Grate** $\frac{1}{4}$ cup of cheese.
    Ralle $\frac{1}{4}$ de taza de queso.
12. **Fold** everything into a tortilla.
    Envuelva todo en una tortilla.
13. **Microwave** for 30 seconds.
    Hornee en microondas durante 30 segundos.

Roast Chicken with Potatoes Recipe
Receta de Pollo Asado con Papas

14. **Season** the chicken with garlic and rosemary.
    Sazone el pollo con ajo y romero.
15. **Roast** at 350°F (175°C). (20 minutes per pound)
    Hornee a 350°F (175°C). (20 minutos por libra)
16. **Baste** frequently with pan juices.
    Bañe frecuentemente con el jugo que suelte.
17. **Boil** the potatoes.
    Cueza las papas.
    ° = degrees
    ° = grados

Pea Soup Recipe
Receta de Sopa de Chícharo

18 **Slice** 1 large onion.
Rebane 1 cebolla grande.

19 **Sauté** the onion in oil.
Saltee / Sofría la cebolla en aceite.

20 **Stir** the onion and 1 pound of split peas into 2 quarts of water.
Revuelva la cebolla y 1 libra de chícharos en mitades en 2 cuartos de galón de agua.

21 **Simmer** for 2 hours.
Cueza a fuego lento durante 2 horas.

22 **Peel** 4 large carrots.
Pele 4 zanahorias grandes.

23 **Chop** the carrots and add to the soup.
Pique las zanahorias y añádaselas a la sopa.

24 **Cook** for 30 minutes more.
Cocine durante 30 minutos más.

25 **Puree** the soup in a blender.
Licue la sopa a punto de puré.

Candy Pecans Recipe
Receta de Dulce de Nueces de Pecana

26 **Grease** a cookie sheet.
Engrase una charola para hornear galletas.

27 **Beat** 1 egg white.
Bata una clara de huevo.

28 **Sift** $^1/_2$ cup of sugar with 2 teaspoons of cinnamon.
Cierna $^1/_2$ taza de azúcar con 2 cucharaditas de canela.

29 **Mix** 3 cups of pecans and the sugar and cinnamon into the egg white.
Mezcle 3 tazas de nueces, el azúcar y la canela con la clara de huevo.

30 **Spread** the mix on a cookie sheet.
Extienda la mezcla sobre la charola para hornear galletas.

31 **Bake** at 250°F (120°C).
Hornee a 250°F (120°C).

Word Partnerships	
bake	bread
	a cake
steam	vegetables
chop	
cook	
peel	potatoes
boil	

Words in Action

1. Which recipe looks the best to you? Why?

2. Write down your favorite recipe. Put your recipe together with your classmates' recipes to make a class cookbook.

Cooking Equipment

Utensilios de Cocina

Words in Context

Every country has its own **cooking equipment.** For example, Italian kitchens usually have a big **pot** for cooking pasta. Many Mexican kitchens have a special **pan** to make tortillas. Asian kitchens often have a **grill** for meat and a special **vegetable steamer.** Many kitchens around the world have a **set of knives,** a **cutting board, measuring cups,** and **measuring spoons.**

1 a cutting board
una tabla para picar

2 a set of knives
un juego de cuchillos

3 a (frying) pan
una sartén (para freír)

4 a grill
una parrilla

5 a pot
una olla

6 a lid
una tapa / tapadera

7 a (kitchen) timer
un cronómetro (de cocina)

8 a food processor
un procesador de alimentos

9 a wooden spoon
una cuchara de madera

10 a saucepan
una cacerola

11 a ladle
un cucharón

12 a mixing bowl
un tazón

13 a grater
un rallador

14 a vegetable peeler
un pelador de verduras

15 a bottle opener
un destapador de botellas

16 a can opener
un abrelatas

17 a (meat) thermometer
un termómetro (para carnes)

18 a strainer
una coladera

Word Partnerships

a cast-iron	pan
an aluminum	pot
a stainless steel	

a bread	knife
a paring	
a carving	
a sharp	
a dull	

19 a (hand) mixer
una batidora (de mano)

20 a whisk
un batidor

21 a cookie sheet
una charola / un molde para horno

22 a rolling pin
un rodillo de amasar

23 measuring cups
tazas medidoras

24 measuring spoons
cucharas medidoras

25 a casserole (dish)
un molde

26 a (vegetable) steamer
una vaporera

27 a colander
un colador / un escurridor

28 a wok
un wok

29 a pie pan
un molde para pay

30 a cake pan
un molde para pastel

31 a spatula
una espátula

Words in Action

1. Which five pieces of cooking equipment do you use most often? What do you use each piece for?

2. What food do you like to cook? What cooking equipment do you need to make it?

Measurements and Containers
Medidas y Recipientes

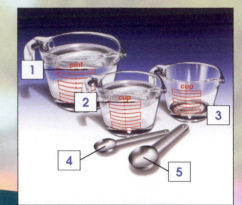

Words in Context

At a farmer's market, you can see a **pile** of ripe tomatoes, smell a warm **loaf** of bread, buy a **jar** of honey, and find a **bunch** of fresh carrots. You can meet the farmers who grow your food and vendors who sell **bars** of homemade soap and **bouquets** of fresh flowers.

Abbreviations

tsp.	=	teaspoon
TBS.	=	tablespoon
c.	=	cup
oz.	=	ounce
qt.	=	quart
pt.	=	pint
gal.	=	gallon
lb.	=	pound
g.	=	gram
kg.	=	kilogram
l.	=	liter

4 qt.	=	1 gal.
3 tsp.	=	1 TBS.
1 qt.	=	.94 l.
1 oz.	=	28 g.
1 lb.	=	.45 kg.

1 a pint
una pinta

2 a cup
una taza

3 an ounce
una onza

4 a teaspoon
una cucharadita

5 a tablespoon
una cucharada

6 a bouquet of flowers
un ramo de flores

7 a bottle of olive oil
una botella de aceite de oliva

8 a bar of soap
una barra de jabón

9 a tube of hand cream
un tubo de crema para las manos

10 a carton of orange juice
un envase de cartón de jugo de naranja

11 a tray of pastries
una charola de pastitas / galletas

12 a pot of coffee
una cafetera

13 a cup of coffee
una taza de café

14 a pitcher of lemonade
una jarra de limonada

15 a piece of cake
una rebanada de pastel

16 a loaf of bread
una barra de pan

17 a liter of water
un litro de agua

18 a quart of milk
un cuarto de galón de leche

19 a pound of cherries
una libra de cerezas

20 a box of strawberries
una canastilla de fresas

21 a gallon of cider
un galón de sidra

22 a bag of potatoes
una arpilla / bolsa de papas

23 a carton of eggs
un cartón de huevos

24 a jar of honey
un frasco de miel

25 a container of yogurt
un bote de yogurt

26 a six-pack of soda
un paquete de seis sodas / refrescos

27 a can of soda
una lata de soda / refresco

28 a pile of tomatoes
una pila / un montón de jitomates

29 a bunch of carrots
un manojo de zanahorias

30 a crate of melons
un guacal / un huacal / una rejilla / una caja de melones

31 a basket of apples
una canasta de manzanas

Word Partnerships

a can of	soup
	tuna
a box of	cereal
	pasta
	cookies
a cup of	tea
	sugar
	flour
a piece of	pie
	bread

Words in Action

1. Imagine you are shopping at a farmer's market. What will you buy? Why?

2. Name five containers you have at home. Tell what is in each container.

Supermarket
Supermercado

Words in Context

The first **supermarket** opened in France in the early 1900s. Before that, people bought **groceries** like **produce, dairy products,** and **canned goods** in small shops and markets. Now there are supermarkets in every country of the world. Besides food, you can find **household cleaners, paper products,** and **pet food** in most supermarkets.

1 produce
   productos agrícolas

2 meats and poultry
   carnes y aves

3 dairy products
   productos lácteos

4 frozen foods
   productos congelados

5 bakery
   panadería / pastelería

6 a deli counter
   la salchichería

7 a scale
   una báscula

8 paper products
   productos de papel

9 household cleaners
   artículos de limpieza para el
   hogar

10 pet food
   alimento / comida para
   mascotas

11 beverages
   bebidas

12 canned goods
   productos enlatados

13 an aisle
   un pasillo

14 a paper bag
   una bolsa de papel

15 a checkout counter
   un mostrador de la caja / una
   caja

16 a cash register
   una caja registradora

17 a shopping cart
   un carrito para compras

18 a bagger
   un cerillo / empacador

19 a barcode scanner
   un escáner de código de
   barras

20 a plastic bag
   una bolsa de plástico

21 a cashier / a checker
   un cajero / una cajera

22 groceries
   abarrotes / víveres y artículos
   comprados

23 a shopper
   un comprador / una
   compradora

24 a shopping basket
   una canasta para compras

Snacks
Bocadillos

25 a candy bar
   una barra de dulce

26 pretzels
   pretzels / galletas saladas en
   forma de moño

27 (potato) chips
   papas fritas

28 popcorn
   palomitas de maíz

BAKERY

DELI

Word Partnerships

the frozen food	aisle
the produce	section
the canned goods	
the bakery	
shop for	groceries
pick up	

Words in Action

1. Where can you find the following items in
   the supermarket: *milk, water, bread, apples,
   paper towels, chicken,* and *ice cream*?
   Work with a partner.
   ▪ *Milk is with the dairy products.*
   ▪ *Water is in the beverages section.*

2. What section do you go to first in a
   supermarket? What do you get there?

Restaurant
Restaurante

Words in Context

The first **restaurant** opened in Paris in 1765. The only thing on the **menu** was soup. There were no **appetizers** and no **desserts.** Restaurants have changed a lot since then. Now you can eat at a Chinese restaurant in Moscow or a Mexican restaurant in Beijing. The biggest restaurant in the world is the Royal Dragon in Bangkok. The dining room seats 5,000 **diners.** The **servers** wear roller skates!

1 a chef
un chef / un jefe de cocina

2 a dishwasher
un lavaplatos

3 an apron
un delantal / un mandil

4 a server / a waitress
una mesera

5 a busser / a busboy
un ayudante de mesero

6 a server / a waiter
un mesero

7 a diner / a customer
un cliente

8 a creamer
una jarrita para crema

9 a vase
un jarrón

10 a sugar bowl
una azucarera

11 a tablecloth
un mantel

12 a saltshaker
un salero

13 a pepper shaker
un pimentero

14 a bowl
un tazón

15 a wine glass
una copa para vino

16 a (water) glass
un vaso (de agua)

17 a high chair
una silla alta para bebés

18 a cup
una taza

19 a saucer
un plato pequeño

20 a menu
un menú

21 a fork
un tenedor

22 a napkin
una servilleta

23 a plate
un plato

24 a knife
un cuchillo

25 a spoon
una cuchara

26 an appetizer
un entremés

27 a main course
un plato principal

28 a dessert
un postre

29 a tray
una charola

30 a salad bar
una barra de ensaladas

31 a check / a bill
una cuenta

Guest Check

TABLE NO.   NO. PERSONS   CHECK NO. 052173   SERVER NO.

1 coffee	$1.75
1 soda	$2.00
1 salad	$4.50
1 dinner special	$9.50

31

TOTAL $17.75

THANK YOU!

Word Partnerships

a steak	knife
a butter	
a salad	fork
a dinner	
a soup	spoon
a dessert	
a serving	
a dinner	plate
a dessert	
a soup	bowl
a salad	

Words in Action

1. Compare your favorite restaurant with this one. How is it the same? How is it different?

2. What is your favorite appetizer? Main course? Dessert?

101

Order, Eat, Pay
Ordene, Coma, Pague

Words in Context

I'm a waiter. I **wait on** lots of customers every night. Some customers are difficult. They **order** things that aren't on the menu. They **spill** their drinks. One customer left and didn't **pay** the check! But most customers are great. Some of them **compliment** me and **leave** a big tip. They're my favorite customers!

1 **make** a reservation
hacer una reservación

2 **pour** water
servir agua

3 **light** a candle
prender una vela

4 **carry** a tray
llevar una charola

5 **set** the table
poner la mesa

6 **wait on** someone
atender / servir una mesa

7 **look at** the menu
ver el menú

8 **butter** the bread
untar mantequilla al pan

9 **spill** a drink
derramar una bebida

10 **order**
ordenar / pedir

11 **take** an order
tomar una orden

12 **drink**
beber

13 **compliment** someone
hacer un cumplido / felicitar

14 **refill** the glass
volver a llenar el vaso

15 **eat**
comer

16 **serve** a meal
servir una comida

17 **ask for** the check
pedir la cuenta

18 **signal** the server
llamar / hacer una seña al mesero / a la mesera

19 **share** a dessert
compartir un postre

20 **offer** a doggie bag
ofrecer una bolsa para las sobras

21 **thank** the server
agradecerle / darle las gracias a la persona que atendió la mesa

22 **wipe** the table
limpiar la mesa

23 **leave** a tip
dejar una propina

24 **pay** the check
pagar la cuenta

25 **clear** the table / **bus** the table
levantar la mesa

Word Partnerships

eat	out
order	breakfast
	lunch
	dinner
	supper
	a meal
	a snack

Words in Action

1. Think about the last time you ate out. Tell your class about five things you did at the restaurant.

2. Work with a partner. Act out a verb from the word list. Your partner will guess what you are doing. Take turns.

Clothes
Ropa

Words in Context

The **clothes** we wear today come from around the world. For example, the **tie** is originally from Croatia. The **poncho** is from South America. The **business suit** originated in France in the 1700s. And a Bavarian immigrant named Levi Strauss made the first **blue jeans** in California in 1873. Now blue jeans are popular around the world.

1 a dress
   un vestido
2 a shirt
   una camisa
3 a sweatshirt
   una sudadera
4 sweatpants
   pants / pantalones deportivos
5 a gown
   un vestido largo
6 a tuxedo
   un esmokin
7 a windbreaker
   un rompevientos
8 shorts
   shorts / pantalones cortos
9 a sari
   un sari
10 a raincoat
   un impermeable

11 a poncho
   un poncho
12 overalls
   overol
13 a uniform
   un uniforme
14 a blouse
   una blusa
15 a skirt
   una falda
16 a jacket
   una chamarra
17 a hat
   un sombrero
18 a scarf
   una bufanda
19 a trench coat
   un impermeable
20 a pullover / a sweater
   un suéter

21 a sports jacket /
   a sports coat
   un saco sport
22 pants / trousers / slacks
   pantalones
23 a shawl
   un chal
24 a maternity dress
   un vestido de maternidad
25 a T-shirt
   una camiseta
26 a vest
   un chaleco
27 (blue) jeans
   unos jeans
28 a tie
   una corbata
29 a (business) suit
   un traje
30 a coat
   un abrigo

Word Partnerships

a leather	jacket
a down	coat
a winter	
a cowboy	hat
a sun	
a straw	
a silk	blouse
	tie

Words in Action

1. Work with a partner. One person says a kind of clothing. The other person points to the clothing in the picture. Take turns.

2. Choose three or four people in your class. Say what each person is wearing.

Sleepwear, Underwear, and Swimwear
Ropa para Dormir, Ropa Interior, y Ropa para Nadar

Words in Context

Socks have a long history. Thousands of years ago, people wore animal skins on their feet. Knit socks appeared in the 3rd century in Egypt. They quickly became popular around the world. **Underwear** has a long history, too. Hundreds of years ago only very rich people wore underwear. However, in the 1700s, cotton became cheap and soon most people began to wear **boxer shorts, briefs,** or **underpants.**

1
2
3
4
5
6
7
8
9
10
11
18
19
20
21
22
23
24
25
26
27
28

1 a clothesline
un tendedero

2 a clothespin
una pinza para tender ropa

3 socks
calcetines

4 tights
mallas

5 pantyhose / nylons
pantimedias

6 stockings
calcetas / medias calcetín

7 a swimsuit /
a bathing suit
un traje de baño

8 a bikini
un bikini

9 (swimming) trunks
traje / shorts de baño

10 flip flops / thongs
sandalias de gallo

11 slippers
pantuflas

12 a nightshirt
un camisón / una camisa de
dormir

13 a (bath)robe
una bata de baño

14 a nightgown
un camisón / una bata
de dormir

15 long underwear
ropa interior de invierno

16 a (blanket) sleeper
un mameluco

17 pajamas
pijama

18 a leotard
un leotardo / unas mallas

19 a bra
un brassiere / un sostén

20 panties / underpants
pantaletas tipo bikini

21 a girdle
una faja

22 a camisole
un corpiño

23 a slip
un fondo

24 an undershirt
una camiseta

25 a tank top
una camiseta sin manga

26 boxer shorts / boxers
boxers / trusas

27 briefs
trusas

28 an athletic supporter /
a jockstrap
un suspensorio

Word Partnerships

a terrycloth	(bath)robe
a silk	
a flannel	
knee	socks
sweat	
ankle	
dress	
a pair of	briefs
	boxer shorts
	socks
	slippers

Words in Action

1. Study the word list for three minutes. Then close your book. Write down as many of the words as you can remember. Write each word under one of these categories: *Sleepwear, Swimwear,* or *Underwear.*

2. Take turns describing an item of sleepwear or swimwear that you own.
   - *I have a blue nightshirt with yellow stars on it.*

107

Shoes and Accessories
Zapatos y Accesorios

Words in Context

Different **shoes** and **accessories** are popular in different cultures. For example, in Guatemala, many women wear **sandals,** long **earrings,** and bright **scarves, necklaces,** and **bracelets.** In India, women often wear a beautiful scarf, called a *dupatta,* and gold **rings.** What kinds of shoes and accessories are popular in your culture?

Word Partnerships

a pair of	shoes
comfortable	shoes
walking	
running	
tennis	
a gold	ring
an engagement	
a wedding	
a diamond	
pierced	earrings
clip-on	
pearl	

1 gloves
guantes

2 a purse /
a handbag
una bolsa / una bolsa de mano

3 mittens
manoplas

4 an umbrella
un paraguas

5 suspenders
tirantes

6 a belt
un cinturón

7 a ring
un anillo

8 a necklace
un collar

9 earrings
aretes

10 a bracelet
una pulsera / un brazalete

11 a (wrist)watch
un reloj de pulsera

12 a pin
un prendedor

13 jewelry
joyería

14 sunglasses
lentes de sol

15 a wallet
una cartera

16 a briefcase
un portafolios

17 a (high) heel
un tacón (alto)

18 a pump
una zapatilla

19 a loafer
un mocasín

20 a clog
un zueco

21 a sandal
una sandalia

22 a sneaker
un tenis / una zapatilla

23 an athletic shoe
un tenis

24 a hiking boot
una bota de excursión

25 a boot
una bota

26 a (knit) hat
un gorro tejido

27 a baseball cap /
a baseball hat
una gorra de béisbol

28 earmuffs
orejeras

29 a key chain
un llavero

Shoes

Words in Action

1. Name a place where you like to go. What shoes and accessories are good to wear to this place?

2. You need to buy three gifts: one for your 80-year-old grandfather, one for your 25-year-old brother, and one for your teenage sister. What shoes or accessories will you buy for each person?

Describing Clothes
Describiendo Ropa

Words in Context

Fashions come and go. For example, sometimes ties are **wide** and sometimes they're **narrow**. The length of **skirts** is always changing too. One year they're **long** and **straight,** and the next year they're **short** and **pleated.** It's hard to keep up with fashion!

1

2

3

4

5

8

9

10

11

12

Word Partnerships

fashionable	clothes
trendy	
designer	
work	
maternity	

7:00
Casual Clothes
24

8:00
Formal Clothes
25

1 a **light** jacket
una chamarra **ligera**

2 a **heavy** jacket
una chamarra **gruesa**

3 a **sleeveless** shirt
una playera **sin manga**

4 a **short-sleeved** shirt
una camisa de **manga corta**

5 a **long-sleeved** shirt
una camisa de **manga larga**

6 a **button-down** shirt
una camisa de **vestir**

7 a **polo** shirt
una playera **tipo polo**

8 a **wide** tie
una corbata **ancha**

9 a **narrow** tie
una corbata **angosta**

10 **flared** jeans
jeans / pantalones de **mezclilla acampanados**

11 **straight leg** jeans
jeans / pantalones de **mezclilla rectos**

12 **baggy** pants /
loose pants
pantalones **holgados**

13 a **V-neck** sweater
un suéter con **cuello V**

14 a **crew neck** sweater
un suéter de **cuello redondo**

15 a **cardigan** sweater
un suéter **abierto**

16 a **turtleneck** sweater
un suéter de **cuello de tortuga**

17 a **tight** skirt
una falda **ajustada**

18 a **straight** skirt
una falda **recta**

19 a **pleated** skirt
una falda **plegada**

20 a **short** skirt
una falda **corta**

21 a **long** skirt
una falda **larga**

22 **high** heels
tacones **altos**

23 **low** heels
tacones **bajos**

24 **informal** clothes /
casual clothes
ropa **informal** / ropa **casual**

25 **formal** clothes /
dress clothes
ropa **formal** / ropa **de vestir**

Words in Action

1. Describe the clothes you and other people in class are wearing.

2. Which items of clothing in the picture are in fashion? Are any of the clothes not in fashion?

Fabrics and Patterns
Telas y Estampados

1

Words in Context

Fabrics can be natural or man-made. **Linen, cotton,** and **silk** are natural fabrics. Linen and cotton come from plants. Silk comes from silk worms. Polyester is a man-made fabric. It is made from chemicals. It is now the most common fabric in the world.

2

3

4

6

7

10

Word Partnerships

a wool	jacket
	sweater
	coat
	scarf
a silk	tie
	robe
	dress

11

112

Fabrics
Telas

1 cotton
  algodón
2 corduroy
  pana
3 velvet
  terciopelo
4 silk
  seda
5 leather
  piel
6 denim
  mezclilla
7 linen
  lino
8 suede
  ante
9 cashmere
  cachemira / casimir
10 nylon
  nylon
11 lace
  encaje
12 wool
  lana

Patterns
Estampados

13 solid
  liso / de un solo color
14 print
  estampado
15 polka dot
  de lunares
16 floral
  de flores / floreado

17 paisley
  paisley
18 checked
  a cuadros
19 plaid
  tartán / escocés
20 striped
  a rayas
21 embroidered
  bordado

5

8

9

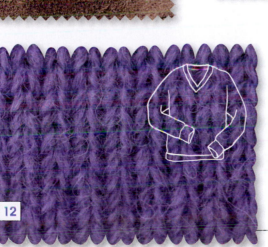

12

Words in Action

1. Work with a partner. Describe your partner's clothes.
   - *You're wearing brown corduroy pants and a blue and white striped cotton shirt.*

2. Design an outfit. Decide on the fabrics and patterns. Draw the outfit and describe it to your class.

Buying, Wearing, and Caring for Clothes

Compra, Uso y Cuidado de la Ropa

Words in Context

Different clothes have different care instructions. Jeans are easy. You can **wash** them in the washing machine and then **dry** them in the dryer. However, a wool shirt needs special care. You shouldn't wash a wool shirt. Instead, you should **dry clean** it. To prevent wrinkles, always **hang up** clothes.

1 go shopping
ir de compras

2 look for a jacket
buscar una chamarra

3 go into a dressing room
entrar al probador

4 try on
probarse

5 buy
comprar

6 take home
llevar a casa

7 cut off
quitar

8 put on
ponerse

9 zip
subir el cierre

10 button
abotonar

11 buckle
abrochar

12 roll up
arremangar / arremangarse

13 wear
usar

14 unbutton
desabotonar

15 unzip
bajar el cierre

16 unbuckle
desabrochar

17 take off
quitarse

18 wash
lavar

19 dry
secar

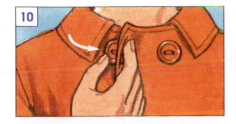

10

11

12

13

14

15

16

17

18

19

20

21

22

23

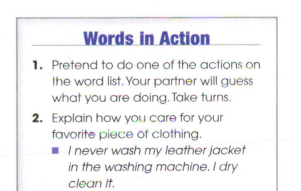

24

20 dry clean
   lavar en seco
21 mend / repair
   zurcir / reparar
22 sew on
   coser
23 iron / press
   planchar
24 hang (up)
   colgar

Word Partnerships

hang it	on a hook
	on a hanger
	in the closet
wash it	in cold water
	in hot water
	by hand
zip	up
button	

Words in Action

1. Pretend to do one of the actions on the word list. Your partner will guess what you are doing. Take turns.

2. Explain how you care for your favorite piece of clothing.
   - *I never wash my leather jacket in the washing machine. I dry clean it.*

Sewing and Laundry
Costura y Lavandería

Words in Context

Fashion designer Josie Natori comes from the Philippines. She sells her clothes all over the world. Her company started very small. At first, Natori worked alone in her living room with a **sewing machine, pins, needles, buttons, thread,** and **scissors.** Now her company has offices in Manila, Paris, and New York.

1 an **ironing board**
una **mesa** / un **burro para planchar**

2 an **iron**
una **plancha**

3 **fabric softener**
suavizante de telas

4 **(laundry) detergent**
detergente (para ropa)

5 **bleach**
blanqueador

6 a **dryer**
una secadora

7 a **washer** / a **washing machine**
una lavadora

8 **wet clothes**
ropa húmeda / mojada

9 **dry clothes**
ropa seca

10 a **laundry basket**
una canasta de lavandería

11 a hanger
un gancho para ropa

12 a collar
un cuello

13 a pocket
una bolsa

14 a buttonhole
un ojal

15 a button
un botón

16 a sleeve
una manga

17 a cuff
un puño

18 a hem
una bastilla / un
dobladillo sastre

19 a tailor
un sastre

20 a sewing machine
una máquina de
coser

21 a pin
un alfiler

22 a pincushion
un alfiletero

23 a (pair of) scissors
unas tijeras

24 a zipper
un cierre

25 a seam
una costura

26 a thimble
un dedal

27 thread
hilo

28 a tape measure
una cinta de medir /
métrica

29 a needle
una aguja

30 a safety pin
un seguro / un alfiler
de seguridad

Word Partnerships

a wire	hanger
a plastic	
a shirt	pocket
a pants	
a jacket	
long	sleeves
short	

Words in Action

1. Find the following things on your classmates' clothes: *a buttonhole, a collar, a cuff, a pocket, a sleeve, a hem.*

2. Which of the items in the picture do you have in your home?

117

Vehicles and Traffic Signs
Vehículos y Señales de Tráfico

Words in Context

Do you need a new car or truck? There is a lot to think about. Do you have children? A **compact car** may be too small. People with children often drive large **vehicles** like **station wagons, sedans,** and **SUVs.** Do you like to camp? An **RV** may be good for you. Do you like adventure? You might like a **motorcycle.** Do you often need to move large things? You may want a **pickup truck.** There are so many vehicles to choose from!

1
ONE WAY

2 STOP

3 H

4 DO NOT PASS

5 DO NOT ENTER

6

7 R R

8

9

10 YIELD

11

Signs
Señales

1 one way
un sentido / una vía

2 stop
alto

3 hospital
hospital

4 do not pass
prohibido el paso

5 do not enter
no entrar

6 no left turn
prohibida vuelta a la izquierda

7 railroad crossing
cruce de ferrocarril

8 school zone
zona escolar

9 pedestrian crossing
cruce de peatones

10 yield
ceda el paso

11 no U-turn
prohibida la vuelta en U

Vehicles
Vehículos

12 a school bus
un camión escolar

13 a tow truck
una grúa

14 a garbage truck
un camión de basura

15 a pickup (truck)
una camioneta de cárga / una pick up

16 an RV
una casa remolque / un vehículo de recreación

17 a minivan
una camioneta de pasajeros

18 a limousine / a limo
una limusina

19 a sedan
un sedán

20 a van
una camioneta

21 a dump truck
un camión de volteo / un volquete

22 an SUV
una camioneta

23 a trailer
un remolque

24 a sports car
un carro deportivo / un coche deportivo

25 a semi / a tractor trailer
un tráiler

26 a police car
una patrulla de policía

27 an ambulance
una ambulancia

28 a fire engine
un camión de bomberos

29 a station wagon
una camioneta / una furgoneta

30 a compact (car)
un carro compacto / un coche compacto

31 a convertible
un convertible

32 a motorcycle
una motocicleta

Word Partnerships

drive	a convertible
	a truck
	an SUV
ride	a motorcycle
ride in	a limousine
ride on	a bus

Words in Action

1. Work with a partner. Make a list of the five largest vehicles in the word list. Make another list of the five smallest vehicles.

2. Imagine you have enough money to buy a new vehicle. What vehicle will you buy? Explain your choice to the class.

Parts of a Car
Partes de un Coche / Carro

1

2

3

4

5

6

7

GGGRJ22

8

9

10

11

14

15

16

13

17

18

19

20

12

21

22

23

24

25

26

27

28

1 a child car seat
un asiento de coche / carro para niño

2 a jack
un gato

3 a trunk
una cajuela

4 a tire
una llanta

5 a taillight
un faro trasero

6 a brake light
un faro de frenos

7 a gas tank
un tanque de gasolina

8 a license plate
una placa

9 a bumper
una defensa

10 an air bag
una bolsa de aire

11 a rearview mirror
un espejo retrovisor

12 a seat belt
un cinturón de seguridad

13 an oil gauge
un marcador / indicador del nivel de aceite

14 a speedometer
un velocímetro

15 a gas gauge
un marcador / indicador del nivel de gasolina

16 a dashboard
un tablero

17 a radio
un radio

18 a glove compartment
una guantera

19 air conditioning
aire acondicionado / acondicionador de aire

20 heater
calentador

21 a horn
un claxon

22 an ignition
un encendido

23 a gearshift
una palanca de velocidades

24 a steering wheel
un volante

25 a clutch
un clutch / un embrague

26 a brake pedal
un pedal de freno

27 an accelerator / a gas pedal
un acelerador

28 an emergency brake
un freno de mano

29 a windshield wiper
un limpiador de parabrisas

30 a hood
un cofre

31 a fender
una salpicadera

32 an engine / a motor
un motor

33 a battery
una batería

34 jumper cables
cables de transmisión de corriente

35 a radiator
un radiador

36 a turn signal
una direccional

37 a headlight
un faro delantero

Word Partnerships

open	the hood
close	the trunk
check	the battery
	the rearview mirror
a spare	tire
a flat	

Words in Action

1. Study the word list for three minutes. Then close your book. Write down as many of the words as you can remember. Write each word under one of these categories: *Inside the car, Outside the car,* and *Under the hood.* Compare your lists with a partner.

2. Draw a car. Label as many parts of the car as you can, without looking at the word list.

Road Trip
Viaje Por Carretera

Words in Context

Here are some tips for a good **road trip.** Before you **leave,** make sure your car is running well. **Get** gas, **check** the oil, and **put** air in your tires. Take plenty of coins to **pay** tolls. Once you are on the road, **turn on** your headlights. Finally, make sure you **get off** the highway for a short break every two or three hours.

24

Toll $1.00

23

WELCOME TO YELLOWSTONE NATIONAL PARK

22

5

6

21

7

Turn On Headlights

13

4

Route 66?

8

SLOW

12

Highway Entrance

3

9

EXIT

2

11

1

10

STOP

1 **pack**
empacar

2 **leave**
salir

3 **drive**
manejar

4 **ask for** directions
pedir información (sobre cómo llegar a un lugar)

5 **speed up**
acelerar

6 **get** a speeding ticket
recibir una multa por exceso de velocidad

7 **turn on** the headlights
encender las luces delanteras

8 **slow down**
reducir la velocidad

9 **get off** the highway
salirse de la autopista

10 **stop**
pararse / detenerse

11 **look at** a map
ver un mapa

12 **get on** the highway
tomar la autopista

13 **pass** a truck
rebasar un camión

14 **honk** (the horn)
tocar el claxon

15 **get** gas
poner gasolina

16 **check** the oil
verificar el aceite

17 **wash** the windshield
lavar el parabrisas

18 **put** air in the tires
poner aire a las llantas

19 **have** an accident
tener un accidente

20 **pull over**
hacerse a un lado / detenerse

21 **have** a flat (tire)
poncharse una llanta

22 **change** the tire
cambiar la llanta

23 **pay** a toll
pagar peaje

24 **arrive at** the destination
llegar al destino

25 **park** (the car)
estacionar (el coche / el carro)

Word Partnerships

pack	a suitcase
	a bag
stop	at a red light
	for gas
turn on	the windshield wipers
	the radio
	the air conditioning

Words in Action

1. Work with a partner. Act out a verb on the list. Your partner will guess the verb. Take turns.

2. Plan your "dream" road trip. Where will you go? What will you do on the trip?

Airport
Aeropuerto

Words in Context

Air travel is changing. **Airports** now have **automated check-in machines**. A **passenger** can quickly check in, choose a **seat,** and get a **boarding pass.** In the future, some **airplanes** will be bigger and some will fly much faster.

Airport
Aeropuerto

1 a terminal
una terminal

2 a ticket
un boleto

3 a photo ID
una identificación con fotografía

4 a ticket counter /
a check-in counter
un mostrador para registro

5 baggage / luggage
equipaje

6 a passenger
un pasajero / una pasajera

7 an automated
check-in machine
una máquina automática para registro

8 a boarding pass
un pase de abordar

TICKETS

AUTOMATED CHECK-IN

AIRLINE TICKET

LOCAL TIME

ARRIVALS
DEPARTURES

CUSTOMS

BAGGAGE CLAIM

FLIGHT 51455

CUSTOMS

9 a metal detector
un detector de metales

10 a security checkpoint
un punto de control / revisión (de seguridad)

11 arrival and departure monitors
monitores de llegadas y salidas

12 a helicopter
un helicóptero

13 a runway
una pista

14 a gate
una puerta

15 a pilot
un piloto

16 a carry-on bag
una bolsa / un maletín de mano

17 customs
aduana

18 a customs (declaration) form
una forma de declaración de aduana

19 the baggage claim (area)
una reclamación de equipaje / área de reclamaciones de equipaje

20 immigration
inmigración

21 a line
una fila / una cola

Airplane / Plane
Avión

22 first class
primera clase

23 economy (class) / coach (class)
clase turista

24 an overhead compartment
un compartimiento arriba de la cabeza

25 an emergency exit
una salida de emergencia

26 a flight attendant
un aeromozo / una aeromoza

27 a seat
un asiento

28 a seat belt
un cinturón de seguridad

29 an aisle
un pasillo

Word Partnerships

an aisle	seat
a middle / a center	
a window	
an electronic / an e-	ticket
a paper	
an arrival	terminal
a departure	
an international	

Words in Action

1. Work with a partner. One person says an airport or airplane word. The other points to the item in the picture. Take turns.

2. Make three lists: *people you see at an airport, areas you see at an airport,* and *things you see at an airport.*

Taking a Flight
Al Tomar un Vuelo

Words in Context

Air Travel Tips

- **Check in** early.
- When you **board** the plane, **stow** your carry-on bag.
- Drink plenty of water.
- **Stretch** often.
- **Ask for** a pillow. Put your seat back, and try to sleep as much as possible.

1 check in
  registrarse

2 show your ID
  presentar su identificación

3 check your baggage
  registrar su equipaje

4 get your boarding pass
  conseguir su pase de abordar

5 go through security
  pasar por seguridad

6 check the monitors
  verificar los monitores

7 wait at the gate
  esperar en la puerta

8 board the plane
  abordar el avión

9 find your seat
  localizar su asiento

10 stow your carry-on bag
  acomodar su bolsa de mano /
  acomodar su maletín de mano

11 turn off your cell phone
  apagar su teléfono celular /
  apagar su celular

12 fasten your seat belt
  abrochar su cinturón de
  seguridad

13 take off
  despegar

14 ask for a pillow
  pedir una almohada

15 turn on the overhead light
  encender la lámpara para
  iluminación individual

16 put on your headphones
  ponerse sus audífonos

17 listen to music
  escuchar música

18 put your tray table down
  bajar la mesa de servicio

19 stretch
  estirarse

20 choose a meal
  escoger una comida

21 land
  aterrizar

22 unfasten your seat belt
  desabrocharse su cinturón de
  seguridad

23 get off the plane
  bajarse del avión

24 claim your bags
  recoger el equipaje

Pillow, please.

Word Partnerships

wait	for a boarding call
	in line
go through	a metal detector
	customs
	immigration

Words in Action

1. Work with a partner. Pretend to do one of the actions on the word list. Your partner will guess what action you are doing. Take turns.
2. Make a list of things you can do on a plane to be safe. Make another list of things you can do to be comfortable.

127

Public Transportation

Transporte Público

Words in Context

There are three ways to get from JFK Airport in New York to Manhattan. The first way is by **cab.** You can get a cab at the **taxi stand.** The **fare** is about $35.00. The second way is by **bus.** You can catch a bus from the **bus stop** outside the airport. The **ticket** is about $13.00. The bus will take you to a Manhattan **train station** or hotel. The third way is by **subway.** Go to the JFK Airport **subway station.** The subway will take you into Manhattan. This is the cheapest way. It costs only $2.00.

1 a taxi stand
una terminal / una base de taxis

2 a meter
un taxímetro

3 the fare
la tarifa

4 a taxi / a cab
un taxi / un carro / una coche de alquiler

5 a taxi driver / a cab driver
un chofer de taxi / una taxista

6 a passenger
un pasajero / una pasajera

7 a bus stop
una parada de autobús

8 a bus driver
un conductor / una conductora de autobús

9 a bus
un autobús

10 a ticket window
una taquilla

11 a ticket
un boleto

12 a train
un tren

13 a conductor
un conductor / una conductora

14 a track
un riel / una vía

15 a strap
un tirante

16 a (subway) line
una ruta / un línea de metro

17 a ferry
un transbordador

18 a subway (train)
un metro

19 a platform
un andén

20 a token
una ficha

21 a fare card
una tarjeta de pasaje

22 a schedule
un horario

23 a turnstile
un torniquete

TICKETS

East River Ferry

TO TRAIN AND SUBWAY

BUS STOP

7

8

9

MTA New York City Bus 827

Word Partnerships

a bus	station
a train	
a subway	
take	a taxi / a cab
	a ferry
	a train
	a bus
catch	a train
miss	a bus

12

13

TRAIN SCHEDULE

22

TOKENS AND
FARE CARDS
HERE

MTA MetroCard

20   21

23

19

Words in Action

1. What kind of public transportation do you use? Where do you get on? What is the fare?

2. One student names a form of public transportation. Other students make up sentences about that form of transportation in your town or city.
   - Student A: *the subway*
   - Student B: *You need a fare card.*
   - Student C: *There's a subway station a block from the school.*

129

Up, Over, Around
Arriba, Sobre, Alrededor

Words in Context

Roller coaster rides are exciting. You go **up** a track very, very slowly. Then suddenly you go **over** the top and race **down** the track. Most roller coaster rides go **around** several sharp curves. Some even go **upside down.** But when the ride is over, people often want to do it again!

1 straight
derecho

2 past the house
más allá de la casa

3 into the tunnel
en el túnel / dentro del túnel

4 through the tunnel
a través del túnel

5 out of the tunnel
fuera del túnel

6 behind the building
detrás del edificio

7 toward the rocks
hacia las rocas

8 between the flags
entre las banderas

9 around the trees
alrededor de los árboles

10 up
arriba

11 down
abajo

12 upside down
al revés

13 under the waterfall
debajo de la cascada

14 over the water
sobre el agua

15 left
izquierda / izquierdo

16 right
derecha / derecho

17 across the river
a través del río / al otro lado del río

18 along the river
por el río / a lo largo del río

19 north
norte

20 east
este

21 south
sur

22 west
oeste

Word Partnerships

go	through
	straight
	across
turn	left
make a	right
take a	

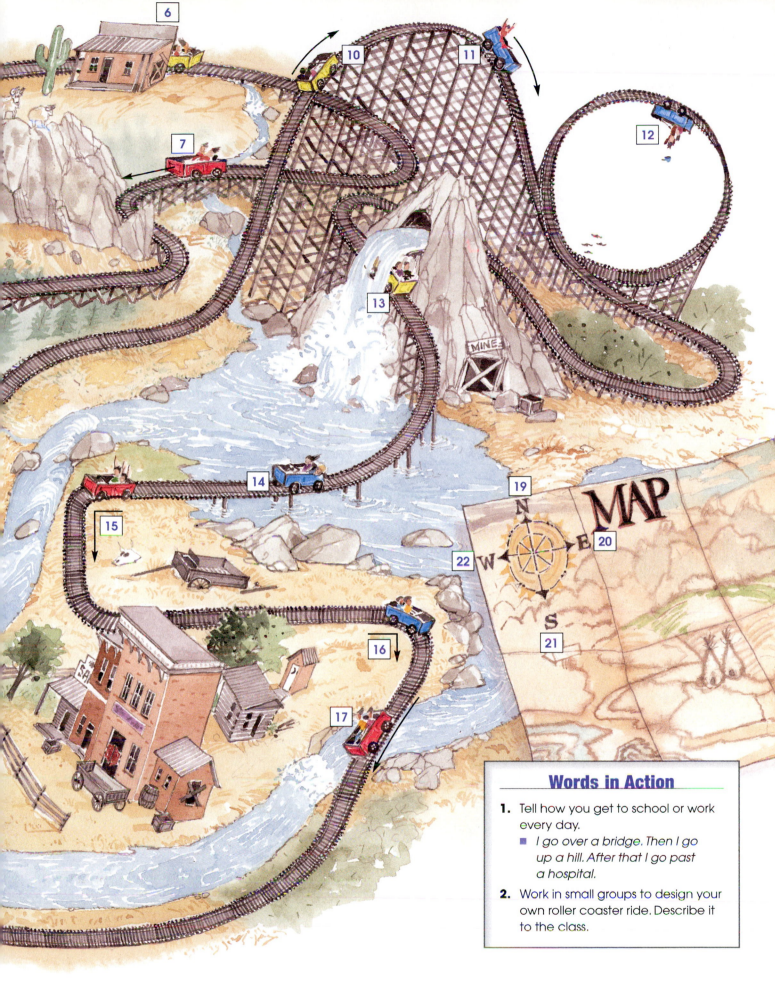

Words in Action

1. Tell how you get to school or work every day.
   - *I go over a bridge. Then I go up a hill. After that I go past a hospital.*

2. Work in small groups to design your own roller coaster ride. Describe it to the class.

The Human Body

El Cuerpo Humano

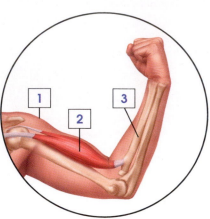

Words in Context

Always prepare for exercise. A ten-minute warm-up will stretch your **muscles** and get your **body** ready. Roll your **head** around in a circle. Move your **shoulders** up and down. Stretch your **arms** out and swing them in a circle. Bend your **knees,** and then stretch out your **legs.** Now you are ready to exercise.

Word Partnerships

ring	finger
index	
pinky	

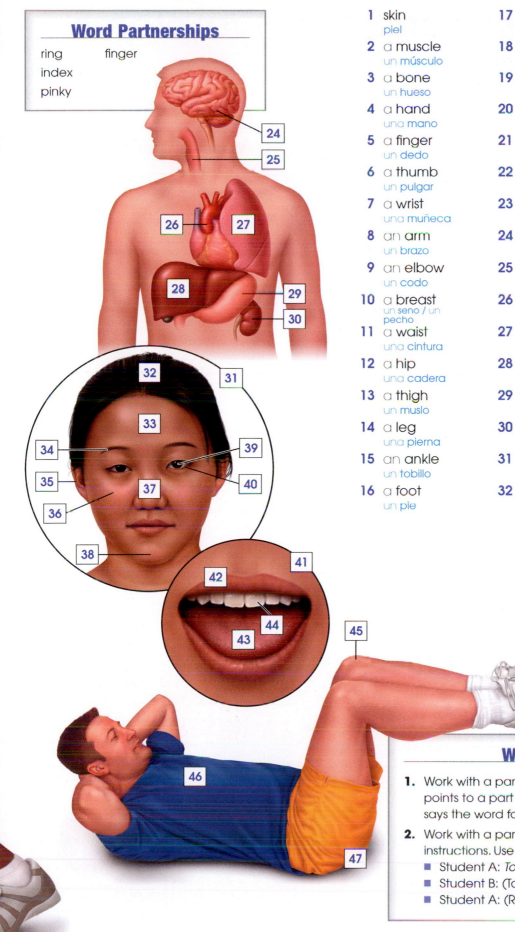

1 skin
piel

2 a muscle
un músculo

3 a bone
un hueso

4 a hand
una mano

5 a finger
un dedo

6 a thumb
un pulgar

7 a wrist
una muñeca

8 an arm
un brazo

9 an elbow
un codo

10 a breast
un seno / un pecho

11 a waist
una cintura

12 a hip
una cadera

13 a thigh
un muslo

14 a leg
una pierna

15 an ankle
un tobillo

16 a foot
un pie

17 a heel
un talón

18 a toe
un dedo del pie

19 a head
una cabeza

20 a neck
un cuello

21 a shoulder
un hombro

22 a back
una espalda

23 a (finger)nail
una uña (del dedo)

24 a brain
un cerebro

25 a throat
una garganta

26 a heart
un corazón

27 a lung
un pulmón

28 a liver
un hígado

29 a stomach
un estómago

30 a kidney
un riñón

31 a face
una cara

32 hair
pelo / cabello

33 a forehead
una frente

34 an eyebrow
una ceja

35 an ear
una oreja

36 a cheek
una mejilla

37 a nose
una nariz

38 a chin
una barbilla / un mentón

39 an eye
un ojo

40 eyelashes
pestañas

41 a mouth
una boca

42 a lip
un labio

43 a tongue
una lengua

44 a tooth
un diente

45 a knee
una rodilla

46 a chest
un pecho / un tórax

47 buttocks
nalgas / glúteos

Words in Action

1. Work with a partner. Cover the word list. One person points to a part of the body in the picture. The other says the word for the part. Take turns.

2. Work with a partner. Take turns giving and following instructions. Use words from the word list.
- Student A: *Touch your head.*
- Student B: (Touches her head.) *Raise your hand.*
- Student A: (Raises her hand.)

Illnesses, Injuries, Symptoms, and Disabilities

Enfermedades, Lesiones, Síntomas y Discapacidades

Words in Context

There are many reasons people visit the doctor's office. In winter, many people get a **sore throat,** a **cough,** or the **flu.** In summer, bad **sunburns** are common. **Earaches, stomachaches,** and **backaches** are common problems all year round.

Word Partnerships

a head	cold
a bad	
catch	a cold
have	a cold
	the flu
	a sore throat
feel	dizzy
	nauseous

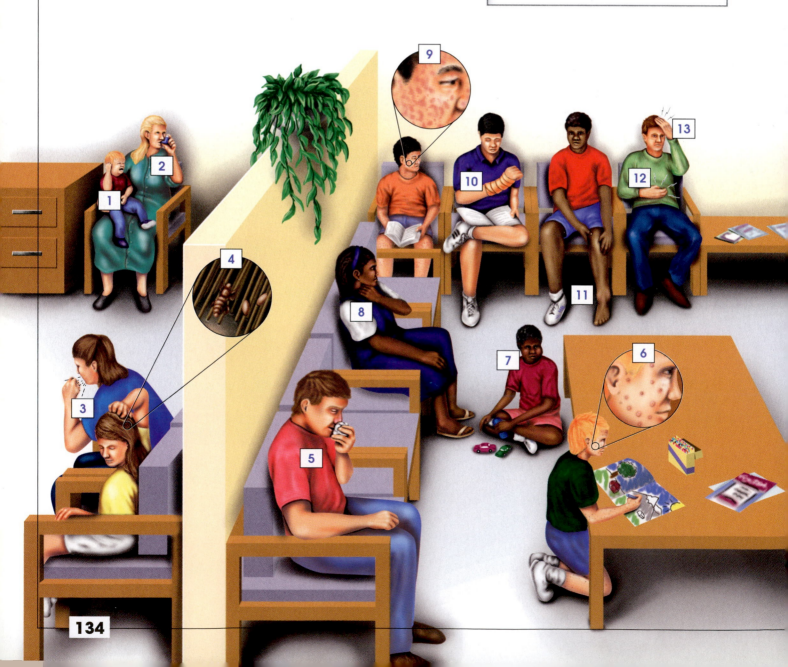

1 an **earache**
un dolor de oído

2 **asthma**
asma

3 a **cough**
tos

4 **lice**
piojos

5 a **cold**
un resfriado / un catarro

6 **chicken pox**
varicela

7 **mumps**
paperas

8 a **sore throat**
tener la garganta irritada

9 **measles**
sarampión

10 a **sprained wrist**
una muñeca torcida

11 a **swollen ankle**
un tobillo inflamado

12 a **stomachache**
un dolor de estómago

13 a **headache**
un dolor de cabeza

14 the **flu**
una gripe / una gripa

15 a **fever** /
a **temperature**
fiebre / temperatura

16 **arthritis**
artritis

17 a **backache**
un dolor de espalda

18 **blind**
ciego / ciega

19 **nauseous**
tener náusea

20 **dizzy**
estar mareado / estar mareada

21 **deaf**
sordo / sorda

22 **acne**
acné

23 a **cut**
una cortada

24 a **burn**
una quemada

25 a **blister**
una ampolla

26 a **rash**
un sarpullido / un salpullido / una erupción

27 a **sunburn**
una quemadura de sol

28 a **bee sting**
una picadura de abeja

29 a **bloody nose**
una hemorragia nasal

30 a **bruise**
una contusión / un moretón

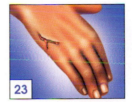

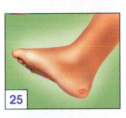

Words in Action

1. Which of the illnesses on the list can you catch from another person?

2. Make a list of three items on the list that are injuries and three that are illnesses.

Dr. Cho
Dr. Weiss
Dr. Aziz

Hurting and Healing
Lesiones y Curaciones

Words in Context

Are you **coughing** and **sneezing**? You probably have a cold. **Drink** plenty of fluids and **rest** as much as possible. Do you feel hot? **Take** your temperature. You might have the flu. **Make** an appointment with your doctor. He will **examine** you. You may need to **take** pills or get a shot. Follow your doctor's instructions. You will soon **feel** better.

1 **be** in pain
tener un dolor

2 **be** unconscious
estar inconsciente

3 **bleed**
sangrar

4 **be** in shock
estar en shock / conmoción

5 **break** a leg
romperse una pierna

6 **burn** yourself
quemarse

7 **choke**
atragantarse / asfixiarse

8 **cut** yourself
cortarse

9 **drown**
ahogarse

10 **swallow** poison
ingerir veneno

11 **overdose** (on drugs)
sobredosis (de drogas)

12 **have** an allergic reaction
tener una reacción alérgica

13 **have** a heart attack
tener un ataque cardiaco / cardíaco

14 **get** a(n electric) shock
tener un electrochoque

15 **fall**
caerse

Word Partnerships

be	injured	
	hurt	
feel	much	better
	a little	

136

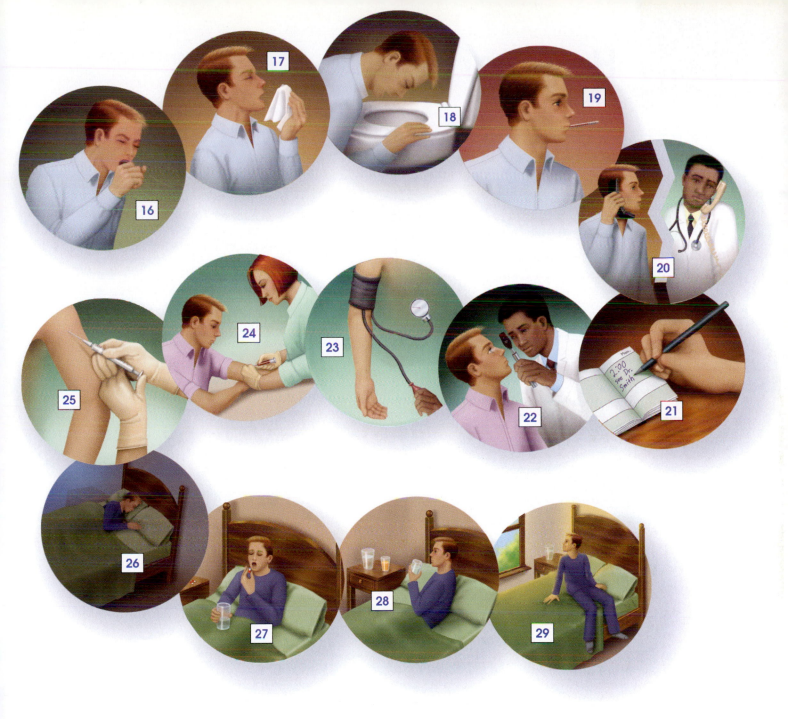

16 **cough**
toser

17 **sneeze**
estornudar

18 **vomit / throw up**
vomitar

19 **take** your temperature
tomarse la temperatura

20 **call** the doctor
llamar al doctor

21 **make** an appointment
hacer una cita

22 **examine** the patient
examinar al paciente

23 **check** his blood pressure
tomar / medir la
presión sanguínea

24 **draw** his blood
sacarle sangre

25 **give** him a shot
ponerle una inyección

26 **rest**
descansar

27 **take** a pill
tomar una pastilla / píldora

28 **drink** fluids
beber líquidos

29 **feel** better
sentirse mejor

Words in Action

1. Look at page 136. Which things on the list are more likely to happen to adults? Which are more likely to happen to children?

2. Work with a partner. One person pretends to have one of the medical problems on the list. The other guesses the problem. Take turns.

137

Hospital

Hospital

Words in Context

Here are some things to look for in a **hospital**:

- Are the **doctors** and **nurses** friendly and helpful?
- Are there plenty of nurses at each **nurses' station**?
- Are the **patients** happy with the hospital?

1 a nurses' station
una central de enfermeros

2 a nurse
un enfermero / una enfermera

3 an intensive care unit
una unidad de cuidado
intensivo

4 an IV / an intravenous drip
un goteo intravenoso

5 an operating room
una sala de operaciones

6 an X-ray
una radiografía

7 an anesthesiologist
un / una anestesista

8 an operating table
una mesa de operaciones

9 blood
sangre

10 a surgeon
un cirujano / una cirujana

11 an operation
una operación

12 latex gloves
guantes de látex

13 a (surgical) mask
una mascarilla quirúrgica

14 a lab / a laboratory
un laboratorio

15 a lab technician
un / una laboratorista, un técnico /
una técnica de laboratorio

16 a doctor
un doctor / una doctora

17 a visitor
un / una visitante

18 a patient
un / una paciente

19 a bedpan
un cómodo / un orinal

20 a hospital gown
una bata de hospital

21 a call button
un timbre

22 an orderly
un / una auxiliar de enfermero /
enfermera

23 a wheelchair
una silla de ruedas

24 CPR / cardiopulmonary
resuscitation
resucitación cardiopulmonar

25 an emergency room
una sala de emergencia

26 a paramedic / an EMT
un / una paramédico

27 a stretcher
una camilla

28 stitches
puntadas / puntos

29 an ambulance
una ambulancia

Word Partnerships

an in-	patient
an out-	
a blood	test
	type
	donor
give	blood
donate	

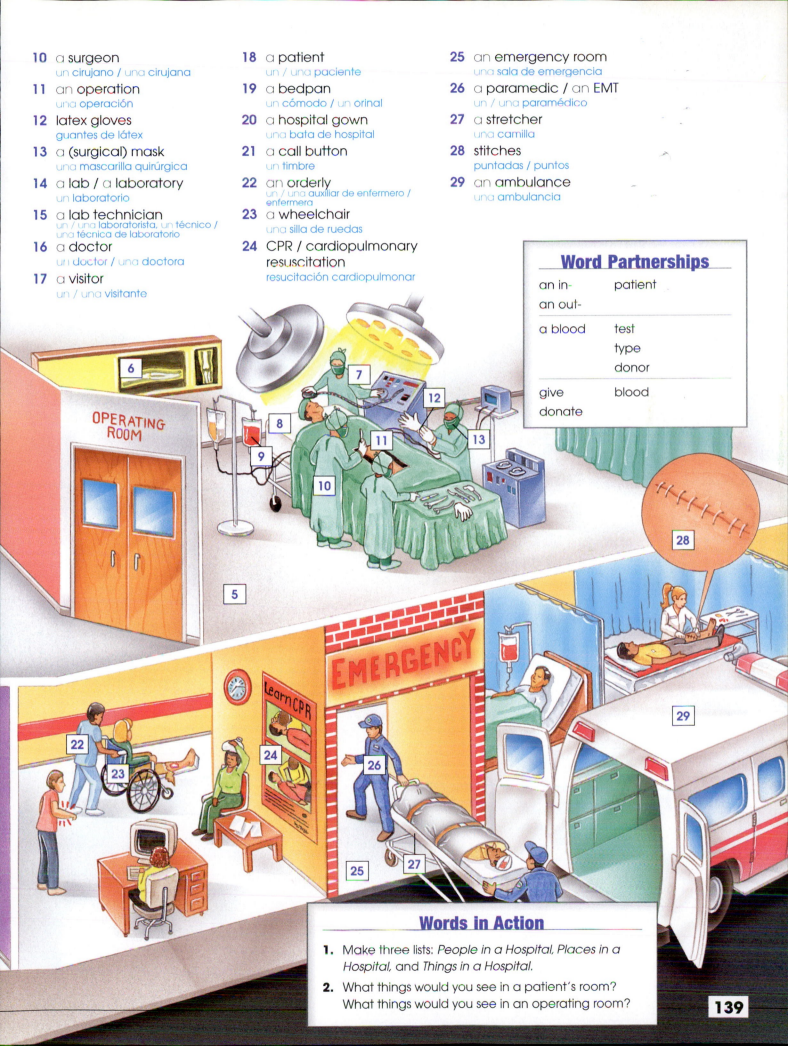

OPERATING ROOM

EMERGENCY

LearnCPR

Words in Action

1. Make three lists: *People in a Hospital, Places in a Hospital,* and *Things in a Hospital.*

2. What things would you see in a patient's room? What things would you see in an operating room?

Medical Center
Centro Médico

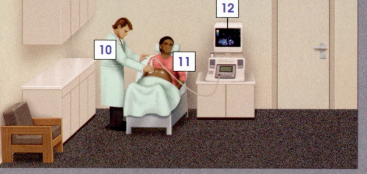

1

2

Words in Context

During a **physical,** a doctor does several tests. She listens to the patient's heart and lungs with a **stethoscope.** She checks the patient's blood pressure with a **blood pressure monitor.** For patients over 40, the doctor may also give the patient an **EKG.**

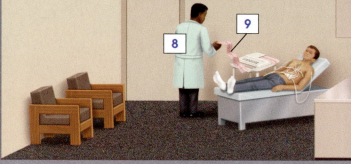

3

4

5

8

9

10

11

12

18

19

20

21

22

23

24

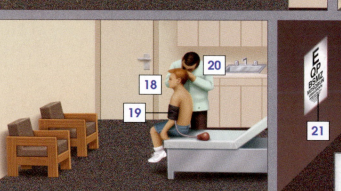

Word Partnerships

hard	contacts / contact lenses
soft	
disposable	
a leg	cast
an arm	
an annual	physical
a dental	checkup

1 a stethoscope
un estetoscopio

2 a medical chart
un expediente médico

3 acupuncture
acupuntura

4 an acupuncturist
un(a) acupuntor(a)

5 a psychologist
un psicólogo / una psicóloga

6 a waiting room
una sala de espera

7 a pediatrician
un / una pediatra

8 a cardiologist
un cardiólogo / una cardióloga

9 an EKG /
an electrocardiogram
un electrocardiograma

10 an obstetrician
un / una obstetra

11 a pregnant woman
una mujer embarazada

12 a sonogram /
an ultrasound
un sonograma / un ultrasonido

13 a sling
un cabestrillo

14 a crutch
una muleta

15 a cast
un vendaje enyesado / un yeso

16 a receptionist
un / una recepcionista

17 an orthopedist
un / una ortopedista

18 a physical (exam) /
a checkup
un examen / un chequeo médico

19 a blood pressure monitor
un monitor de presión arterial / presión sanguínea

20 a GP /
a general practitioner
un médico general

21 an eye chart
un optotipo

22 a contact (lens)
un lente de contacto

23 an optometrist
un / una optometrista

24 (eye)glasses
lentes (para los ojos) / anteojos

25 a (dental) hygienist
un / una higienista dental

26 a dentist
un / una dentista

27 a filling
un empaste / una amalgama

28 a tooth
un diente

29 braces
frenos

30 gums
encías

31 a drill
una fresa

32 a cavity
una caries

Words in Action

1. Work with a partner. Cover the word list. One person points to a person or object in the picture. The other says the word for the person or object. Take turns.

2. Work with a group. Make three lists. Who in your group has had a cast? Who has had a sling? Who has had crutches?

Pharmacy
Farmacia

Words in Context

Follow these steps to treat a cut.

- Press **gauze** on the cut. This will help stop the bleeding.
- Lift the cut above the heart.
- Clean the cut with soap and water. Then put **antibacterial ointment** on it.
- Cover the cut with a **sterile pad** and **sterile tape**.

Remember—accidents happen. Always keep a **first-aid kit** in your home.

1 a tablet
una tableta

2 a capsule
una cápsula

3 a pill
una píldora

4 prescription medicine
medicina de prescripción /
medicamento recetado

5 a pharmacist
un farmacéutico / una
farmacéutica

6 over-the-counter
medication
medicamentos en los mostradores /
medicamentos sin receta

7 cough syrup
jarabe para la tos

8 an antacid
un antiácido

9 (throat) lozenges
pastillas (para la garganta)

10 cough drops
pastillas para la tos

11 an inhaler
un inhalador

12 a nasal (decongestant)
spray
un spray nasal
descongestionante

13 eyedrops
gotas para los ojos

14 antihistamine
antihistamínico /
antihistamínica

15 a prescription
una prescripción / una receta
médica

16 a warning label
una etiqueta de advertencia

17 a cane
un bastón

18 a knee brace
una rodillera

19 an elastic bandage
una venda elástica

20 vitamins
vitaminas

21 a heating pad
un cojín eléctrico

22 hydrogen peroxide
agua oxigenada

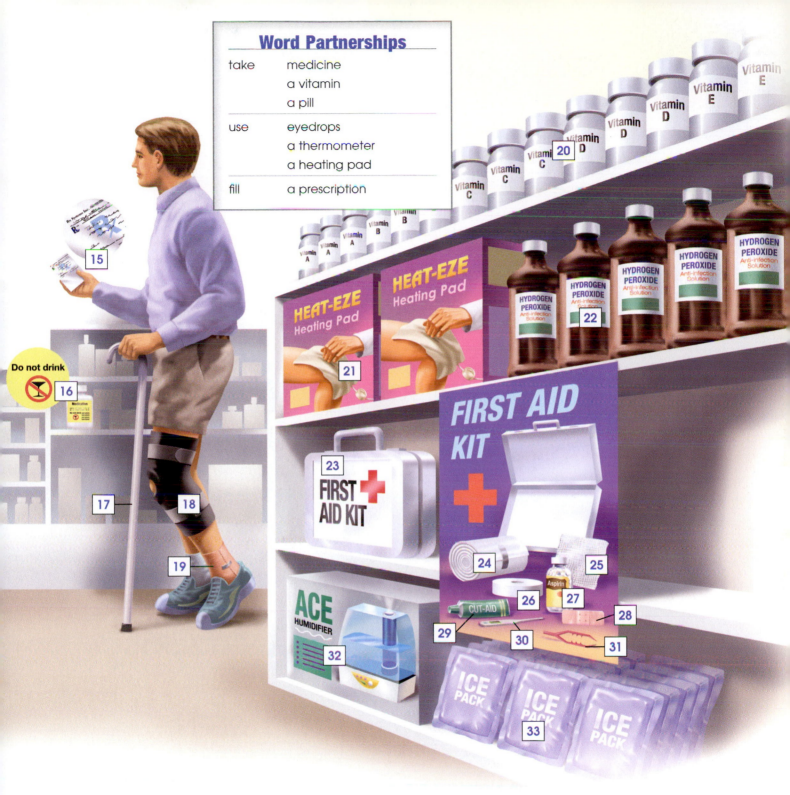

take	medicine
	a vitamin
	a pill
use	eyedrops
	a thermometer
	a heating pad
fill	a prescription

Do not drink

23 a first-aid kit
un botiquín de primeros auxilios

24 gauze
gasa

25 a sterile pad
almohadilla estéril

26 sterile tape
cinta estéril

27 aspirin
aspirina

28 an adhesive bandage
una venda adhesiva

29 antibacterial ointment / antibacterial cream
ungüento antibacteriano / crema antibacterianal

30 a thermometer
un termómetro

31 tweezers
pinzas

32 a humidifier
un humidificador

33 an ice pack
un compresa de hielo

Words in Action

1. Which pharmacy items on the word list do you have in your home?

2. Which pharmacy items are good for a cold? Which are good for a cut? Which are good for a sprain? Discuss with a partner.

Soap, Comb, and Floss

Jabón, Peine, Hilo Dental

1 hairspray
spray para el pelo

2 shampoo
shampú

3 conditioner
acondicionador

4 hair gel
gel para pelo

5 a curling iron
unas pinzas eléctricas

6 a blow dryer /
a hair dryer
una secadora de pelo

7 a barrette
un pasador

8 a comb
un peine

9 rollers / curlers
tubos / rulos

10 a (hair)brush
un cepillo (para pelo)

11 nail polish
esmalte para uñas

12 a nail clipper
un cortauñas

13 dental floss
hilo dental

14 toothpaste
pasta de dientes

15 a toothbrush
un cepillo de dientes

16 shaving cream
crema para afeitar

17 aftershave
loción para después de
afeitar

18 a razor
una rasuradora

19 an electric shaver /
an electric razor
una rasuradora
eléctrica

20 deodorant
desodorante

21 perfume
perfume

22 sunscreen
protector solar

23 lotion
loción

24 soap
jabón

25 tissues
pañuelos deshechables

Makeup
Maquillaje

26 face powder
polvo facial

27 lipstick
lápiz labial

28 blush / rouge
rubor

29 eye shadow
sombra para los ojos

30 mascara
máscara para pestañas /
rimel

31 eyeliner
delineador de ojos

16

17

18

19

32 wash
lavar

33 rinse
enjuagar

34 comb
peinar

35 (blow) dry
secar
(con pistola)

36 brush
cepillar

37 cut
cortar

20

21

22

sun
screen

23

Silken
Skin

25

24

SOAP

27

26

28

29

30

MASCARA

31

EYELINER

Word Partnerships

a disposable	razor
a dull	
nail polish	remover
hand	soap
face	
antibacterial	
hand	lotion
body	
put on	aftershave
wear	mascara
	lipstick

Words in Action

1. What things from the list do you use every day?

2. Work with a partner. One person pretends to use one of the items from the list. The other guesses what it is. Take turns.

145

Jobs 1
Trabajos 1

Words in Context

What kind of work is right for you? Do you like to work with your hands? You could be a **carpenter,** an **assembler,** or a **construction worker.** Do you want to help people? You could be a **babysitter,** a **home health aide,** or a **doctor.** Are you creative? You could be a **hairstylist,** a **florist,** or an **architect.** Are you good with numbers? You could be an **accountant** or an **engineer.**

1 **an accountant**
un contador / una contadora

2 **a dentist**
un dentista / una dentista

3 **an artist**
un artista / una artista

4 **a cook**
un cocinero / una cocinera

5 **a hairstylist / a hairdresser**
un estilista / una estilista

6 **a construction worker**
un trabajador de la construcción / una trabajadora de la construcción

7 **a graphic artist**
un artista gráfico / una artista gráfica

8 **a gardener**
un jardinero / una jardinera

9 **a delivery person**
un repartidor / una repartidora

10 **a computer technician**
un técnico en computación / una técnica en computación

11 **a janitor / a custodian**
un conserje / una conserje

12 **a doctor**
un doctor / una doctora

13 **a homemaker**
una ama de casa

14 **a florist**
un florista / una florista

15 **a housekeeper**
una ama de llaves

16 **an editor**
un editor / una editora

17 **a barber**
un peluquero / una peluquera

18 **an assembler**
un ensamblador / una ensambladora

19 **an architect**
un arquitecto / una arquitecta

20 **a butcher**
un carnicero / una carnicera

21 **a (home) health aide / a (home) attendant**
un ayudante / una ayudante

22 **an engineer**
un ingeniero / una ingeniera

23 **a businessman / a businesswoman**
un hombre de negocios / una mujer de negocios

Word Partnerships

a	part-time	job
	well-paid	
	blue-collar	
	white-collar	
look for	a job	
apply for		
get		
lose		

24 a **cashier**
un cajero / una cajera

25 an **actor**
un actor

26 a **carpenter**
un carpintero / una carpintera

27 an **electrician**
un electricista / una electricista

28 a **firefighter**
un bombero / una bombera

29 a **garment worker**
una costurera

30 a **babysitter**
una niñera

Words in Action

1. Look at the list. What are the best five jobs to have? Why?

2. Which jobs are done in offices? Which are done in shops? Which are done outdoors? Make three lists.

Jobs 2
Trabajos 2

Words in Context

There are many **jobs** in my family. I'm a **reporter** for a newspaper. My sister is a **musician.** My brother likes to work with animals, so he is a **veterinarian.** My other brother travels a lot. He's a **truck driver.** Our parents are **teachers.** They taught us to love work.

1 a reporter
  un(a) reportero(a)

2 a manicurist
  un(a) manicurista

3 a lawyer
  un(a) abogado(a)

4 a soldier
  un(a) soldado

5 a receptionist
  un(a) recepcionista

6 a physical therapist
  un(a) fisioterapeuta

7 a locksmith
  un(a) cerrajero(a)

8 a security guard
  un(a) guardia de seguridad

9 a teacher /
  an instructor
  un(a) maestro(a) /
  un(a) instructor(a)

10 a mechanic
   un(a) mecánico(a)

11 a police officer
   un(a) oficial de policía

12 a photographer
   un(a) fotógrafo(a)

13 a stockbroker
   un(a) corredor(a) de bolsa

14 a (house)painter
   un(a) pintor(a)
   (de casas)

15 a plumber
   un(a) plomero(a)

16 a scientist
   un(a) científico(a)

17 a taxi driver
   un(a) taxista

18 a server
   un(a) camarero(a)

19 a nurse
   un(a) enfermero(a)

20 a realtor
   un(a) corredor(a) de bienes raíces

21 a salesperson
   un(a) vendedor(a)

22 a tour guide
   un(a) guía de recorridos turísticos

23 a pilot
   un(a) piloto

24 a musician
   un(a) músico(a)

25 a writer
   un(a) escritor(a)

26 a truck driver
   un(a) chofer de camión

27 a travel agent
   un(a) agente de viajes

28 a veterinarian / vet
   un(a) veterinario(a)

HOME FOR SALE

Word Partnerships

a fashion	photographer
a wedding	
a registered	nurse
a school	
a commercial	pilot
a private	
a fighter	

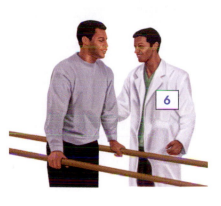

3

6

4

5

8

SECURITY

HOMEWORK PAGE 98

9

10

11

16

TAXI

17

18

24

Book
Signing
TODAY

25

26

Words in Action

1. Look at the list. Which are the five most difficult jobs? Why? Which are the five easiest? Why?

2. Look at the list. Which people use vehicles in their jobs? What vehicles do they use? Which people use equipment in their jobs? What equipment do they use?

ISLAND
FUN

27

28

Working
Trabajar

Words in Context

Needed: Office Assistant

Can you answer phones, **take** messages, **schedule** appointments, and **file**? Can you **use** a computer and a fax machine? Can you **type** 50 words per minute? You may be the right person for this job. Call 555-9389 to schedule an appointment for an interview.

1 cook
cocinar

2 examine
examinar

3 speak
hablar

4 arrest
arrestar

5 open mail
abrir la correspondencia

6 load
cargar

7 deliver
entregar

8 type
escribir en máquina / escribir en computadora

9 take care of
cuidar

10 act / perform
actuar

11 sing
cantar

12 take a message
tomar un mensaje

13 hire
contratar

14 sell
vender

15 repair / fix
reparar / arreglar

16 plan
planear

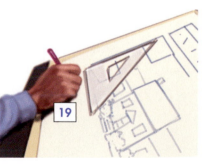

17 staple
engrapar
18 manage
administrar / dirigir
19 design
diseñar
20 make copies
sacar copias
21 use a computer
usar una computadora
22 call in sick
reportarse enfermo / reportarse enferma
23 manufacture
manufacturar

24 file
archivar
25 drive
conducir
26 make a decision
tomar una decisión

... and then ...

Word Partnerships

attend	a weekly	meeting
	a company	
take	a short	break
	a coffee	
make	a tough	decision
	an easy	
	a good	
	a bad	

Words in Action

1. Which of the things on the list can you do?
2. Choose five verbs on the list. Look at the jobs on pages 146–149. Can you find one or more jobs that match the verb?

Farm
Granja

Words in Context

Jimmy Carter was the 39th president of the U.S. He grew up on a **farm** full of animals. There were **dogs, turkeys, horses,** and **cows** on the farm. Carter did many jobs around the farm. He **milked** the cows each day after school. He also **picked** cotton and peanuts in the **fields.**

1. an orchard
   un huerto
2. a silo
   un silo
3. a barn
   un granero
4. a tractor
   un tractor
5. a plow
   un arado
6. a farmworker /
   a farmhand
   un agricultor / un
   trabajador de granja
7. a bull
   un toro
8. a vineyard
   un viñedo / una
   viña
9. a field
   un campo

10. soil
    suelo / tierra
11. a crop
    una cosecha / un
    cultivo
12. a scarecrow
    un espantapájaros
13. hay
    heno
14. a farmer
    un granjero / un
    agricultor
15. a farmhouse
    una casa de
    granja
16. a dog
    un perro / una
    perra
17. a cat
    un gato / una
    gata
18. a rabbit
    un conejo / una
    coneja
19. a goose
    un ganso / una
    gansa

20. a rooster
    un gallo
21. a goat
    un macho cabrío /
    una cabra
22. a horse
    un caballo
23. a sheep
    un carnero / una
    oveja
24. a donkey
    un burro / una burra /
    un asno
25. a pig
    un puerco / una
    puerca
26. a cow
    una vaca
27. a turkey
    un(a) pavo(a) /
    un guajolote
28. a chicken
    un pollo / una
    polla

Verbs
Verbos

29 plant
plantar

30 water
regar

31 pick
recoger

32 milk
ordeñar

33 feed
alimentar

Animal	Baby Animal
dog	puppy
cat	kitten
chicken	chick
pig	piglet
sheep	lamb
cow	calf
goat	kid

Words in Action

1. Study the word list for three minutes. Then close your book. Write down as many of the words as you can remember. Write each word under one of these categories: *People and animals on a farm, Things on a farm, Places on a farm.*

2. Choose a word and draw a picture of it on the board. The first classmate to guess the word gets a point and draws the next picture on the board.

Office
Oficina

Words in Context

Offices are very different today than they were 100 years ago. Back then there were no **computers, fax machines,** or **photocopiers.** People used **typewriters** to write letters. However, some things are the same. Most offices still have **file cabinets** and use supplies like **staplers, paper clips,** and **rubber bands.**

Employee of the Month

JOHN LOPEZ
45 Lawrence Street • Brooklyn, New York 11203 • (718) 555-0303

Executive Assistant

QUALIFICATIONS

• A highly organized and detail-oriented Executive Assistant providing skillful administrative support.
• Able to prioritize tasks and achieve goals.
• A self-motivated professional.
• Excellent research and writing skills.
• Computer skills include: MS Word, PowerPoint, Excel

EXPERIENCE

KEMCORP, New York, N.Y.

• Executive Assistant to the CEO, 2003-present
• Coordinated conference calls.
• Created effective filing systems, including quick indexing, fili...
• Conducted exhaustive research on competitors.
• Updated and maintained CEO's calendar.
• ...duled appointments with important clients an...
• ...systems and procedures which s...

1 2 3 4 5 6 7 8 9 10 11 12 13 14 15 16 17

1 a typewriter
una máquina de escribir

2 a binder
una libreta / carpeta de argollas

3 a fax machine
un fax

4 a (photo)copier /
a copy machine
una fotocopiadora / una copiadora

5 a (photo)copy
una fotocopia / una copia

6 an office manager
un gerente de oficina

7 a desk
un escritorio

8 a computer
una computadora

9 tape
cinta adhesiva

10 a stapler
una engrapadora

11 a calculator
una calculadora

12 a telephone
un teléfono

13 letterhead
membrete

14 an appointment book /
a date book
una libreta de citas

15 a business card file
un tarjetero

16 a (paper) shredder
una trituradora (de papel)

17 a resume
un curriculum vitae

18 a file cabinet
un archivero

19 an office assistant /
a secretary
un(a) asistente de oficina / un secretario

20 a (file) folder
un folder / una carpeta

21 an (electric) pencil
sharpener
un sacapuntas (eléctrico)

22 a supply cabinet
un gabinete / una cómoda

23 a thumbtack
una chinche / una tachuela

24 a rubber band
una liga

25 glue
goma

26 sticky notes
notas autoadhesivas

27 staples
grapas

28 correction fluid
líquido corrector

29 a paper clip
un clip

30 a hole punch
una perforadora

31 a pad
una libreta de notas

32 a label
una etiqueta

Word Partnerships

double sided	tape
packing	
hook up	a fax machine
turn on	a computer
turn off	

Words in Action

1. Which items on the list do you have at home?

2. Work with a partner. One student describes an office item. The other student guesses the item.
   - Student A: *You use this to add numbers.*
   - Student B: *A calculator.*

Factory

Fábrica

Words in Context

Making a chair is a process. There are many steps. The **designer** creates a design. **Parts** for the chair arrive at the **factory's loading dock.** Then **assembly line workers** put the chair together. It travels down a **conveyor belt** and gets a new part at each area. At the end of the assembly line, **packers** put the chair into a box. It goes into a **warehouse.** Then a **shipping clerk** sends it to a store near you!

1 a designer
un diseñador / una diseñadora

2 a front office
una oficina principal

3 an assembly line
una línea de ensamble

4 a worker
un trabajador / una trabajadora

5 a robot
un robot

6 a conveyor belt
una línea transportadora

7 a packer
un empacador / una empacadora

8 a hard hat
un casco

9 a supervisor
un supervisor / una supervisora

30 biohazard
peligro de infección

31 electrical hazard
peligro de alta tensión

32 explosive materials
materiales explosivos

33 flammable materials
materiales inflamables

34 poisonous materials
materiales venenosos

35 radioactive materials
materiales radioactivos

10 a forklift
un elevador de carga

11 a time card
una tarjeta para registrar llegada y salida

12 a time clock
un reloj marcador / checador

13 parts
repuestos (para ensamble)

14 a machine operator
un operador / una operadora

15 a warehouse
una bodega

16 a shipping clerk
un encargado / una encargada de embarque

17 a fire extinguisher
un extinguidor

18 a loading dock
un andén / una plataforma de embarque

19 a hand truck / a dolly
una carretilla

20 a hairnet
una red para el cabello / pelo

21 a safety visor
una visera para protección de la cara

22 a respirator
un respirador

23 safety goggles
gafas de protección de la vista

24 earplugs
tapones para los oídos

25 safety glasses
lentes de seguridad

26 a particle mask
un tapabocas

27 a safety vest
un chaleco de seguridad

28 safety boots
unas botas de seguridad

29 safety earmuffs
orejeras de seguridad

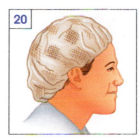

Word Partnerships

a factory	worker
an assembly line	
a forklift	operator
a shift	supervisor
	worker
punch	a time card

Words in Action

1. Make a list of the people in this factory. Which job is the most interesting to you? Which is the least interesting? Why?

2. What part of the body do each of these pieces of safety equipment protect: earplugs, a hard hat, safety boots, safety goggles, a safety visor, safety earmuffs, safety glasses, a particle mask, a hairnet.

Hotel

Hotel

Words in Context

There's a **hotel** in Sweden made completely of ice! You **check in** at the ice **lobby.** All the **rooms** and **suites** are made of ice, too. **Room service** brings you a hot drink in the morning. You can go to the **sauna** to warm up. Room rates are high, but the Ice Hotel is very popular. Be sure to **make** a reservation before you go!

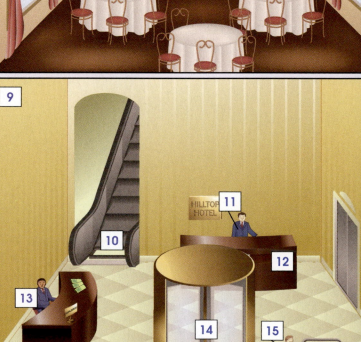

Verbs
Verbos

24 make a reservation
hacer una reservación

25 check in
registrarse

26 order room service
pedir servicio al cuarto

27 check out
pagar la cuenta y dejar el hotel

1 a housekeeper
una ama de llaves

2 a housekeeping cart
un carro de servicio de una ama de llaves

3 room service
servicio de habitación

4 a (hotel) guest
un huésped (de hotel) / una huésped (de hotel)

5 a suite
una suite

6 a meeting room
una sala de juntas / un salón de juntas

7 a business center
un centro de negocios

8 a ballroom
un salón de baile

9 a lobby
un lobby / un vestíbulo

10 an escalator
una escalera mecánica

11 a desk clerk
un recepcionista / una recepcionista

12 a registration desk
un escritorio de recepción

13 a concierge
un conserje / una conserje, un portero / una portera

14 a revolving door
una puerta giratoria

15 a bellhop
un botones

16 a luggage cart
un carro para equipaje

17 a (double) room
un cuarto (doble)

18 a (single) room
un cuarto (sencillo)

19 a fitness center
un gimnasio

20 a sauna
un sauna

21 a (swimming) pool
una alberca

22 a gift shop
una tabaquería / una tienda de regalos

23 valet parking
un estacionamiento con valet

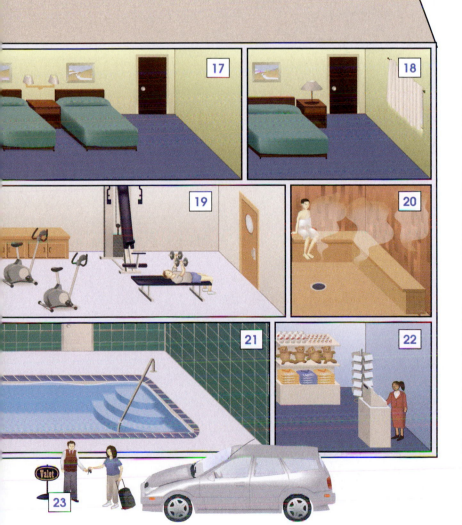

Word Partnerships

a luxury	hotel
a budget	
room	rates
an indoor	(swimming) pool
an outdoor	
a heated	

Words in Action

1. Make three lists: *People in a Hotel*, *Places in a Hotel*, and *Things in a Hotel*.

2. Role-play with a partner. One of you is the desk clerk at a hotel. The other is calling with questions about the hotel.
   - Student A: *How much is a double room?*
   - Student B: *It's $50 a night for a double.*
   - Student A: *Is there a swimming pool?*

Tools and Supplies 1

Herramientas y Utensilios 1

Words in Context

I go to hardware stores a lot because I work in construction. I keep my **wrench,** my **hammer,** and my **screwdriver** in my **tool belt.** Those are the **tools** I use the most.

Hand Tools

1 a utility knife
una cuchilla

2 a C-clamp
una abrazadera C

3 a sledgehammer
un marro

4 a shovel
una pala

5 an ax
un hacha

6 a handsaw
una sierra de mano

7 a file
una lima

8 a caulking gun
una pistola de silicón

9 a hammer
un martillo

10 a wrench
una llave de tuercas

11 a hacksaw
una sierra de arco

12 a tool belt
un chaleco para herramientas

13 a vise
una prensa de tornillo

14 a chisel
un escoplo

15 pliers
pinzas

16 a level
un nivel

17 a ruler
una regla

18 a screwdriver
un desarmador / destornillador

19 electrical tape
cinta aislante

20 an extension cord
una extensión / un cable para extensión

21 wire
cable

22 a lightbulb
un foco

23 a wire stripper
un despuntador de cable

24 (pipe) fittings
conexiones (de tubería)

Electrical

19
20
21
22
23

Plumbing

24
25
26

Power Tools

27
28
29
30
31
32

25 a pipe wrench
una llave perica

26 a pipe
un tramo de tubería

27 a router
una ranuradora

28 a drill
un taladro

29 a drill bit
una broca

30 a blade
un disco de corte

31 a circular saw
una sierra circular

32 a power sander
una lijadora eléctrica

Word Partnerships

a tool	bench
	box
a Phillips	screwdriver
a flathead	
an electric	drill
a cordless	

Words in Action

1. Which items on the list have you used? What job did you do with each item?

2. Which tools would you use to:
- build a bookcase?
- wire a house?
- install a sink?

Tools and Supplies 2

Herramientas y Utensilios 2

Words in Context

How to Hang a Picture on a Wall

- With a **tape measure** or ruler, measure 66 to 68 **inches** above the floor.

- Put a small piece of **masking tape** on the wall.

- Put a **nail** through a picture **hook,** and pound it in through the masking tape.

- Hang your picture.

12 inches	=	1 foot
3 feet	=	1 yard
1 inch	=	2.54 centimeters
1 foot	=	30.5 centimeters
1 mile	=	1.6 kilometers

Building Material

Paint Supplies

Hardware

Lumber / Wood

1 an inch una pulgada	**14** paint pintura	**27** a hook un gancho
2 a centimeter un centímetro	**15** a paint tray una charola para pintura	**28** plywood madera contrachapada / laminada
3 a tape measure una cinta métrica	**16** a (paint) roller un rodillo (para pintar)	**29** molding molduras
4 drywall un muro prefabricado / un muro de tablarroca	**17** steel wool fibra metálica	**30** board lumber tablas de madera / laminada
5 shingles tablillas	**18** an anchor un taquete	**31** duct tape cinta para conductos
6 insulation aislante	**19** an eye hook una armella	**32** a chain una cadena
7 tile baldosa / azulejo	**20** a nail un clavo	**33** a battery una batería
8 a flashlight una linterna	**21** a bolt un tornillo sin punta	**34** a padlock un candado
9 a rope una soga	**22** a screw un tornillo con punta	
10 a paintbrush una brocha	**23** a nut una tuerca	
11 a scraper una espátula	**24** a wing nut una tuerca de mariposa	
12 sandpaper papel de lija	**25** a hinge una bisagra	
13 masking tape cinta / masking tape	**26** a washer una rondana	

Words in Action

1. Name one of the items on the list, then think of as many uses for the item as you can.

2. Imagine you need to paint some windows in an old house. Which items will you need to prepare the windows and paint them?

Drill, Sand, Paint

Taladrar, Lijar, Pintar

Word Partnerships

paint	a wall
	a room
	a house
install	a phone line
	a water heater
shovel	gravel
	snow

1 **put up** drywall
levantar un muro / poner un muro

2 **plaster** a wall
fijar una pared / enyesar una pared

3 **paint** a wall
pintar un muro / pintar una pared

4 **drill** a hole
taladrar un agujero

5 **lay** bricks
colocar ladrillos

6 **pull** a rope
jalar una soga / jalar una cuerda

7 **pour** concrete
vaciar concreto

8 **wire** a house
cablear una casa / hacer las conexiones de una casa

9 **hammer** a nail
clavar un clavo

10 **saw** wood
serrar madera / aserrar madera / cortar madera

11 **measure**
medir

12 **weld**
soldar

13 **install** a window
instalar una ventana

14 **climb** a ladder
subir una escalera

15 **operate** a backhoe
operar una retroexcavadora

16 **tear down** a wall
derribar un muro / derribar una pared

17 **read** blueprints
leer planos

18 **carry** a bag
cargar un saco

19 **shovel** sand
traspalar arena

20 **push** a wheelbarrow
empujar una carretilla

21 **cut** a pipe
cortar un tubo

22 **dig** a trench
cavar una zanja

23 **plane** wood
cepillar madera

24 **glue** wood
pegar madera

25 **sand** wood
lijar madera

Words in Action

1. Check off the things on the list you have done.

2. Pretend to be doing one of the actions on the word list. Your partner will guess what you are doing.

Weather
Clima

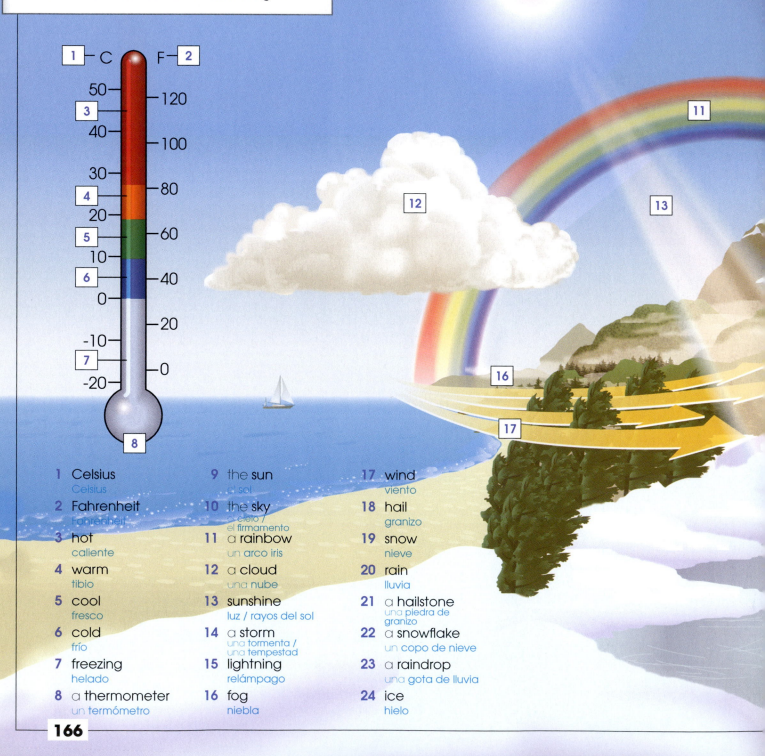

1	Celsius	9	the sun	17	wind
	Celsius		el sol		viento
2	Fahrenheit	10	the sky	18	hail
	Fahrenheit		el cielo / el firmamento		granizo
3	hot	11	a rainbow	19	snow
	caliente		un arco iris		nieve
4	warm	12	a cloud	20	rain
	tibio		una nube		lluvia
5	cool	13	sunshine	21	a hailstone
	fresco		luz / rayos del sol		una piedra de granizo
6	cold	14	a storm	22	a snowflake
	frío		una tormenta / una tempestad		un copo de nieve
7	freezing	15	lightning	23	a raindrop
	helado		relámpago		una gota de lluvia
8	a thermometer	16	fog	24	ice
	un termómetro		niebla		hielo

25 It's **sunny.**
Está soleado. / Hace sol.

26 It's **cloudy.**
Está nublado. / Hay nubes.

27 It's **windy.**
Está airoso. / Hace viento. / Hace aire.

28 It's **snowing.**
Está nevando.

29 It's **foggy.**
Está brumoso. / Hay bruma. / Hay niebla.

30 It's **raining.**
Está lloviendo.

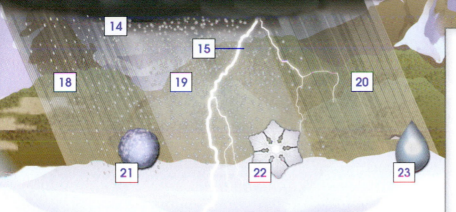

Word Partnerships

25	degrees	Celsius
77		Fahrenheit
a cold	wind	
a bitter		
a heavy	rain	
a light		
a blue	sky	
a gray		
a cloudless		

Words in Action

1. Describe the weather today. Then describe yesterday's weather.
   - *It's rainy and cool today. Yesterday was sunny and warm.*

2. What is your favorite kind of weather? Why?
   - *I like sunny weather because I can go to the beach.*

The Earth's Surface
La Superficie de la Tierra

Words in Context

The land changes across the United States. There are **mountains** in the West, **hills** in the East, and wide **plains** in between. There are **deserts, canyons,** miles of coastline, and thousands of **lakes.**

1
2
3
4
5
9
6
7
8
16
20
19
18
17

1 a peak
una cima

2 a mountain
una montaña

3 a volcano
un volcán

4 a glacier
un glaciar

5 a valley
un valle

6 a stream
un arroyo

7 a lake
un lago

8 an island
una isla

9 a waterfall
una cascada

10 a crater
un cráter

11 a desert
un desierto

12 a plateau
un altiplano / una altiplanicie

13 a canyon
un cañón

14 a cave
una cueva

15 a mesa
una meseta

16 a forest
un bosque

17 a peninsula
una península

18 a shore
una costa / una orilla

19 the mouth of the river
la boca de un río

20 a riverbank
un margen de un río / una orilla de un río

21 a river
un río

22 a hill
una colina

23 a beach
una playa

24 an ocean
un océano

25 a bay
una bahía

26 plains
llanuras

27 a cliff
un acantilado

Word Partnerships

a sandy	beach
a rocky	
a deep	river
a shallow	
a mountain	peak
	range
an active	volcano
a steep	hill

Words in Action

1. Plan a vacation. Pick five things from the list that you want to see on your vacation. Write them down, then share your list with a classmate.

2. Make lists of all of the oceans, rivers, and lakes you know. Use a map to add more to your list. Share your list with a classmate.

169

Energy, Pollution, and Natural Disasters

Energía, Contaminación y Desastres Naturales

Words in Context

Automobile exhaust creates air pollution. Air pollution can turn into acid rain. Acid rain kills plants and animals. Some new cars run on solar energy. These cars don't create air pollution.

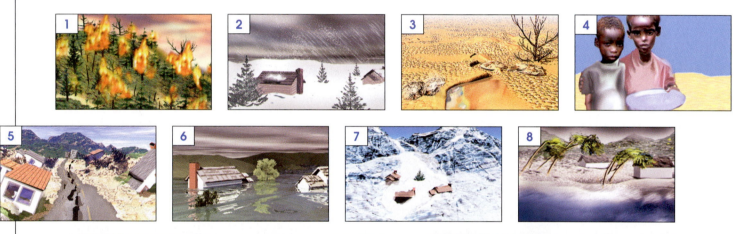

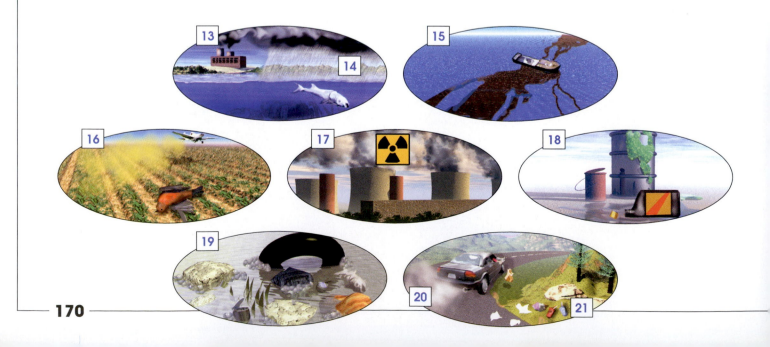

Natural Disasters
Desastres Naturales

1 a forest fire
un incendio forestal

2 a blizzard
una ventisca

3 a drought
una sequía

4 a famine
una hambruna

5 an earthquake
un terremoto / un sismo

6 a flood
una inundación

7 an avalanche
una avalancha

8 a hurricane
un huracán

9 a mudslide
un deslave / derrumbe

10 a tsunami / a tidal wave
un maremoto

11 a tornado
un tornado

12 a volcanic eruption
una erupción volcánica

Pollution
Contaminación

13 air pollution / smog
contaminación del aire / smog

14 acid rain
lluvia ácida

15 an oil spill
un derrame de petróleo

16 pesticide poisoning
intoxicación / envenenamiento por pesticida

17 radiation
radiación

18 hazardous waste
residuos peligrosos

19 water pollution
contaminación del agua

20 automobile exhaust
emisión de gases de combustión / de escape de automóviles

21 litter
basura

Energy
Energía

22 natural gas
gas natural

23 oil / petroleum
petróleo

24 wind
viento

25 geothermal energy
energía geotérmica

26 coal
carbón

27 solar energy
energía solar

28 nuclear energy
energía nuclear

29 hydroelectric power
energía hidroeléctrica

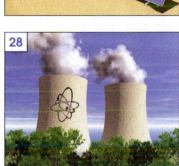

Word Partnerships

a long a severe	drought
a flash	flood
a minor a major	earthquake
environmental	disasters pollution

Words in Action

1. Work with a group. Choose two or three natural disasters. In what parts of the world has each disaster happened? Make a list for each disaster.

2. Which kind of energy source do you use to heat your home? Which do you use to cook? Which do you use to dry your clothes? Discuss with a group.

The United States and Canada
Los Estados Unidos y Canadá

Words in Context

There are fifty states in the **United States.** The capital is **Washington, D.C.** The U.S. city with the most people is **New York City. Canada** is much larger than the U.S., but it has far fewer people. The capital of Canada is **Ottawa** and the city with the most people is **Toronto.**

Regions of Canada
Regiones de Canadá

1 Northern Canada
   Canadá del norte
2 British Columbia
   Columbia Británica
3 the Prairie Provinces
   las provincias de la planicie / pradera
4 Ontario
   Ontario
5 Quebec
   Quebec
6 the Atlantic Provinces
   las provincias del Atlántico

Regions of the United States
Regiones de los Estados Unidos

7 the West Coast
   la costa occidental
8 the Rocky Mountain States
   los estados de las Montañas Rocosas
9 the Midwest
   el medio oeste
10 the Mid-Atlantic States
   los estados del Atlántico medio
11 New England
   Nueva Inglaterra
12 the Southwest
   el suroeste
13 the South
   el sur

ARCTIC OCEAN

St. John's ★

6 Newfoundland & Labrador

5 Québec

Iqaluit ★

4 Ontario

Manitoba

Saskatchewan

3

Alberta

Edmonton ★

2 British Columbia

Nunavut

Northwest Territories

Yellowknife ★

1

Yukon

Whitehorse ★

Word Partnerships

United States	government
	history
	passport
	citizen

Words in Action

1. Work with a partner. Say the name of a state or province. Your partner will point to the state or province and say what region it is in. Take turns.

2. Which states or provinces do you want to visit? Why? Tell your classmates.

Brunswick
Charlottetown
Halifax
Nova Scotia
Fredericton
Maine
Augusta
New Hampshire
Massachusetts
Concord
Boston
Providence
Rhode Island
Connecticut
New Jersey
Hartford
Delaware
Maryland
Trenton
Dover
Québec City
Vermont
Montpelier
New York
Albany
11
10
Pennsylvania
Harrisburg
Annapolis
Washington, D.C.
Ottawa
Toronto
West Virginia
Charleston
Virginia
Richmond
Raleigh
North Carolina
Columbia
South Carolina
Florida
Tallahassee
Ohio
Columbus
Indianapolis
Frankfort
Kentucky
Nashville
Atlanta
Georgia
13
Michigan
Lansing
Indiana
Illinois
Springfield
Tennessee
Alabama
Montgomery
Mississippi
Jackson
Wisconsin
Madison
Iowa
Des Moines
Missouri
Jefferson City
9
Mississippi R.
Arkansas
Little Rock
Louisiana
Baton Rouge
Minnesota
St. Paul
Winnipeg
North Dakota
Bismarck
South Dakota
Pierre
Nebraska
Lincoln
Topeka
Kansas
Oklahoma
Oklahoma City
Texas
Austin
12
Regina
Montana
Helena
8
Wyoming
Cheyenne
Denver
Colorado
Santa Fe
New Mexico
MEXICO
Salt Lake City
Utah
Arizona
Phoenix
Idaho
Boise
Carson City
Nevada
Washington
Victoria
Olympia
Salem
Oregon
7
Sacramento
California

Gulf of Mexico

Hawaii
Honolulu
PACIFIC OCEAN

ARCTIC OCEAN
Juneau
Alaska
PACIFIC OCEAN

PACIFIC OCEAN

The World
El Mundo

Words in Context

There are seven **continents** and almost 200 countries in the **world. Russia** and **Canada** are the biggest countries. **China** and **India** are the countries with the most people.

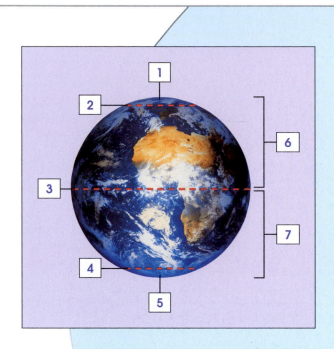

NORTH AMERICA

8 CANADA

UNITED STATES

ATLANTIC OCEAN

MEXICO

BAHAMAS

CUBA
HAITI
DOMINICAN REPUBLIC
Puerto Rico (U.S.)
JAMAICA
ST. KITTS AND NEVIS
BELIZE
HONDURAS
ANTIGUA AND BARBUDA
DOMINICA
GUATEMALA
ST. VINCENT AND THE GRENADINES
ST. LUCIA
GRENADA
BARBADOS
EL SALVADOR
TRINIDAD AND TOBAGO
GUYANA
NICARAGUA
VENEZUELA
SURINAME
COSTA RICA
PANAMA
FRENCH GUYANA
COLOMBIA

ECUADOR

9 BRAZIL

SOUTH AMERICA

PERU

BOLIVIA

SAMOA

TONGA

PACIFIC OCEAN

PARAGUAY

N
W E
S

CHILE

ARGENTINA

URUGUAY

1 the **North Pole**
el Polo Norte

2 the **Arctic Circle**
el Círculo Ártico

3 the **Equator**
la línea del ecuador

4 the **Antarctic Circle**
el Círculo Antártico

5 the **South Pole**
el Polo Sur

6 the **Northern Hemisphere**
el Hemisferio Norte

7 the **Southern Hemisphere**
el Hemisferio Sur

Continents
Continentes

8 **North America**
América del Norte / Norteamérica

9 **South America**
América del Sur / Sudamérica

10 **Europe**
Europa

11 **Asia**
Asia

12 **Africa**
África

13 **Australia**
Australia

14 **Antarctica**
Antártica

Words in Action

1. Go around the room saying the name of a country for each letter of the alphabet. (There are no countries that start with the letters *w* or *x*.)

2. Work with a partner. Say the name of a country. Your partner will point to the country on the map and say the name of the continent it is in. Take turns.

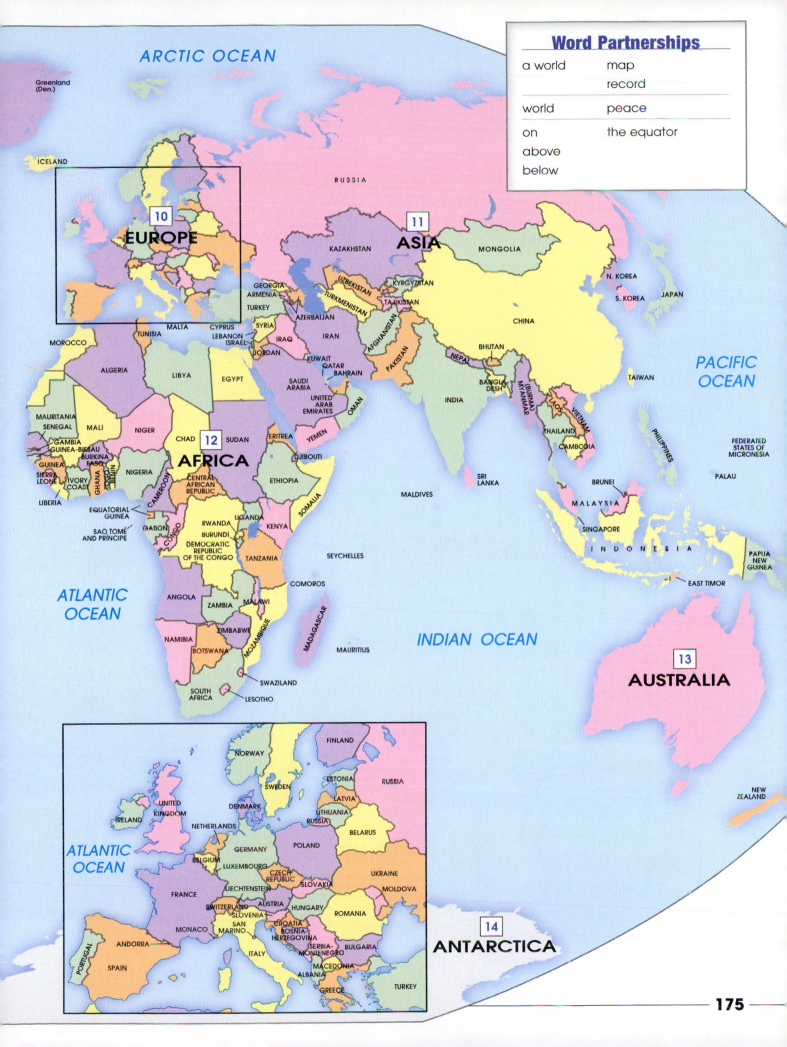

Word Partnerships

a world	map
	record
world	peace
on	the equator
above	
below	

ARCTIC OCEAN

Greenland (Den.)

ICELAND

10 EUROPE

RUSSIA

11 ASIA

KAZAKHSTAN

MONGOLIA

N. KOREA
S. KOREA
JAPAN

GEORGIA
ARMENIA
TURKEY
AZERBAIJAN

UZBEKISTAN
KYRGYZSTAN
TURKMENISTAN
TAJIKISTAN

CHINA

TAIWAN

PACIFIC OCEAN

TUNISIA
MALTA
CYPRUS
LEBANON
ISRAEL
SYRIA
JORDAN
IRAQ

MOROCCO

ALGERIA

LIBYA

EGYPT

IRAN
AFGHANISTAN
PAKISTAN
NEPAL
BHUTAN
BANGLA-DESH
(BURMA) MYANMAR
LAOS
VIETNAM
THAILAND
CAMBODIA

PHILIPPINES

FEDERATED STATES OF MICRONESIA

PALAU

KUWAIT
QATAR
BAHRAIN
SAUDI ARABIA
UNITED ARAB EMIRATES
OMAN

INDIA

MAURITANIA
SENEGAL
GAMBIA
GUINEA-BISSAU
GUINEA
SIERRA LEONE
LIBERIA

MALI

NIGER

CHAD

SUDAN

ERITREA
YEMEN
DJIBOUTI

SRI LANKA

MALDIVES

BRUNEI

MALAYSIA

SINGAPORE

BURKINA FASO
IVORY COAST
GHANA
BENIN
TOGO
NIGERIA

12 AFRICA

CENTRAL AFRICAN REPUBLIC

ETHIOPIA

SOMALIA

INDONESIA

PAPUA NEW GUINEA

EQUATORIAL GUINEA
GABON
SAO TOMÉ AND PRINCIPE
CONGO
CAMEROON

DEMOCRATIC REPUBLIC OF THE CONGO

RWANDA
BURUNDI
UGANDA
KENYA

TANZANIA

SEYCHELLES

EAST TIMOR

ATLANTIC OCEAN

ANGOLA

ZAMBIA

MALAWI

COMOROS

MADAGASCAR

INDIAN OCEAN

13 AUSTRALIA

NAMIBIA
BOTSWANA
ZIMBABWE
MOZAMBIQUE

MAURITIUS

SOUTH AFRICA
SWAZILAND
LESOTHO

NEW ZEALAND

Europe inset

FINLAND

NORWAY

SWEDEN

ESTONIA

RUSSIA

UNITED KINGDOM

DENMARK

LATVIA
LITHUANIA

IRELAND

NETHERLANDS

RUSSIA

BELARUS

ATLANTIC OCEAN

BELGIUM
LUXEMBOURG

GERMANY

POLAND

FRANCE

CZECH REPUBLIC
SLOVAKIA

UKRAINE

LIECHTENSTEIN

MOLDOVA

SWITZERLAND
AUSTRIA
SLOVENIA

HUNGARY

ROMANIA

MONACO
SAN MARINO

CROATIA
BOSNIA-HERZEGOVINA
SERBIA-MONTENEGRO

PORTUGAL

ANDORRA

ITALY

BULGARIA

MACEDONIA
ALBANIA
GREECE

14 ANTARCTICA

TURKEY

SPAIN

175

The Universe
El Universo

1 a space station
una estación espacial

2 a constellation
una constelación

3 a star
una estrella

4 a rocket
un cohete

5 an eclipse
un eclipse

6 an orbit
una órbita

7 a galaxy
una galaxia

8 an observatory
un observatorio

9 a telescope
un telescopio

10 an astronomer
un(a) astrónomo(a)

11 space
espacio

12 the moon
la luna

13 a satellite
un satélite

14 an astronaut
un(a) astronauta

15 Earth's atmosphere
atmósfera terrestre

16 a meteor
un meteoro

17 a space shuttle
un transbordador espacial

18 the sun
el sol

19 a comet
un cometa

The Planets
Los Planetas

20 Pluto
Plutón

21 Neptune
Neptuno

22 Uranus
Urano

23 Saturn
Saturno

24 Júpiter
Júpiter

25 Mars
Marte

26 Earth
Tierra

27 Venus
Venus

28 Mercury
Mercurio

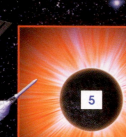

29 a new moon
una luna nueva

30 a crescent moon
media luna

31 a quarter moon
cuarto creciente

32 a full moon
una luna llena

3

24

23

18

27

28

26

25

19

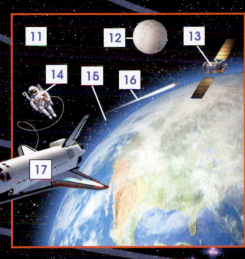

11

12

13

14

15

16

17

Word Partnerships

space	travel
	exploration
a distant	star
a shooting	
a bright	
a solar	eclipse
a lunar	

Words in Action

1. Imagine you are an astronaut. You can go to any one place in the solar system. Where will you go? Why? Share your answer with the class.

2. Look at the sky tonight and report back to your class. Was it a new moon, a crescent moon, a quarter moon, or a full moon? Does everyone in the class agree?

Garden
Jardín

Words in Context

There are 350,000 kinds of plants. Most plants grow from a **seed.** First **roots** grow from seeds, then **stems,** and then **leaves.** In **pine trees,** seeds come from the **pinecones.** In **lilacs, poppies, sunflowers,** and many other plants, seeds come from inside the **flowers.**

1

2

3

4

10

11

13

12

Parts of a Tree
Partes de un Árbol

14

16

15

17

18

Parts of a Flower
Partes de una Flor

25

26

21

19

22

20

23

24

1 a pine (tree)
un pino

2 a willow (tree)
un sauce

3 a birch (tree)
un abedul

4 a maple (tree)
un arce

5 an oak (tree)
un roble

6 an elm (tree)
un olmo

7 a lilac bush
una lila

8 a greenhouse
un invernadero

9 a pinecone
una piña

10 a branch
una rama

11 a trunk
un tronco

12 roots
raíces

13 a leaf
una hoja

14 a flower
una flor

15 a stem
un tallo

16 a petal
un pétalo

17 a bud
un brote

18 a bulb
un bulbo /
un tubérculo

19 irises
lirios

20 lilies
azucenas

21 chrysanthemums
crisantemos

22 daffodils
narcisos

23 violets
violetas

24 a seed
una semilla

25 tulips
tulipanes

26 marigolds
caléndulas

27 ivy
hiedra

28 roses
rosas

29 sunflowers
girasoles

30 geraniums
geranios

31 daisies
margaritas

32 poppies
amapolas

Word Partnerships

a shade	tree
an evergreen	
send	flowers
give	
get / receive	
a bouquet of	roses
a dozen	
long-stem	

Words in Action

1. Which of the flowers and trees grow in your area? Make a list with your class.

2. Describe a flower or tree to a partner. Your partner will guess the flower or tree. Take turns.
   - Student A: *It has a yellow center and white petals. It doesn't really have a smell.*
   - Student B: *It's a daisy.*

Desert
Desierto

1

2

3

5

4

12

Word Partnerships

a red	ant
a black	
a fire	
a carpenter	
a swarm of	ants
	flies
a poisonous	snake
	spider

11

14

13

1	a hawk	7	a palm tree	13	a rat	**Insects / Bugs**

1 a hawk
un halcón

2 an owl
un búho

3 a boulder
una piedra grande

4 a coyote
un coyote

5 a mountain lion
un puma

6 a sand dune
una duna

7 a palm tree
una palmera

8 a camel
un camello

9 a vulture
un buitre

10 a lizard
una lagartija

11 a rock
una roca

12 a tortoise
una tortuga

13 a rat
una rata

14 a snake
una serpiente

15 an oasis
un oasis

16 a cactus
un cactus

17 a pebble
un guijarro

Insects / Bugs
Insectos

18 a spider
una araña

19 a grasshopper
un saltamontes

20 a fly
una mosca

21 a moth
una polilla

22 a cricket
un grillo

23 a scorpion
un escorpión

24 an ant
una hormiga

Words in Action

1. One student chooses a word from the word list. The other students ask "Yes / No" questions to gather information and try to guess the word.
   - Student A: *Is it an animal?*
     Student B: *No.*
   - Student C: *Is it an insect?*
     Student B: *Yes.*
   - Student D: *Does it have wings?*
     Student B: *Yes.*
   - Student D: *Is it a fly?*
     Student B: *Yes!*

2. Imagine you are taking a trip to the desert. What things do you want to see? Discuss this with your class.

181

Rain Forest
Bosque Tropical

Words in Context

Many plants and animals live in **rain forests**. Colorful **parrots** and playful **monkeys** live there. Beautiful **orchids** and long **vines** grow there. At night, **tigers** and **panthers** hunt in the rain forest.

1 a parakeet
un perico / un periquito,
una perica / una periquita

2 a vine
una enredadera

3 a chimpanzee
un chimpancé / una chimpancé

4 a bat
un murciélago

5 a parrot
un papagayo

6 a monkey
un mico / una mica, un mono / una mona

7 a gorilla
un / una gorila

8 a peacock
un pavo real

9 a tiger
un tigre

10 a hummingbird
un colibrí

11 an orchid
una orquídea

12 a frog
una rana

13 an orangutan
un orangután / una orangutana

14 an aardvark
un oso hormiguero

15 a flamingo
un flamenco

16 a fern
un helecho

17 a panther
una pantera

18 an alligator
un caimán

19 a crocodile
un cocodrilo

20 a caterpillar
una oruga

21 a butterfly
una mariposa

22 a snail
un caracol

23 a wasp
una avispa

24 a beetle
un escarabajo

25 a tarantula
una tarántula

Word Partnerships

frogs	hop
wasps	sting
tigers	leap
monkeys	swing

26 swing
columpiarse

27 hop
saltar

28 hang
colgarse

Words in Action

1. Work with a partner. Put the words into groups of *plants*, *animals*, and *insects*.

2. Choose one of the animals on the list that makes a noise. Make that animal's noise. Your partner will guess the animal. Take turns.

Grasslands

Pastizales

Words in Context

Animals in the **grasslands** have different sources of food. **Giraffes** and **elephants** graze on the tallest trees. **Buffalo** and **gazelles** graze on grasses. The large cats, like **lions, leopards,** and **cheetahs,** feed on other animals.

1

2

5

6

7

8

10

11

12

13

14

15

16

20

21

22

23

24

25

1 a bee
una abeja

2 a fossil
un fósil

3 a koala
un koala

4 a kangaroo
un canguro

5 a hyena
una hiena

6 a giraffe
una jirafa

7 a hippopotamus
un hipopótamo

8 a rhinoceros
un rinoceronte

9 an antelope
un antílope

10 an elephant
un elefante

11 a leopard
un leopardo

12 a zebra
una cebra

13 a cheetah
un guepardo

14 an ostrich
un avestruz

15 a gazelle
una gacela

16 a shrub / a bush
un arbusto

17 a buffalo
un búfalo

18 a sparrow
un gorrión

19 a gopher
una tuza

20 a lion
un león

21 an antler
una cornamenta /
un cuerno / una asta

22 a hoof
una pezuña

23 a horn
un cuerno

24 a tusk
un colmillo

25 a trunk
una trompa

26 a mane
una melena

27 a paw
una zarpa

28 fur
piel

29 a tail
una cola

Word Partnerships

a herd of	antelope
	buffalo
	elephants
lions	roar
bees	buzz
hyenas	laugh

Words in Action

1. Which animals on the list have fur?
Which have a tail? Which have paws?
Make lists with a partner.

2. Describe an animal to a partner. Your
partner says the name and points to the
correct picture.
   - Student A: *It's big and it has two
   horns on its head.*
   - Student B: (pointing to the
   rhinocerous) *It's a rhinoceros.*

Polar Lands
Tierras Polares

Words in Context

Many animals live on the ice or in the waters near the North Pole. They stay warm in different ways. The **whale** and the **walrus** have thick layers of body fat. The arctic **fox** and the **polar bear** stay warm in their thick, white fur. Even **moss** finds a way to stay warm. It grows over rocks facing the sun.

2

3

6

8

11

7

9

Word Partnerships

a humpback	whale
a blue	
a Canada	goose
a wild	
a pack of	wolves
a flock of	birds

10

1 a goose
un ganso / una gansa

2 a moose
un alce

3 a reindeer
un reno

4 a wolf
un lobo / una loba

5 a (grizzly) bear
un oso gris / una osa gris

6 moss
musgo

7 an otter
una nutria

8 a (polar) bear
un oso (polar) / una osa (polar)

9 a (bear) cub
un cachorro / un osezno

10 an iceberg
un iceberg

11 a fox
un zorro / una zorra

12 a seal
una foca

13 a penguin
un pingüino

14 a whale
una ballena

15 a walrus
un morsa

16 whiskers
bigotes

17 a tusk
un colmillo

18 a flipper
una aleta

19 a falcon
un halcón

20 a beak
un pico

21 a wing
una ala

22 a claw
un garra

23 a feather
una pluma

Parts of a Bird

Partes de una Ave

Words in Action

1. Which polar animals eat meat? Which eat plants? Discuss these questions with your classmates.

2. In a group, make one list of the polar animals with wings, a second list of the animals with flippers, and a third list of the animals with claws. Compare lists among groups.

Sea

Mar

2

Words in Context

There are more than 15,000 kinds of **fish** in the **sea.** The largest fish is the **shark.** The great white shark can grow to over 7 meters*. There are also some very fast fish in the sea. For example, the **swordfish** swims at about 90 kilometers** per hour, and the **tuna** swims at about 70 kilometers*** per hour. The slowest fish is the **sea horse.** It only swims about 0.001 kilometers per hour!

* 7 meters = 23.1 feet   ** 90 kilometers = 55.8 miles   *** 70 kilometers = 43.4 miles

7

4   5   6

Parts of a Fish   **Partes de un Pez**

9

10

11

13

14

Word Partnerships

a school of	fish
a freshwater	
a saltwater	
a sea	turtle
a snapping	
a hammerhead	shark
a great white	

15   16

23

21

20

22

24

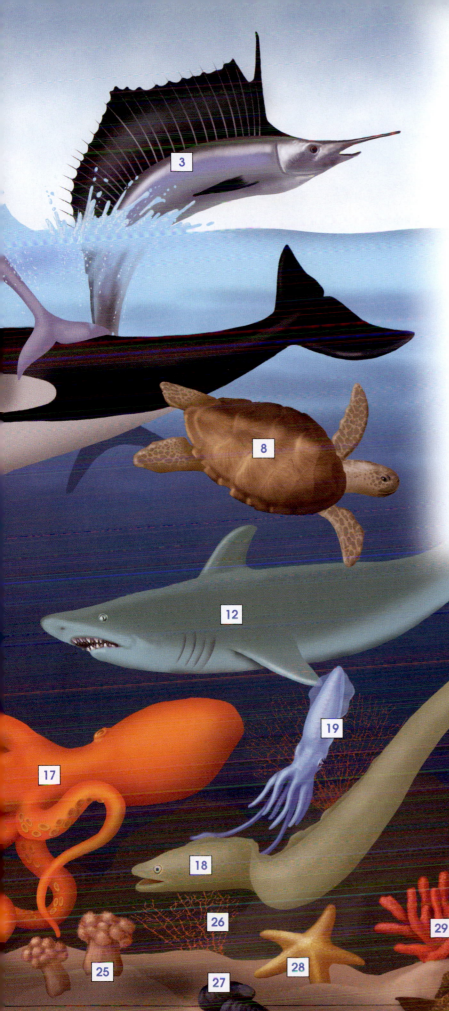

1 a seagull
una gaviota

2 a dolphin
un delfín

3 a swordfish
un pez espada

4 gills
agallas

5 a fin
una aleta

6 scales
escamas

7 a killer whale /
an orca
una ballena
asesina / una orca

8 a turtle
una tortuga

9 seaweed
una alga marina

10 a tuna
un atún

11 a jellyfish
una medusa

12 a shark
un tiburón

13 a (scuba) diver
un buzo

14 a sea horse
un caballo de mar

15 a bass
un róbalo / una
lobina

16 a cod
un bacalao

17 an octopus
un pulpo

18 an eel
una anguila

19 a squid
un calamar

20 a stingray
una raya

21 a shrimp
un camarón

22 a sea urchin
un erizo de mar

23 an angelfish
un pez ángel

24 a crab
un cangrejo

25 a sea anemone
una anémona de
mar

26 a coral reef
un banco de coral /
un arrecife

27 a mussel
un mejillón

28 a starfish
una estrella de mar

29 a sponge
una esponja

30 a halibut
un halibut

Words in Action

1. Make a list of all the sea animals you have seen. Then compare your list with your classmates' lists.

2. Study the spread for five minutes. Close your books. With a group, make a list of as many sea animals as you can remember. Take turns describing what each one looks like. You may want to draw pictures on the board.

Woodlands
Bosques

1 a robin
un petirrojo

2 a cardinal
un cardenal

3 a nest
un nido

4 a blue jay
una urraca

5 an eagle
una águila

6 a bobcat
un lince

7 an opossum
una zarigüeya

8 a squirrel
una ardilla

9 a deer
un venado

10 a groundhog
una marmota

11 a porcupine
un puerco espín

12 a turkey
un pavo

13 a woodpecker
un pájaro carpintero

14 a duck
un pato

15 a beaver
un castor

16 a mole
un topo

17 a salamander
una salamandra

18 a worm
un gusano

19 a raccoon
un mapache

20 a toad
un sapo

21 a chipmunk
una ardilla listada

22 a skunk
un zorrillo

23 a dragonfly
una libélula

24 a mosquito
un mosquito

25 a tick
una garrapata

26 a hornet
un avispón

27 a ladybug
una mariquita

28 a rabbit
un conejo

29 a mouse
un ratón

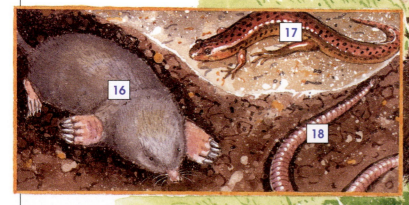

2 **3** **4** **5** **7** **8** **9** **12** **13** **14** **15** **21** **22** **23** **24** **25** **26** **27** **28** **29**

Word Partnerships

as quiet as a mouse

as busy as a beaver

as prickly as a porcupine

as scared as a rabbit

Words in Action

1. What animals live on or near water? What animals live on land? Make lists with a partner.

2. Choose three animals on the list. Write a list of at least three things you know about each of the animals.

Ducks
1. They have wings.
2. They live on water.
3. Baby ducks follow their mother.

Math

Matemáticas

Words in Context

You use **math** every day. You use **subtraction** to balance your checkbook. You use **fractions** to cook. You use **addition** to add up the total on a restaurant bill. You may even use **geometry** to decorate your home. Geometry can help you figure out how much wallpaper you need for your walls and how much carpet you need for your floors.

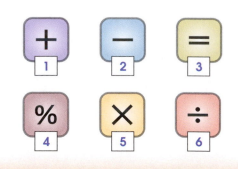

26	$6 + 3 = 9$
27	$6 - 3 = 3$
28	$6 \times 3 = 18$
29	$3 \div 6 = \frac{1}{2}$

Word Families

Noun	Verb
addition	add
subtraction	subtract
multiplication	multiply
division	divide

1 plus más	**9** an angle un ángulo	**17** an oval un óvalo	**25** a cylinder un cilindro
2 minus menos	**10** a side un lado	**18** a rectangle un rectángulo	**26** addition adición / suma
3 equals igual a	**11** perpendicular lines líneas perpendiculares	**19** a triangle un triángulo	**27** subtraction substracción / resta
4 percent por ciento	**12** parallel lines líneas paralelas	**20** a square un cuadrado	**28** multiplication multiplicación
5 multiplied by / times multiplicado por / por	**13** the circumference la circunferencia	**21** a pyramid una pirámide	**29** division división
6 divided by dividido entre	**14** the radius el radio	**22** a cube un cubo	**30** a fraction una fracción
7 a straight line una línea recta	**15** the diameter el diámetro	**23** a sphere una esfera	**31** geometry geometría
8 a curved line una línea curva	**16** a circle un círculo	**24** a cone un cono	**32** algebra álgebra

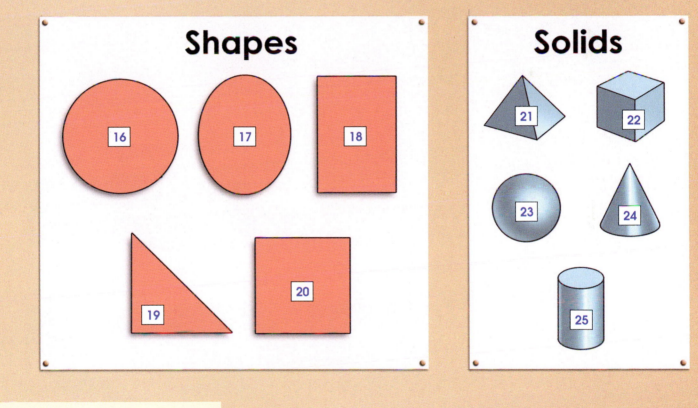

Shapes

Solids

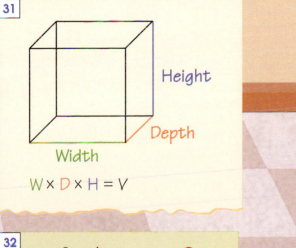

$$W \times D \times H = V$$

Height

Depth

Width

32

$$ax^2 + bx + c = 0$$

Words in Action

1. Look around your classroom. Find an example of each of the shapes on the list. Share your ideas with the class.
   - *My desk is a rectangle and the clock is a circle.*

2. Work with a partner. One student writes down a math problem. The other student figures out the answer, then reads the problem and the answer out loud.
   - Student A: (writes: *3 + 3*)
   - Student B: *Three plus three equals six.*

Science
Ciencia

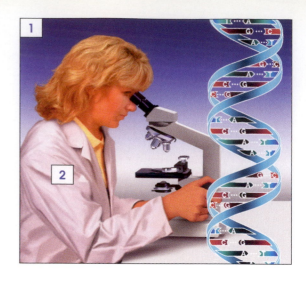

1 biology
biología

2 a biologist
un biólogo / una bióloga

3 chemistry
química

4 a chemist
un químico / una química

5 physics
física

6 a physicist
un físico / una física

7 a prism
un prisma

8 forceps
fórceps

9 a balance
una balanza

10 a solid
un sólido

11 a liquid
un líquido

12 a gas
un gas

13 a test tube
un tubo de ensayo

14 a Bunsen burner
un mechero de Bunsen

15 the periodic table
la tabla periódica

16 an element
un elemento

17 an atom
un átomo

18 a molecule
una molécula

19 a formula
una fórmula

20 a graduated cylinder
una probeta graduada

21 a dropper
un gotero

22 a stopper
un tapón

23 a beaker
un vaso de precipitado

24 a flask
un matraz

25 a microscope
un microscopio

26 a magnifying glass
una lupa

27 a funnel
un embudo

28 a slide
un portaobjeto

29 a petri dish
una caja de petri

30 a magnet
un imán

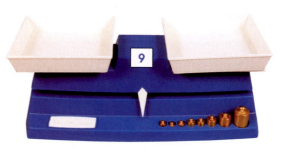

Word Partnerships

a biology	class
a chemistry	lab / laboratory

Word Families

Noun	Adjective
atom	atomic
magnet	magnetic
microscope	microscopic
liquid	liquid
solid	solid

PERIODIC TABLE OF THE ELEMENTS

$E=mc^2$

PERIODIC TABLE AND ATOMIC DATA
WITH ILLUSTRATED TEXT OF NUCLEAR TERMS

$E=mc^2$

Words in Action

1. Work with a partner. One person describes a laboratory object from the list. The other guesses the object. Take turns.
   - Student A: *You use this to pour liquid into a beaker.*
   - Student B: *A funnel.*

2. Put the items on the word list into three groups: items you find in a physics lab, items you find in a biology lab, and items you find in a chemistry lab. Compare lists with another student. (Note: Some items can be on more than one list.)

Writing
Escribir

Words in Context

Writing an **essay** is a process. First you **brainstorm** ideas. Next you **write** an outline, and then you write a draft. Before you **edit,** you **get** feedback. Are you ready to write the final draft? Before you do, make sure the **punctuation** is correct. Have you used **capital letters** for the first letter of each **word** in the **title**? Have you indented each **paragraph**? If so, now you are ready to write the final draft.

1 a letter
una carta

2 a word
una palabra

3 a sentence
una oración

4 a paragraph
un párrafo

5 a paper / an essay
un ensayo

6 an indentation
una sangría

7 a margin
un margen

8 a title
un título

9 punctuation
puntuación

10 a period
un punto

11 a comma
una coma

12 a question mark
un signo de interrogación

13 an exclamation point /
an exclamation mark
un signo de admiración

14 an apostrophe
un apóstrofe

15 parentheses
paréntesis

16 quotation marks
comillas

17 a colon
dos puntos

18 a semicolon
punto y coma

19 a hyphen
un guión

Verbs
Verbos

20 brainstorm ideas
lluvia de ideas

21 write an outline
escribir un resumen

22 write a draft
escribir un borrador

23 get feedback
recibir retroalimentación

24 edit your essay
revisar su ensayo

25 type your final draft
escribir en la máquina su borrador final /
escribir en la computadora su borrador final

1 W

2 Writing

3 Writing an essay is a process.

4 Writing an essay is a process. There are four stages to this process: prewriting, drafting, revising, and editing. Each of these stages is an important part in the process that leads a writer to create a well thought out and well organized paper.

5

Megan Purdum
English 1A

8 The Writing Process

6 Writing an essay is a process. There are four stages to this process: prewriting, drafting, revising, and editing. Each of these stages is an important part in the process that leads a writer to create a well thought out and well organized paper.

7 Prewriting consists of things the writer does before writing a draft of a paper. This is the stage in which the writer gathers and organizes ideas for the paper. This stage can include thinking, talking to others, gathering information, brainstorming, and making an outline of the paper.

In the next stage, the writer writes a draft. While writing a draft, the writer puts ideas into sentences and paragraphs. Each paragraph must have a topic sentence. The topic sentence is what that paragraph is about. The rest of the paragraph should explain and support the topic sentence. It is not important to focus on things like grammar and spelling at this stage.

9

10 •

11 ,

12 ?

13 !

14 '

15 ( )

16 " "

17 :

18 ;

19 -

Word Partnerships

a capital / an uppercase	letter
a lowercase	
a vocabulary	word
a slang	
a one-syllable	
a two-syllable	
a term	paper
a research	

Words in Action

1. Look at a magazine or newspaper article. Find and circle the following:
   - a comma
   - an apostrophe
   - a sentence
   - a paragraph

2. What are the steps in writing a paper? Discuss with a partner.

Explore, Rule, Invent
Explorar, Gobernar, Inventar

Words in Context

Humans have achieved amazing things. We have **composed** operas and poetry. We have **discovered** cures for diseases. We have **sailed** the world's oceans and **explored** the continents. We have **launched** rockets into space and **reached** the moon.

1 Humans **migrate** from Asia to the Americas.
Los humanos **emigran** de Asia a las Américas.

2 Mesopotamians **produce** the first wheel.
Los mesopotámicos **hacen** la primera rueda.

3 The Egyptians **build / construct** pyramids.
Los egipcios **construyen** pirámides.

4 The Vikings **sail** to present-day Canada.
Los vikingos **navegan** al actual Canadá.

5 The Chinese **grow** tea.
Los chinos **cultivan** té.

6 Joan of Arc **defends** France.
Juana de Arco **defiende** Francia.

7 Montezuma I **rules** the Aztecs.
Moctezuma I **gobierna** a los aztecas.

8 Amerigo Vespucci **explores** the Amazon.
Américo Vespucio **explora** el Amazonas.

9 Sir Isaac Newton **discovers** gravity.
Sir Isaac Newton **descubre** la gravedad.

10 Ludwig von Beethoven **composes** his first symphony.
Ludwig von Beethoven **compone** su primera sinfonía.

11 The Suez Canal **opens**.
Se **abre** el Canal de Suez.

12 Thomas Edison **invents** the lightbulb.
Thomas Edison **inventa** el foco.

13 The Wright brothers **fly** the first plane.
Los hermanos Wright **vuelan** el primer aeroplano.

14 World War II **ends**.
Termina la Segunda Guerra Mundial.

15 The Soviet Union **launches** the first satellite.
La Unión Soviética **lanza** el primer satélite.

16 Martin Luther King Jr. **wins** the Nobel Peace Prize.
Martin Luther King Jr. **gana** el Premio Nobel de la Paz.

17 Japan **introduces** the high-speed "bullet" train.
Japón **presenta** su tren "bala" de alta velocidad.

18 Apollo 11 astronauts **reach** the moon.
Los astronautas del Apolo 11 **llegan** a la luna.

19 The Berlin Wall **falls**.
Cae el Muro de Berlín.

20 South Africa **elects** Nelson Mandela president.
Sudáfrica **elige** a Nelson Mandela como presidente.

15,000 B.C. *3800 B.C.* *2485 B.C.–2*

Word Partnerships

win	a war
	a contest
compose	a song
	a letter
elect	a prime minister
	a president
	a mayor
build	a road
	a bridge

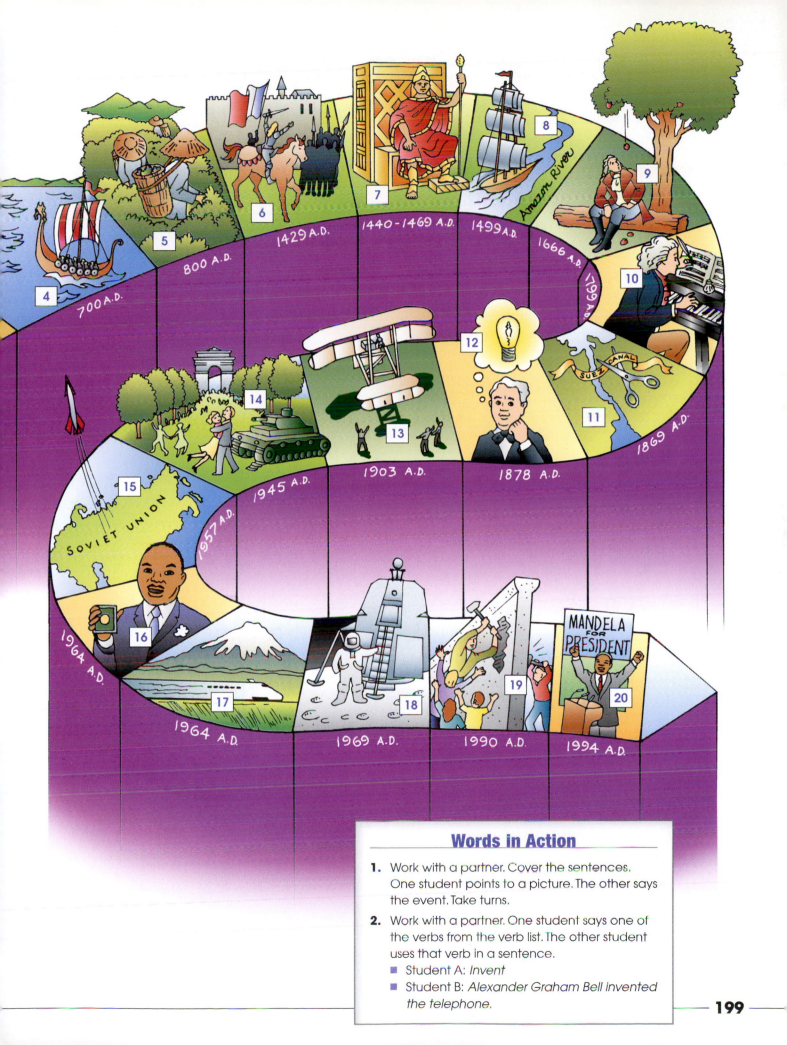

Words in Action

1. Work with a partner. Cover the sentences. One student points to a picture. The other says the event. Take turns.

2. Work with a partner. One student says one of the verbs from the verb list. The other student uses that verb in a sentence.
   - Student A: *Invent*
   - Student B: *Alexander Graham Bell invented the telephone.*

U.S. Government and Citizenship

El Gobierno de Estados Unidos y la Ciudadanía

The U.S. **government** has three parts. These parts are called *branches*. The executive branch includes the **president** and the **vice president**. The legislative branch includes the **House of Representatives** and the **Senate**. There are 100 **senators** in the Senate and 435 **congressmen** and **congresswomen** in the House of Representatives. The judicial branch includes nine **Supreme Court justices**.

1 a (political) candidate
   un candidato (político) /
   una candidata (política)

2 a ballot
   una votación

3 a voting booth
   una casilla para votar

4 a citizen
   un ciudadano / una ciudadana

5 the U.S. Constitution
   la Constitución de Estados Unidos

6 the Capitol (Building)
   el (edificio del) Capitolio

7 the White House
   la Casa Blanca

8 the Supreme Court
   la Suprema Corte

9 a congresswoman /
   a congressman
   una congresista / un congresista

10 a senator
   un senador / una senadora

11 the president
   el presidente

12 the vice president
   el vicepresidente

13 the justices
   los jueces

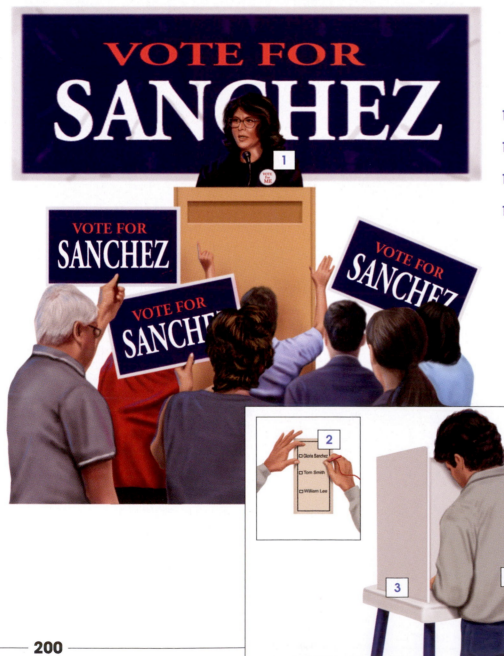

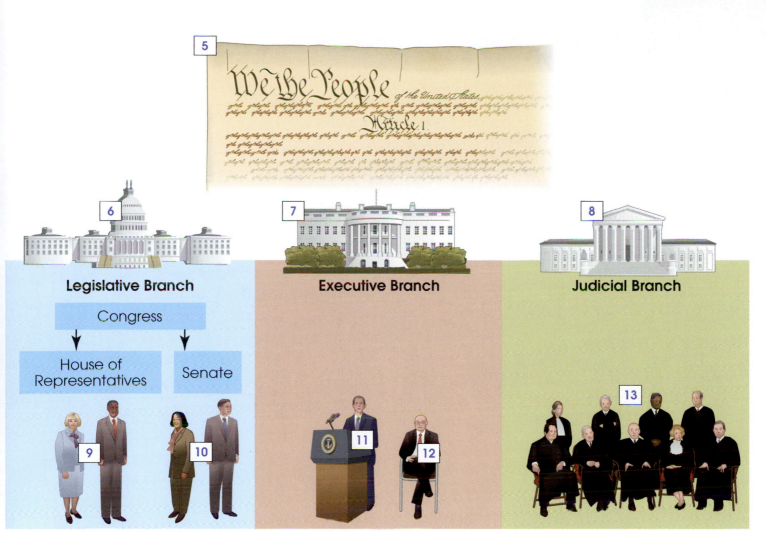

5 We the People of the United States, ... Article I.

6 Legislative Branch

Congress

House of Representatives   Senate

9   **10**

7 Executive Branch

11   **12**

8 Judicial Branch

13

Verbs

14 vote
votar

16 pay taxes
pagar impuestos

18 protest / demonstrate
protestar

15 obey the law
obedecer la ley

17 serve on a jury
ser miembro de un jurado

19 serve in the military
pertenecer al ejército

Word Partnerships

a United States   citizen

senator

congressman

Words in Action

1. Compare the U.S. government with the government of another country. How are they similar? How are they different?

2. Discuss which branch of the U.S. government you think is most important. Explain your reasons.

Fine Arts
Bellas Artes

Words in Context

Pablo Picasso is probably the most famous artist of the last 100 years. His **portraits** and **still lifes** hang in the world's great museums. Picasso worked as a **painter, sculptor,** and **potter.** He **painted** with oils and watercolors, and he sculpted in **clay.**

1

3

2

7

15

4

6

5

8

9

16

17

10

11

12

13

14

1 a frame
un marco

2 a still life
una naturaleza muerta

3 a portrait
un retrato

4 a landscape
un paisaje

5 a model
un modelo / una modelo

6 a palette
una paleta

7 a painting
una pintura

8 a paintbrush
un pincel

9 a painter
un pintor / una pintora

10 paint
pintar

11 an easel
un caballete

12 a canvas
un lienzo

13 a sketchpad
un boceto

14 a sketch
un cuaderno de bocetos

15 a mural
un mural

16 a sculpture
una escultura

17 a sculptor
un escultor / una escultora

18 pottery
alfarería / cerámica

19 a potter
un alfarero / una alfarera, un ceramista / una ceramista

20 a potter's wheel
un torno de alfarero

21 clay
arcilla / barro

22 a photograph
una fotografía

23 a photographer
un fotógrafo / una fotógrafa

Verbs
Verbos

24 draw
dibujar

25 paint
pintar

26 photograph / take a photograph
sacar / tomar una foto

Word Partnerships

modern	art
a work of	
oil	paint
acrylic	
watercolor	
a watercolor	painting
an oil	

Words in Action

1. Work with a group. Make a list of famous artists. Answer the following questions about each:
   - What kind of artist is he/she?
   - What materials did/does this artist use?
   - Do you know the names of any of the artist's works?

2. What is your favorite kind of art? Why? Discuss with a partner.

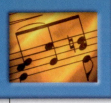

Performing Arts

Artes Escénicas

Words in Context

Different **performing arts** began in different countries around the world. For example, theater began in ancient Greece. The **actors** wore **masks** and performed **plays** in large outdoor theaters. **Opera** began in Italy at the end of the 16th century, and soon became popular in France and Germany. **Ballet** also began in Italy at the end of the 16th century, and it became very popular in France while Louis XIV was king.

1 a ballet
   un ballet

2 a balcony
   una galería

3 a dancer
   un bailarín / una bailarina

4 a mask
   una máscara

5 a costume
   un disfraz

6 a stage
   un escenario

7 a conductor
   un director

8 an orchestra
   una orquesta

9 an audience
   un público

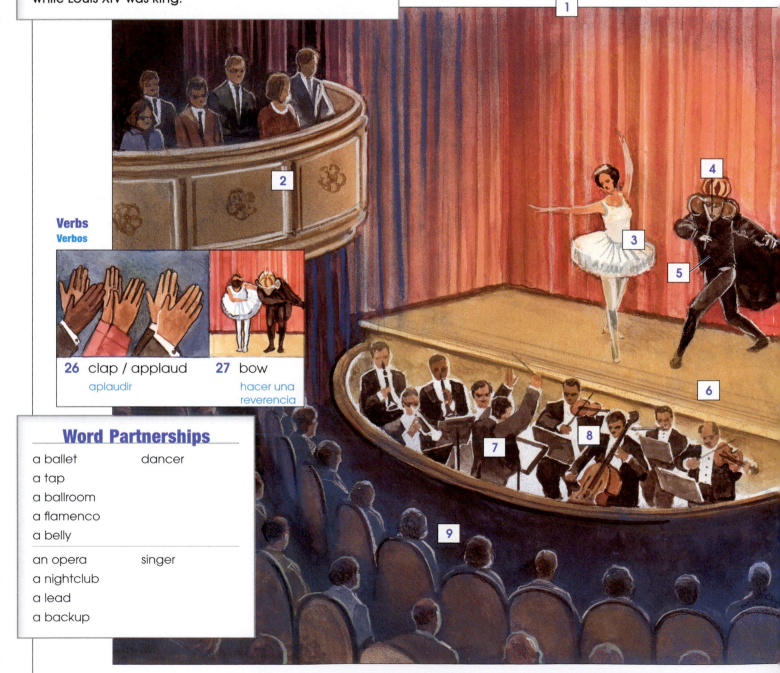

Verbs
Verbos

26 clap / applaud
   aplaudir

27 bow
   hacer una reverencia

Word Partnerships

a ballet	dancer
a tap	
a ballroom	
a flamenco	
a belly	
an opera	singer
a nightclub	
a lead	
a backup	

10	a (rock) concert	18	an actor
	un concierto (de rock)		un actor / una actriz
11	a spotlight	19	a set
	un reflector		un foro
12	a drummer	20	a seat
	un baterista / una baterista		un asiento
13	a microphone	21	an usher
	un micrófono		un acomodador
14	a singer	22	a ticket
	un cantante / una cantante		un boleto
15	a guitarist	23	a program
	un guitarrista / una guitarrista		un programa
16	backup singers	24	a box office
	cantantes del coro		una taquilla
17	a play	25	an opera
	una obra de teatro		una ópera

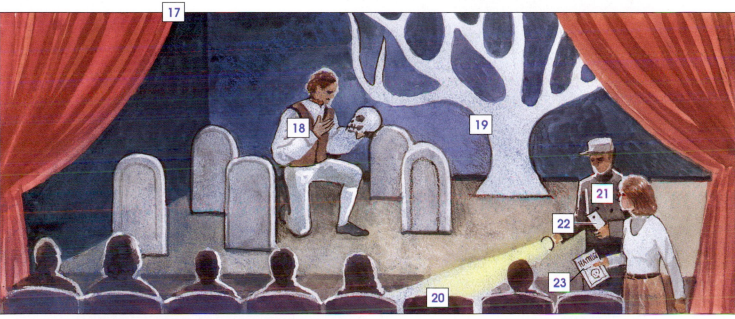

Words in Action

1. Have you ever seen a ballet? An opera? A play? Choose your favorite and tell a partner about it.

2. Imagine you are the directors of a new arts center. What kinds of concerts, plays, and other performances will you present this year? Discuss with your group.

Instruments
Instrumentos

Words in Context

Percussion instruments are thousands of years old. **Drums** are one of the oldest percussion instruments. They were part of African culture as early as 6000 B.C. The **tambourine** is also thousands of years old. Many countries, from Japan to Morocco to England, use tambourines in their music. Other percussion instruments include **maracas,** from Latin America, and **cymbals,** from China.

Word Partnerships

play	an instrument
tune	
practice	the piano
	the violin
	the cello
an acoustic	guitar
an electric	
a bass	

Percussion
Percusión

1 drums
  batería

2 cymbals
  címbalos / platillos

3 a tambourine
  un pandero / una pandereta

4 a marimba
  una marimba

5 maracas
  maracas

Brass
Metal

6 a tuba
  una tuba

7 a French horn
  un corno francés

8 a trombone
  un trombón

9 a trumpet
  una trompeta

10 a bugle
  un clarín

Woodwind
Madera / Viento

11 a saxophone
  un saxofón

12 a flute
  una flauta

13 an oboe
  un oboe

14 a clarinet
  un clarinete

15 a bassoon
  un fagot

16 pan pipes
  flauta de Pan

17 a harmonica
  una armónica

String
Cuerda

18 a sitar
  una cítara

19 a bass
  un contrabajo

20 a cello
  un chelo / un violonchelo

21 a violin
  un violín

22 a guitar
  una guitarra

23 a banjo
  un banjo

24 a harp
  una arpa

Keyboard
Teclado

25 an electric keyboard
  un teclado eléctrico

26 a piano
  un piano

27 an organ
  un órgano

28 an accordion
  un acordeón

Words in Action

1. Make a list of famous musicians and the instruments they play.

2. Work with a partner. Pretend to play an instrument. Your partner will guess the instrument. Take turns.

Film, TV, and Music
Filme, Televisión y Música

AGENT 009

OFFICER BABY

THE RAMIREZ FILES

A CLUE

Love in Paris

STARDATE 2075

Dragon Story

MIDNIGHT

COWBOY

A FISH Story

HISTORY OF THE PYRAMIDS

Films / Movies
Filmes / Películas

1 action / adventure
   acción / aventura
2 comedy
   comedia
3 mystery / suspense
   misterio / suspenso
4 drama
   drama
5 romance
   romance
6 science fiction
   ciencia ficción
7 western
   oeste
8 fantasy
   fantasía
9 horror
   horror
10 documentary
   documental
11 animated
   animado

Word Partnerships

an independent	film
a foreign	
a funny	movie
a scary	
satellite	TV
cable	
a TV	station
	commercial
loud	music
soft	

TV programs
Programas de televisión

12 news
noticias

13 sitcom
telecomedia (de situación)

14 cartoon
caricatura

15 game show
programa de juegos

16 soap opera
telenovela

17 talk show
programa de entrevistas

18 nature program
programa sobre la naturaleza

19 children's program
programa para niños

20 sports
deportes

21 reality show
reality show

Music
Música

22 pop
pop

23 jazz
jazz

24 rock
rock

25 blues
blues

26 R&B / soul
soul

27 hip hop
hip hop

28 classical
clásica

29 country and western
country

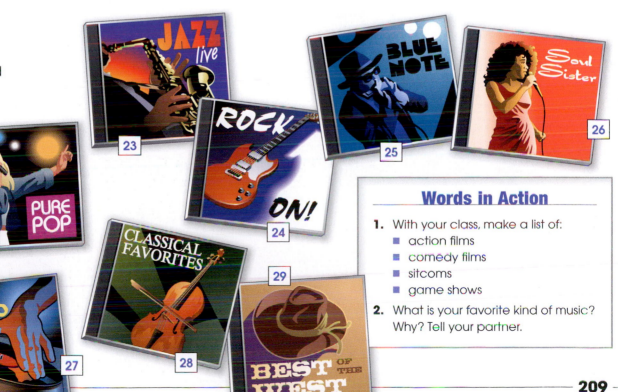

Words in Action

1. With your class, make a list of:
- action films
- comedy films
- sitcoms
- game shows

2. What is your favorite kind of music? Why? Tell your partner.

Beach

Playa

Words in Context

There is a **beach** in Japan with perfect weather every day of the year. How is it possible? The beach at Ocean Dome is indoors! **Sunbathers** put their beach towels on the **sand** and relax. There is no sun, but it feels warm and sunny inside. **Swimmers swim** in a man-made **ocean,** and **surfers surf** on man-made **waves!**

Verbs
Verbos

30 surf
hacer surf

31 dive
saltar de clavado

32 swim
nadar

33 float
flotar

210

1 a sailboat
un velero / un barco de vela

2 a pier
un malecón

3 a water-skier
un esquiador acuático / una esquiadora acuática

4 a motorboat
una lancha motora

5 the ocean / the water
el océano / el mar

6 a ship
un barco

7 a lighthouse
un faro

8 a swimmer
un nadador / una nadadora

9 a wave
una ola

10 a snorkeler
una persona con esnórquel

11 a snorkel
un esnórquel

12 a sailboard
una tabla de windsurf

13 a sailboarder
un windsurfista / una windsurfista

14 a life jacket
un chaleco salvavidas

15 a surfer
un surfista / una surfista

16 a surfboard
una tabla de surf

17 a lifeguard
un salvavidas / una salvavidas

18 a cooler
una hielera

19 a sunbather
una persona que toma el sol

20 a beach ball
una pelota para la playa

21 sand
arena

22 a (sea)shell
una concha (marina)

23 a water wing
un flotador

24 sunscreen
crema de protección solar

25 a sand castle
un castillo de arena

26 a (diving) mask
un visor

27 fins
aletas

28 a pail
un balde / una cubeta

29 a shovel
una pala

Word Partnerships

a public	beach
a private	
a tropical	
a beach	umbrella
	chair
	towel
	house
a bottle of	sunscreen
a tube of	
apply / put on	sunscreen
use	

Words in Action

1. Plan a day at the beach. What will you take to the beach? What will you do there?

2. Think of different ways to group the words in the word list. For example, *Things children play with* or *People and things you see in the water.*

211

Camping

Excursionismo

Words in Context

The Appalachian Trail is a 2,174-mile* **trail** in the U.S. It starts in Maine and goes all the way to Georgia. Some people **hike** a small part of the trail for a day. Others hike longer portions of the trail. These **hikers** usually bring a **backpack,** a **tent,** and a **sleeping bag,** along with other camping equipment like a **trail map,** a **compass,** a **water bottle,** and a **pocket knife.** Hiking the whole trail takes an entire season!

*3,478.4 kilometers

1

2

5

7

11

6

12

13

10

8

9

14

15

16

20

17

19

21

18

22

23

Word Partnerships

a camping	trip
	site
a fishing	boat
a ski	
a street	map
a city	
a road	

1 a compass
una brújula

2 a rock climber
un montañista

3 a horseback rider
un jinete

4 a hiker
un excursionista

5 a fishing pole
una caña de pescar

6 a fisherman
un pescador

7 a (row)boat
una lancha de paseo / un bote de paseo

8 a canoe
una canoa

9 a paddle
un remo

10 a raft
una balsa

11 a backpack
una mochila

12 a backpacker
un mochilero

13 a water bottle
una botella para agua

14 a (hiking) trail
un sendero

15 a camping stove
una estufa de excursión

16 a lantern
una linterna

17 a rope
una cuerda / una soga

18 a (trail) map
un mapa de veredas

19 a canteen
una cantimplora

20 binoculars
binoculares

21 a pocket knife
una navaja de bolsillo

22 insect repellent
repelente de insectos

23 matches
cerillos / fósforos

24 a tent
una tienda de campaña

25 a sleeping bag
una bolsa para dormir

26 an air mattress
un colchón inflable

27 a camper
un campista

28 a (camp)fire
una fogata

Verbs
Verbos

29 camp
acampar

30 fish
pescar

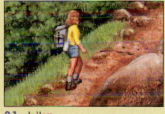

31 hike
ir de caminata

Words in Action

1. Imagine you are going on a camping trip. What will you do? What will you take?

2. You are lost on a hiking trail. You can only bring five of the items on the list. Which items will you bring? Explain why you need each one.

City Park
Parque de la Ciudad

Words in Context

Central Park is a beautiful **park** in the middle of New York City. It is about two miles* long and has something for everyone. For adults, there are bicycle and jogging paths. For children, there is a **playground** with a **sandbox, monkey bars,** and **swings.** There is even an old **carousel,** an ice rink, and a zoo.

*3.218 kilometers

1 a kite
   una cometa / un papalote

2 swings
   columpios

3 monkey bars
   un pasamanos

4 a playground
   un campo de juegos

5 a slide
   una resbaladilla

6 a jungle gym
   un trepador

7 a seesaw
   un sube y baja

8 a sandbox
   una caja de arena / un arenero

9 a trash can /
   a garbage can
   un bote de basura

10 a puppet show
   un teatro de títeres

11 a picnic
   un día de campo

12 a picnic basket
   una canasta para día de campo

13 a picnic table
   una mesa para día de campo

14 a carousel /
   a merry-go-round
   un carrusel

15 a Ferris wheel
   una rueda de la fortuna

16 a roller coaster
   una montaña rusa

17 a bridge
   un puente

18 a (park) bench
   una banca (de parque)

19 a pond
   un estanque

20 a jogger
   un corredor

21 a skateboard
   una patineta

22 a skateboarder
   un patinador / una patinadora

23 a skater
   un patinador / una patinadora

24 (in-line) skates
   patines (en línea)

25 a cyclist
   un ciclista / una ciclista

26 a bicycle / a bike
   una bicicleta

27 a path
   un sendero

28 a street vendor
   un vendedor ambulante / una vendedora ambulante

29 a pigeon
   un pichón

Word Partnerships

a local	park
a national	
an amusement	
ride	a bike
	a carousel
have	a picnic
go on	
fly	a kite

Words in Action

1. Work with your class. Discuss your dream park. Draw a picture of the park on the board. Each student adds an item to the park and labels this item.

2. When did you last go to a park? What did you do? What did you see? Tell a partner.

Places to Visit
Lugares para Visitar

Words in Context

Try a new activity this weekend. Do you like shopping? You could go to a flea market or a **garage sale.** Do you enjoy nature? You could walk on a **hiking trail** or ride your bicycle on a **bicycle path.** Do you like animals? You could go to a **zoo** or an **aquarium.**

1 a café
un café

2 a zoo
un zoológico

3 a planetarium
un planetario

4 a nursery
un vivero

5 a bowling alley
una pista de boliche

6 a sporting event
un evento deportivo

7 a pool hall
una sala de billar

8 an aquarium
un acuario

9 a garage sale
una venta de cochera /
una venta de garaje

10 an amusement park
un parque de diversiones

11 a (hiking) trail
un sendero para
excursionistas

12 a lecture
una conferencia

13 a botanical garden
un jardín botánico

14 a gym
un gimnasio

15 a circus
un circo

16 miniature golf
golfito

17 a bicycle path
una ciclopista

18 a video arcade
una sala de videojuegos

19 a carnival
un carnaval / una feria

20 a museum
un museo

21 a water park
un parque acuático

22 a movie theater
una sala de cine

23 a rodeo
un rodeo

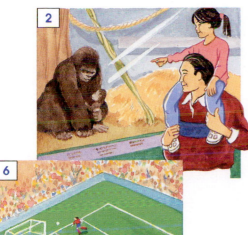

2

3

4

7

6

12

11

13

16

15

20

19

23

22

1 SILLY MOVIE 3
2 BLUE COYOTE

Tickets

Word Partnerships

a petting	zoo
a traveling	circus
a three-ring	
an outdoor	café
a sidewalk	
an internet	

Words in Action

1. What are your five favorite places to visit from this list? Compare your favorite places with your classmates'. Can you find another student with the same favorite places?

2. Work with a group. Make a list of famous:
   - zoos
   - amusement parks
   - museums

Indoor Sports and Fitness

Deportes Bajo Techo y Buena Condición Física

Words in Context

Different sports and fitness activities help in different ways. **Yoga** and **martial arts** can help you relax. **Aerobics** and the **treadmill** can help you lose weight. **Push-ups** and free weights can help you become stronger.

1 martial arts
artes marciales

2 yoga
yoga

3 basketball
básquetbol / baloncesto

4 a referee
un árbitro / un réferi

5 a basketball court
una cancha de básquetbol /
una cancha de baloncesto

6 a (basketball) player
un jugador (de básquetbol /
de baloncesto)

7 a basketball
una pelota de básquetbol / una
pelota de baloncesto

8 ping-pong
pimpón / ping-pong

9 a ping-pong paddle
una raqueta de pimpón /
una raqueta de ping-pong

10 a ping-pong table
una mesa de pimpón/
una mesa de ping-pong

11 a chin-up
una dominada

12 a push-up
una lagartija

13 a sit-up
un abdominal

14 a (stationary) bike
una bicicleta (estacionaria) /
una bicicleta (fija)

15 a treadmill
una caminadora

16 boxing
boxeo

17 a boxer
un boxeador / una
boxeadora

18 a boxing glove
un guante de boxeo

19 a boxing ring
un cuadrilátero de
boxeo

20 a punching bag
un saco de boxeo

21 wrestling
lucha

22 a wrestler
un luchador / una
luchadora

23 gymnastics
gimnasia

24 a gymnast
una gimnasta / un
gimnasta

25 weightlifting
levantamiento de pesas

26 a weightlifter
un levantador de pesas /
una levantadora de pesas

27 a bench
un banco

28 a barbell
una barra de pesas

29 a dartboard
una diana

30 darts
dardos

31 aerobics
aerobics

32 a diving board
un trampolín

33 a diver
un clavadista / una
clavadista

34 a (swimming) pool
una alberca / una
piscina

35 a locker room
un vestidor

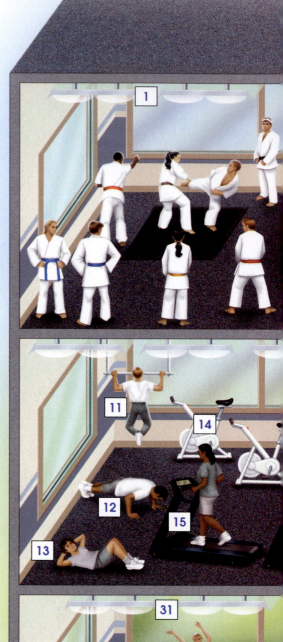

Word Partnerships

sports	club
	team
	equipment
	injury
a yoga	instructor
an aerobics	class
a martial arts	

218

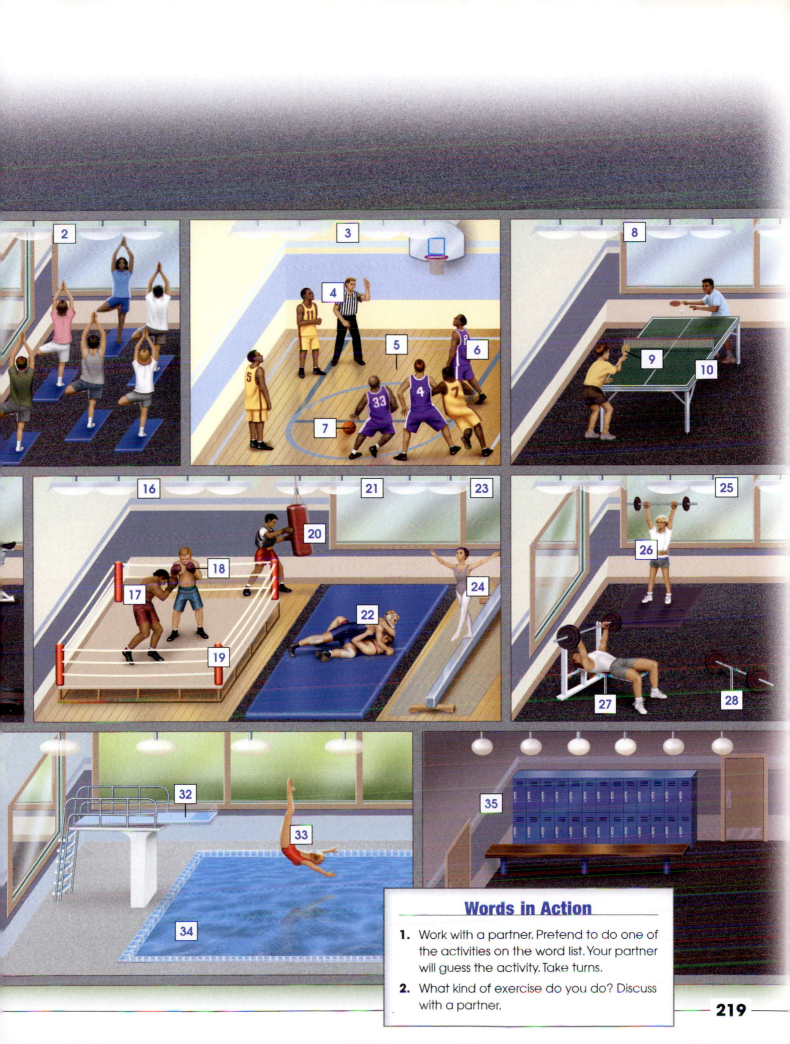

Words in Action

1. Work with a partner. Pretend to do one of the activities on the word list. Your partner will guess the activity. Take turns.

2. What kind of exercise do you do? Discuss with a partner.

19

Outdoor Sports and Fitness
Deportes al Aire Libre y Buena Condición Física

Words in Context

Tennis is one of the most popular sports in the world. The rules are simple. A player uses a racket to hit a tennis ball over the net. The other player tries to hit the ball back. The first player to win four points wins the game.

1 tennis
tenis

2 a (tennis) racket
una raqueta (de tenis)

3 a (tennis) ball
una pelota (de tenis)

4 baseball
béisbol

5 a baseball
una pelota de béisbol

6 a batter
un bateador

7 a bat
un bate

8 a catcher
un catcher

9 volleyball
voleibol

10 a volleyball
un balón de voleibol

11 a (volleyball) net
una red de voleibol

12 golf
golf

13 a (golf) club
un club de golf / un palo de golf

14 a golfer
un golfista / una golfista

15 a golf course
un campo de golf

16 track
atletismo

17 a runner
un corredor / una corredora

18 a track
una pista

19 soccer
fútbol

20 a fan
un fanático / una fanática / un aficionado / una aficionada

21 a soccer field
un campo de fútbol

22 a uniform
un uniforme

23 football
fútbol americano

24 a goalpost
una portería

25 a (football) helmet
un casco (de fútbol americano)

26 a cheerleader
una porrista / una animadora

27 a football
un balón de fútbol americano

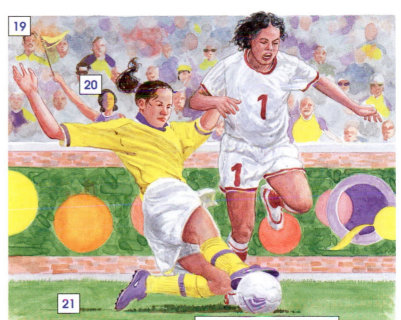

Words in Action

1. Which of these sports do you like to play? Which do you like to watch? Discuss with a partner.

2. Work with a partner. One person pretends to play one of these sports. The other guesses the sport. Take turns.

Winter Sports
Deportes de Invierno

Words in Context

Skiing began in Norway in the 1700s. Early **skiers** used long wooden cross-country **skis** and wooden **ski poles.** Today there is a new kind of **winter sport** called **snowboarding. Snowboarders** don't use ski poles. They slide down the slopes with both feet on a **snowboard.**

Word Partnerships

a hockey	team
	game
	arena
	rink
a skiing	injury
	lesson

1 a snowmobile un trineo motorizado	**6** ski poles palos para esquiar	**11** (cross country) skiing esquí a campo traviesa
2 snowshoes raquetas (para andar en la nieve)	**7** a toboggan un tobogán	**12** (downhill) skiing patinaje cuesta abajo
3 a sled un trineo	**8** a chairlift una telesilla	**13** a skier un esquiador / una esquiadora
4 skis esquíes	**9** ice skating patinaje sobre hielo	**14** snowboarding esquí con tabla
5 ski boots botas para esquiar	**10** an ice skater un patinador sobre hielo / una patinadora sobre hielo	**15** a snowboarder un esquiador de tabla / una esquiadora de tasla

16 a snowboard una tabla para esquiar	**21** a goal una portería
17 (ice) hockey hockey sobre hielo	**22** a (hockey) player un jugador de hockey / una jugadora de hockey
18 a scoreboard un tablero de resultados	**23** a hockey stick un palo de hockey
19 a score un resultado	**24** a (hockey) puck un disco de hockey
20 an ice (skating) rink una pista de hielo	**25** (ice) skates patines para hielo

Words in Action

1. Which winter sports are the most fun? Which are the most dangerous? Discuss with your class.

2. One student names a winter sport. The other students take turns naming clothing and equipment for that sport.
   - Student A: *Hockey.*
   - Student B: *Ice skates.*
   - Student C: *A hockey stick.*

Games, Toys, and Hobbies
Juegos, Juguetes y Pasatiempos

Words in Context

Playing **cards** are popular in countries around the world. The French style deck is the most common. This deck has 52 cards and four suits—**spades, hearts, diamonds,** and **clubs.** There are 13 cards in each suit: **ace, king, queen, jack,** and numbers 2 through 10. People use these cards to play different **games** around the world, like *bridge* and *gin rummy* in the U.S., *king* in Brazil, and *dai hin min* in Japan.

1 **cards**
cartas

2 an **ace**
un **as**

3 a **king**
un **rey**

4 a **queen**
una **reina**

5 a **jack**
una **jota**

6 a **joker**
un **comodín**

7 a **spade**
una **pica**

8 a **diamond**
un **diamante**

9 a **club**
un **trébol**

10 a **heart**
un **corazón**

11 **backgammon**
backgammon

12 **chess**
ajedrez

13 **mah-jongg**
majong

14 **dominoes**
dominó

15 **checkers**
damas

16 a **puzzle**
un **rompecabezas**

17 **dice**
dados

18 **crayons**
crayolas

19 a **doll**
una **muñeca**

20 **knitting needles**
agujas para tejer

21 **yarn**
estambre

22 a **crochet hook**
un **gancho para tejer**

23 (**embroidery**) **thread**
hilo para bordar

24 a **needle**
una **aguja**

Verbs
Verbos

25 **knit**
tejer con agujas

26 **crochet**
tejer con gancho

27 **embroider**
bordar

28 **build** a model
armar un modelo

Word Partnerships

a board	game
a card	
a chess	board
a checker	piece
a deck of	cards
a hand of	
play	cards
	a game
king of	hearts
nine of	spades

Words in Action

1. Make a list of your three favorite games from the list. Put the list in order, with the game you like best at the top. Share your list with a partner.

2. Take a poll to find out the favorite games of the students in your class.
   - Which is the most popular game?
   - Which is the least popular game?

225

Camera, Stereo, and DVD
Cámara, Estéreo y DVD

Words in Context

Audio equipment keeps changing. Until the 1980s, most people listened to music on **records** or **tapes.** Then in 1983, **CD players** and **CDs** became available. By 1998, more people bought CDs than records. By the late 1990s, MP3 technology became popular. Now **MP3 players** are becoming one of the most popular items at electronics stores.

1 (a roll of) film
un rollo de película

2 a zoom lens
una lente zoom

3 a camera
una cámara

4 a camcorder
una grabadora de video

5 a tripod
un trípode

6 a plug
una clavija

7 an adapter (plug)
un adaptador (de clavija)

8 a record
un disco

9 an MP3 player
un reproductor MP3

10 a (personal) CD player
un reproductor portátil de CD's

11 headphones
audífonos

12 a CD player
un reproductor de CD's

13 a CD / a compact disc
un CD / un disco compacto

14 a speaker
un parlante

15 a stereo (system)
un (sistema) estéreo

16 a tape / a cassette
una cinta de audio / un cassette de audio

17 a boom box
una grabadora

18 a satellite dish
una antena satelital de disco

19 a television / a TV
una televisión / una TV

20 a (video) game system
un aparato de videojuegos

21 a VCR / a videocassette recorder
una reproductora de videos / una videograbadora

22 a video(cassette)
un cassette de video

23 a remote control
un control remoto

24 a DVD player
un reproductor de DVD's

25 a DVD
un DVD

Word Partnerships

a digital	camera
a 35-millimeter	
a disposable	
shoot	(a roll of) film
develop	
turn up	the TV
turn down	the stereo

26 play
reproducir

27 fast forward
avanzar rápidamente

28 rewind
rebobinar

29 pause
poner pausa

30 stop
detener

31 eject
expulsar

Words in Action

1. Which three items on the list would you most like to get as gifts? Why? Discuss with a partner.

2. Which items on the list could help you learn English? How? Discuss with your class.

Holidays and Celebrations
Días Festivos y Celebraciones

Words in Context

People celebrate the **New Year** in different ways around the world. In Brazil, many people have **parties.** They often go to the beach after midnight and watch **fireworks.** It is also traditional to throw **flowers** into the sea. The Chinese New Year happens between January 17 and February 19. Chinese people all over the world celebrate with **parades** and **firecrackers.**

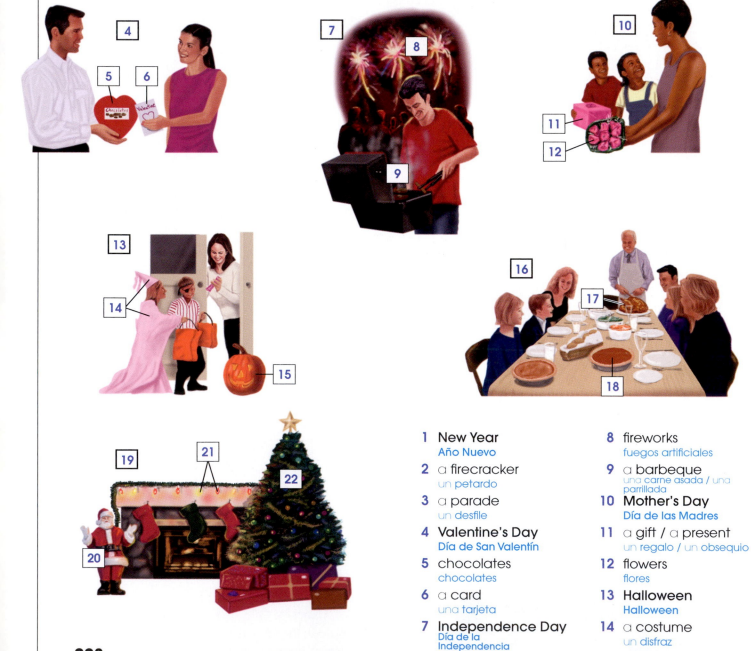

1 New Year Año Nuevo	**8 fireworks** fuegos artificiales
2 a firecracker un petardo	**9 a barbeque** una carne asada / una parrillada
3 a parade un desfile	**10 Mother's Day** Día de las Madres
4 Valentine's Day Día de San Valentín	**11 a gift / a present** un regalo / un obsequio
5 chocolates chocolates	**12 flowers** flores
6 a card una tarjeta	**13 Halloween** Halloween
7 Independence Day Día de la Independencia	**14 a costume** un disfraz

Verbs
Verbos

29 wrap
a present
envolver un regalo /
envolver un obsequio

30 light
candles
encender velas

31 blow out
candles
apagar velas

32 open
a present
abrir un regalo /
abrir un obsequio

Word Partnerships

a birthday	party
a retirement	
a New Year's Eve	
a birthday	gift
a wedding	cake
a birthday	card
a Valentine's Day	
a Mother's Day	

Words in Action

1. Work with a group. Choose a holiday on the list. What are the different ways the people in your group celebrate this holiday? Discuss with your group.

2. Plan a birthday party for a friend.
   - What will you eat?
   - How will you decorate?
   - What gift will you give?

Index

Index Guide

All entries in the index are followed by a phonetic listing and a translation. Following the phonetic listing and translation, most entries have two numbers. The first number, in bold type, is the page number on which the entry item is found. The second number corresponds to the item's number in the word list. See the example below.

Some entries have two numbers in bold type. In this case, the entry is a topic covered in a two-page lesson, and the numbers indicate the page numbers of this lesson.

If the entry is in capital letters, it is a unit title, and the two numbers in bold type indicate the pages on which this unit begins and ends.

If an entry is followed by only a single number in bold type, then the entry appears on this page number as a subhead in the word list, or it appears somewhere else on the page.

Verb and verb phrase entries appear in bold type in the index. Some entries appear twice in the index—once in bold and once in regular type. In these cases, the bold type entry is a verb, and the regular type entry is a noun.

Guide to Pronunciation Symbols

Vowels			Consonants		
Symbol	Key Word	Pronunciation	Symbol	Key Word	Pronunciation
/a/	hot	/hat/	/b/	boy	/bɔɪ/
	far	/far/	/d/	day	/deɪ/
/æ/	cat	/kæt/	/ʤ/	just	/ʤʌst/
/aɪ/	fine	/faɪn/	/f/	face	/feɪs/
/aʊ/	house	/haʊs/	/g/	get	/gɛt/
/ɛ/	bed	/bɛd/	/h/	hat	/hæt/
/eɪ/	name	/neɪm/	/k/	car	/kar/
/i/	need	/nid/	/l/	light	/laɪt/
/ɪ/	sit	/sɪt/	/m/	my	/maɪ/
/oʊ/	go	/goʊ/	/n/	nine	/naɪn/
/ʊ/	book	/bʊk/	/ŋ/	sing	/sɪŋ/
/u/	boot	/but/	/p/	pen	/pɛn/
/ɔ/	dog	/dɔg/	/r/	right	/raɪt/
	four	/fɔr/	/s/	see	/si/
/ɔɪ/	toy	/tɔɪ/	/t/	tea	/ti/
/ʌ/	cup	/kʌp/	/ʧ/	cheap	/ʧip/
/ɛr/	bird	/bɛrd/	/v/	vote	/voʊt/
/ə/	about	/əˈbaʊt/	/w/	west	/wɛst/
	after	/ˈæftər/	/y/	yes	/yɛs/
			/z/	zoo	/zu/
			/ð/	they	/ðeɪ/
			/θ/	think	/θɪŋk/
			/ʃ/	shoe	/ʃu/
			/ʒ/	vision	/ˈvɪʒən/

Stress

/ˈ/	city	/ˈsɪti/	used before a syllable to show primary (main) stress
/ˌ/	dictionary	/ˈdɪkʃəˌnɛri/	used before a syllable to show secondary stress

general practitioner /ˈʤɛnərəl prækˈtɪʃənər/ *médico general,* **141**–20

geometry /ʤiˈɑmətri/ *geometría,* **193**–31

geothermal energy /ˌʤioʊˈθɜrməl ˈɛnərʤi/ *energía geotérmica,* **171**–25

geraniums /ʤəˈreɪniəmz/ *geranios,* **179**–30

German /ˈʤɜrmən/ *alemán, alemana,* **44**–11

get /gɛt/
  ... a speeding ticket /ə ˈspidɪŋ ˈtɪkɪt/ *recibir una multa por exceso de velocidad,* **123**–6
  ...a job /ə ʤɑb/ *conseguir un trabajo,* **31**–8
  ...a(n electric) shock /ə(n ɪˈlɛktrɪk) ʃɑk/ *tener un electrochoque,* **136**–14
  ...feedback /ˈfidˌbæk/ *recibir retroalimentación,* **196**–23
  ...gas /gæs/ *poner gasolina,* **123**–15
  ...the key /ðə ki/ *conseguir la llave,* **64**–8
  ...your boarding pass /yər ˈbɔrdɪŋ pæs/ *conseguir su pase de abordar,* **126**–4

get dressed /gɛt drɛsd/ *vestirse,* **34**–8

get engaged /gɛt ɛnˈgeɪʤd/ *comprometerse,* **31**–11

get in /gɛt ɪn/ *entrar,* **37**–6

get married /gɛt ˈmærid/ *casarse,* **31**–12

get off /gɛt ɔf/ *salir, bajar de,* **37**–14
  ...the highway /ðə ˈhaɪˌweɪ/ *salirse de la autopista,* **123**–9
  ...the plane /ðə pleɪn/ *bajar del avión,* **126**–23

get on /gɛt ɑn/ *subirse,* **37**–12
  ...the highway /ðə ˈhaɪˌweɪ/ *tomar la autopista,* **123**–12

get out (of) /gɛt aʊt (ʌv)/ *salir de,* **37**–5

get sick /gɛt sɪk/ *enfermarse,* **31**–18

get up /gɛt ʌp/ *levantarse,* **34**–2

gift /gɪft/ *regalo, obsequio,* **228**–11
  give a... /gɪv ə/ *dar un regalo,* **40**–7

gift shop /gɪft ʃɑp/ *tienda de regalos,* **48**–4, **159**–22

gills /gɪlz/ *agallas,* **189**–4

giraffe /ʤəˈræf/ *jirafa,* **185**–6

girdle /ˈgɜrdl/ *faja,* **107**–21

girl /gɜrl/ *niña,* **57**–13

give /gɪv/
  ...a gift /ə gɪft/ *dar un regalo,* **40**–7
  ...a shot /ə ʃɑt/ *ponerle una inyección,* **137**–25

glacier /ˈgleɪʃər/ *glaciar,* **169**–4

glass /glæs/ *vaso,* **70**–25
  refill the... /ˈriˌfɪl ðə/ *volver a llenar el vaso,* **102**–14
  water... /ˈwɔtər/ *vaso de agua,* **101**–16

glass cleaner /glæs ˈklinər/ *limpiador de vidrios,* **80**–11

glasses /ˈglæsɪz/ *lentes,* **33**–28, **141**–24
  safety... /ˈseɪfti/ *seguridad,* **157**–25

globe /ˈgloʊb/ *globo terráqueo,* **19**–9

glove compartment /glʌv kəmˈpɑrtmənt/ *guantera,* **121**–18

gloves /glʌvz/ *guantes,* **109**–1

glue /glu/ *goma,* **155**–25

glue /glu/ *pegar,* **165**–24

go /goʊ/
  ...home /hoʊm/ *ir a casa,* **34**–14
  ...to bed /tə bɛd/ *irse a la cama,* **34**–23
  ...to college /tə ˈkɑlɪʤ/ *ir a la universidad,* **31**–6
  ...to the board /tə ðə bɔrd/ *pasar al pizarrón,* **20**–16
  ...to work /tə wɜrk/ *ir a trabajar,* **34**–11

goal /goʊl/ *portería,* **223**–21

goalpost /ˈgoʊlˌpoʊst/ *portería,* **220**–24

goat /goʊt/ *macho cabrío, cabra,* **152**–21

go down /goʊ daʊn/ *bajar, bajarse,* **37**–19

goggles /ˈgɑgəlz/
  safety... /ˈseɪfti/ *lentes de seguridad,* **157**–23

go in /goʊ ɪn/ *entrar,* **37**–3

go into /goʊ ˈɪntu/ *entrar*
  ...a dressing room /ə ˈdrɛsɪŋ rum/ *entrar al vestidor,* **114**–3

gold /goʊld/ *oro,* **10**–13

golf /gɑlf/ *golf,* **220**–12

golf club /gɑlf klʌb/ *club de golf, palo de golf,* **220**–13

golf course /gɑlf kɔrs/ *campo de golf,* **220**–15

golfer /gɑlfər/ *un golfista, una golfista,* **220**–14

goose /gus/ *un ganso, una gansa,* **152**–19, **187**–1

gopher /ˈgoʊfər/ *tuza,* **185**–19

gorilla /gəˈrɪlə/ *gorila,* **182**–7

go shopping /goʊ ˈʃɑpɪŋ/ *ir de compras,* **114**–1

go through /goʊ θru/
  ...security /səˈkyʊrəti/ *pasar por seguridad,* **126**–5

go up /goʊ ʌp/ *subir, subirse,* **37**–20

gown /gaʊn/ *vestido largo,* **104**–5

GP /ʤi pi/ *médico general,* **141**–20

grade /greɪd/ *calificación,* **19**–28

graduate /ˈgræʤuˌeɪt/ *graduarse*
  ...from high school /frəm haɪ skul/ *graduarse de preparatoria,* **31**–5

graduated cylinder /ˈgræʤuˌeɪtɪd ˈsɪləndər/ *probeta graduada,* **194**–20

graduation /ˌgræʤuˈeɪʃən/ *graduación,* **23**–19

graffiti /grəˈfiti/ *grafito,* **61**–8

gram /græm/ *gramo,* **96**

grandchildren /ˈgrænˌʧɪldrən/ *nietos,* **27**–23

grandfather /ˈgrænˌfɑðər/ *abuelo,* **27**–1

grandmother /ˈgrænˌmʌðər/ *abuela,* **27**–2

grandparent /ˈgrænˌpɛrənt/ *abuelo, abuela*
  become a... /bɪˈkʌm ə/ *ser un abuelo, ser una abuela,* **31**–21

grandparents /ˈgrænˌpɛrəntz/ *abuelos,* **27**–24

grapefruit /ˈgreɪpˌfrut/ *toronja,* **83**–9

grapes /greɪps/ *uvas,* **83**–5

graphic artist /ˈgræfɪk ˈɑrtɪst/ *artista gráfico, artista gráfica,* **146**–7

grass /græs/ *césped,* **69**–8
  mow the... /moʊ ðə/ *cortar el césped,* **79**–17

grasshopper /ˈgræsˈhɑpər/ *saltamontes,* **181**–19

grasslands /ˈgræsˌlændz/ *pastizales,* **184–185**

grate /greɪt/ *ralle,* **92**–11

grater /ˈgreɪtər/ *rallador,* **94**–13

gray /greɪ/ *gris,* **10**–23

gray hair /greɪ hɛr/ *pelo gris, cabello gris, pelo canoso, cabello canoso,* **33**–5

grease /gris/ *engrase,* **93**–26

Greek /grik/ *griego(a),* **44**–15

green /grin/ *verde,* **10**–5

green beans /grin binz/ *ejotes,* **85**–28

green card /grin kard/ *tarjeta verde,* **43**–17

greenhouse /ˈgrinˌhaʊs/ *invernadero,* **179**–8

green onions /grin ˈʌnyənz/ *cebollines,* **85**–27

greet /grit/ *saludar,* **40**–2

greeting card /ˈgritɪŋ kard/ *tarjeta de felicitación,* **52**–3

grill /grɪl/ *ase,* **92**–6

grill /grɪl/ *asador, parrilla,* **69**–6, **94**–4

grizzly bear /ˈgrɪzli bɛr/ *oso gris, osa gris,* **187**–5

groceries /ˈgroʊsəriz/ *abarrotes, víveres y artículos comprados,* **99**–22

ground beef /graʊnd bif/ *carne de res molida,* **87**–8

groundhog /ˈgraʊndˌhɔg/ *marmota,* **190**–10

group /grup/
  talk with a... /tɔk wɪð ə/ *hable en un grupo,* **21**–20

grow /groʊ/ *crecer, cultivan,* **29**–26, **198**–5

grow up /groʊ ʌp/ *crecer,* **29**–27

guest /gɛst/ *huésped*
  hotel... /hoʊˈtɛl/ *huésped de hotel,* **159**–4

guidance counselor /ˈgaɪdns ˈkaʊnslər/ *asesor, asesora,* **23**–17

guitar /gɪˈtar/ *guitarra,* **207**–22

guitarist /gɪˈtarɪst/ *guitarrista,* **205**–15

gums /gʌmz/ *encías,* **141**–30

gun /gʌn/
  caulking... /ˈkɔkɪŋ/ *pistola de silicón,* **160**–8

gym /ʤɪm/ *gimnasio,* **23**–4, **48**–13, **67**–15, **216**–14

laundry room /ˈlɔndri rum/ cuarto de lavandería, 67-18
law /lɔ/
    obey the... /ouˈbei ðə/ obedecer la ley, 201-15
lawn /lɔn/ césped, 69-8
    mow the... /mou ðə/ cortar el césped, cortar el pasto, 79-17
    water the... /ˈwɔtər ðə/ regar el césped, regar el pasto, 79-18
lawn mower /lɔn mouər/ cortadora de pasto, podadora de pasto, 69-9
lawyer /ˈlɔyər/ abogado(a), 61-24, 148-3
lay /lei/
    ...bricks /ˈbriks/ colocar ladrillos, 165-5
lead /lid/ guiar, dirigir, 37-18
leaf /lif/ hoja, 179-13
leaks /liks/ gotea, 77-3
learn /lɜrn/ aprender, 31-2
lease /lis/
    sign the... /sain ðə/ firmar el contrato de arrendamiento, 64-6
leather /ˈlɛðər/ piel, 113-5
leave /liv/ irse, salir, 37-2, 123-2
    ...a tip /ə tip/ dejar una propina, 102-23
leaves /livz/
    rake the... /reik ðə/ recoger las hojas con el rastrillo, 79-20
lecture /ˈlɛktʃər/ conferencia, 216-12
left /lɛft/ izquierdo, izquierda, 130-15
leg /lɛg/ pierna, 133-14
    break a... /breik ə/ romperse una pierna, 136-5
Legislative branch /ˈlɛdʒisˌleitiv bræntʃ/ Poder Legislativo, 201
leg of lamb /lɛg ʌv læm/ pierna de cordero, 87-2
legs /lɛgz/ piernas, 87-33
lemon /ˈlɛmən/ limón, 83-14
lemonade /ˌlɛmənˈeid/
    pitcher of... /ˈpitʃər ʌv/ jarra de limonada, 97-14
lens /lɛnz/
    contact... /ˈkɑnˌtækt/ lentes de contacto, 141-22
leopard /ˈlɛpərd/ leopardo, 185-11
leotard /ˈliəˌtard/ leotardo, 107-18
letter /ˈlɛtər/ carta, 52-2, 196-1
    write a... /rait ə/ escribir una carta, 40-8
letter carrier /ˈlɛtər ˈkæriər/ mensajero, mensajera, 52-10
letterhead /ˈlɛtərˌhɛd/ membrete, 155-13
lettuce /ˈlɛtəs/ lechuga, 84-5
level /ˈlɛvəl/ nivel, 160-16
librarian /laiˈbrɛriən/ bibliotecario, bibliotecaria, 55-11
library /ˈlaiˌbrɛri/ biblioteca, 47-18, **54-55**
    school... /skul/ biblioteca escolar, 23-7
library card /ˈlaiˌbrɛri kard/ tarjeta de biblioteca, 55-12
lice /lais/ piojos, 135-4
license plate /ˈlaisəns pleit/ placa, 121-8
lid /lid/ tapa, tapadera, 94-6
life events /laif iˈvɛnts/ eventos en la vida, **30-31**
lifeguard /ˈlaifˌgard/ salvavidas, 211-17
life jacket /laif ˈdʒækit/ chaleco salvavidas, 211-14
light /lait/ prender, 102-3
    ...candles /ˈkændls/ encender velas, 229-30
light /lait/ ligero(a), 14-24
    ...jacket /ˈdʒækit/ chamarra ligera, 111-1
lightbulb /ˈlaitˌbʌlb/ foco, 160-22
    ...is burned out /iz ˈbɜrnd aut/ el foco está fundido, 77-6
lighthouse /ˈlaitˌhaus/ faro, 211-7
lightning /ˈlaitnin/ relámpago, 166-15
lights /laits/ luces, 229-21
light switch /lait switʃ/ interruptor de luz, 72-24
lilac bush /ˈlaiˌlæk buʃ/ lila, 179-7
lilies /ˈliliz/ azucenas, 179-20
lima beans /ˈlaimə binz/ habas, 84-21
lime /laim/ lima, 83-20
lime green /laim grin/ verde limón, 10-7

limo /ˈlimou/ limusina, 118-18
limousine /ˌliməˈzin/ limusina, 118-18
line /lain/ fila, cola, 125-21
    curved... /kɜrvd/ línea curva, 193-8
    straight... /streit/ línea recta, 193-7
    subway... /ˈsʌbˌwei/ línea del metro, 128-16
    wait in... /weit in/ esperar en, 51-23
linen /ˈlinən/ lino, 113-7
lines /lainz/
    parallel... /ˈpærəˌlɛl/ líneas paralelas, 193-12
    perpendicular... /ˌpɜrpənˈdikyələr/ líneas perpendiculares, 193-11
lion /ˈlaiən/ león, 185-20
lip /lip/ labio, 133-42
lipstick /ˈlipˌstik/ lápiz labial, 144-27
liquid /ˈlikwid/ líquido, 194-11
listen /ˈlisən/ escuchar, 20-12, 126-17
liter /ˈlitər/ litro, 97-17
liter /ˈlitər/ litro, 96
litter /ˈlitər/ basura, 171-21
little /ˈlitl/ pequeño(a), 14-1
liver /ˈlivər/ hígado, 87-12, 133-28
living room /ˈlivin rum/ sala, 72-73
lizard /ˈlizərd/ lagartija, 181-10
load /loud/ cargar, 150-6
    ...a van or truck /ə væn ɔr trʌk/ cargar una camioneta o camión, 64-10
loading dock /ˈloudin dak/ andén, plataforma de embarque, 157-18
loaf /louf/ barra, 97-16
loafer /ˈloufər/ mocasín, 109-19
loan /loun/ préstamo, 65-22
loan documents /loun ˈdakyəmənts/
    sign the... /sain ðə/ firmar los documentos del préstamo, 65-24
loan officer /loun ˈɔfəsər/ funcionario / funcionaria de préstamos, 51-9
lobby /ˈlabi/ vestíbulo, 67-22, 159-9
lobster /ˈlabstər/ langosta, 87-14
local call /ˈloukəl kɔl/ llamada local, 16-9
lock /lak/
    dead-bolt... /dɛd-boult/ chapa de seguridad, 67-28
    ...is jammed /iz dʒæmd/ está trabada, 77-11
locker /ˈlækər/ gaveta, 23-14
locker room /ˈlækər rum/ vestidor, 218-35
locksmith /ˈlakˌsmiθ/ cerrajero(a), 77-22, 148-7
log cabin /lɔg ˈkæbin/ cabaña, 63-4
lonely /ˈlounli/ solitario(a), solo(a), 39-17
long /lɔn/
    ...skirt /skɜrt/ falda larga, 111-21
long-distance call /lɔn-ˈdistəns kɔl/ llamada de larga distancia, 16-10
long hair /lɔn hɛr/ pelo largo, cabello largo, 33-13
long-sleeved /lɔn-slivd/
    ...shirt /ʃɜrt/ camisa de manga larga, 111-5
long underwear /lɔn ˈʌndərˌwɛr/ ropa interior de invierno, 107-15
look at /luk ət/
    ...a map /ə mæp/ ver un mapa, 123-11
    ...houses /hausəz/ ver casas, 65-17
    ...the menu /ðə ˈmɛnyu/ ver el menú, 102-7
look for /luk fər/
    ...a book /ə buk/ buscar un libro, 54-26
    ...a jacket /ə dʒækit/ buscar una chamarra, 114-2
    ...an apartment /ən əˈpartmənt/ buscar un apartamento, 64-1
look up /luk ʌp/
    ...a word /ə wɜrd/ buscar una palabra, 20-8
loose /lus/
    ...pants /pænts/ pantalones holgados, 111-12

New England /nu ˈɪŋglænd/ *Nueva Inglaterra*, **172**-11
new moon /nu mun/ *luna nueva*, **177**-29
news /nuz/ *noticias*, **209**-12
newspaper /ˈnuzˌpeɪpər/ *periódico*, **55**-17
newsstand /ˈnuzˌstænd/ *puesto de periódico*, **59**-25
New Year /nu yɪr/ *Año Nuevo*, **228**-1
next-day mail /nɛkst-deɪ meɪl/ *correo expreso*, **52**-19
next to /nɛkst tə/ *junto(a)*, **13**-11
nickel /ˈnɪkəl/ *níque*, **8**-2
niece /nis/ *sobrina*, **27**-19
Nigerian /naɪˈʤɪriən/ *nigeriano(a)*, **44**-20
night /naɪt/ *noche*, **5**
nightgown /ˈnaɪtˌgaʊn/ *camisón, bata de dormir*, **107**-14
nightshirt /ˈnaɪtˌʃɜrt/ *camisón, camisa de dormir*, **107**-12
night table /naɪt ˈteɪbəl/ *buró*, **74**-10
nine /naɪn/ *nueve*, **2**
911 /naɪn wʌn wʌn/ *asistencia de emergencia*, **16**-5
nineteen /ˌnaɪnˈtin/ *diecinueve*, **2**
nineteenth /ˌnaɪnˈtinθ/ *decimonoveno*, **3**
ninety /ˈnaɪnti/ *noventa*, **2**
ninth /naɪnθ/ *noveno*, **3**
nipple /ˈnɪpəl/ *mamila*, **57**-1
noisy /ˈnɔɪzi/ *ruidoso(a)*, **15**-35
no left turn /noʊ lɛft tɜrn/ *prohibida vuelta a la izquierda*, **118**-6
nonfiction section /ˌnanˈfɪkʃən ˈsɛkʃən/ *sección de libros fuera de la novela* , **55**-8
noon /nun/ *mediodía*, **5**
north /nɔrθ/ *norte*, **130**-19
North America /nɔrθ əˈmɛrɪkə/ *América del Norte, Norteamérica*, **174**-8
Northern Canada /ˈnɔrðərn ˈkænədə/ *Canadá del Norte*, **172**-1
Northern Hemisphere /ˈnɔrðərn ˈhɛməˌsfɪr/ *Hemisferio Norte*, **174**-6
North Pole /nɔrθ poʊl/ *Polo Norte*, **174**-1
nose /noʊz/ *nariz*, **133**-37
    bloody... /ˈblʌdi/ *hemorragia nasal*, **135**-29
note /noʊt/
    absence... /ˈæbsəns/ *justificante*, **23**-27
notebook /ˈnoʊtbʊk/ *cuaderno*, **19**-27
notebook (computer) /ˈnoʊtbʊk (kəmˈpyutər)/ *computadora portátil*, **25**-23
no U-turn /noʊ ˈyu-ˌtɜrn/ *prohibida la vuelta en U*, **118**-11
novel /ˈnavəl/ *novela*, **55**-20
November /noʊˈvɛmbər/ *noviembre*, **7**-26
nuclear energy /ˈnukliər ˈɛnərʤi/ *energía nuclear*, **171**-28
number /ˈnʌmbər/
    dial a... /ˈdaɪəl ə/ *marcar un número*, **17**-25
numbers /ˈnʌmbərz/ *números*, **1-2**
nurse /nɜrs/ *amamantar*, **29**-2
nurse /nɜrs/ *enfermero, enfermera*, **138**-2, **148**-19
    school... /skul/ *escuela*, **23**-8
nursery /ˈnɜrsəri/ *vivero*, **216**-4
nurses' station /ˈnɜrsɪz ˈsteɪʃən/ *central de enfermeros*, **138**-1
nut /nʌt/ *tuerca*, **163**-23
    wing... /wɪŋ/ *tuerca de mariposa*, **163**-24
nuts /nʌts/ *nueces*, **82-83**
nylon /ˈnaɪˌlan/ *nylon*, **113**-10
nylons /ˈnaɪˌlanz/ *pantimedias*, **107**-5
oak (tree) /oʊk (tri)/ *roble*, **179**-5
oasis /oʊˈeɪsɪs/ *oasis*, **181**-15
obey /oʊˈbeɪ/ *obedecer*, **201**-15
oboe /ˈoʊboʊ/ *oboe*, **207**-13
observatory /əbˈzɜrvəˌtɔri/ *observatorio*, **176**-8
obstetrician /ˌabstəˈtrɪʃən/ *un obstetra, una obstetra*, **141**-10
ocean /ˈoʊʃən/ *océano*, **169**-24, **211**-5
October /akˈtoʊbər/ *octubre*, **7**-25
octopus /ˈaktəpəs/ *pulpo*, **189**-17
off /ɔf/ *hacia fuera de*, **13**-7
offer /ˈɔfər/ *ofrecer*, **102**-20

offer /ˈɔfər/
    make an... /meɪk ən/ *hacer una oferta*, **65**-19
office /ˈɔfɪs/ *oficina*, **154-155**
office assistant /ɔfɪs əˈsɪstənt/ *asistente de oficina*, **155**-19
office building /ˈɔfɪs ˈbɪldɪŋ/ *edificio de oficinas*, **47**-15
office manager /ˈɔfɪs ˈmænɪʤər/ *gerente de oficina*, **155**-6
oil /ɔɪl/ *petróleo*, **171**-23
    check the... /ˈtʃɛk ðə/ *verificar el aceite*, **123**-16
oil gauge /ɔɪl geɪʤ/ *marcador, indicador del nivel de aceite*, **121**-13
oil spill /ɔɪl spɪl/ *derrame de petróleo*, **171**-15
old /oʊld/ *viejo(a)*, **14**-21, **15**-32
olive green /ˈalɪv grin/ *verde olivo*, **10**-6
olive oil /ˈalɪv ɔɪl/
    bottle of... /ˈbatl ʌv/ *botella de aceite de olivo*, **97**-7
    measure... /ˈmɛʒər/ *mida*, **92**-1
olives /ˈalɪvz/ *aceitunas*, **83**-23
on /an/ *sobre*, **13**-3
one /wʌn/ *uno, una*, **2**
one-bedroom apartment /wʌn-ˈbɛdˌrum əˈpartmənt/ *apartamento de una recámara*, **67**-13
one cent /wʌn sɛnt/ *un centavo*, **8**-1
one dollar /wʌn ˈdalər/ *un dólar*, **8**-6
one-dollar bill /wʌn-ˈdalər bɪl/ *un billete de un dólar*, **8**-6
one-half /wʌn-hæf/ *un medio*, **3**
one hundred /wʌn ˈhʌndrɪd/ *cien*, **2**
one hundred-dollar bill /ˈwʌn ˈhʌndrɪd-ˈdalər bɪl/ *un billete de cien dólares*, **8**-11
one hundred dollars /ˈwʌn ˈhʌndrɪd ˈdalərz/ *cien dólares*, **8**-11
one hundred thousand /ˈwʌn ˈhʌndrɪd ˈθaʊzənd/ *cien mil*, **2**
one million /wʌn ˈmɪlyən/ *un millón*, **2**
one-quarter /wʌn-ˈkwɔrtər/ *un cuarto*, **3**
one thousand /wʌn ˈθaʊzənd/ *mil*, **2**
one way /wʌn weɪ/ *un sentido, una vía*, **118**-1
onion /ˈʌnyən/ *cebolla*, **84**-15
    slice... /slaɪs/ *rebane*, **93**-18
online /ˌanˈlaɪn/
    be... /bi/ *estar en línea*, **24**-30
online catalog /ˌanˈlaɪn ˈkætlˌɔg/ *catálogo electrónico*, **55**-6
Ontario /anˈtɛrioʊ/ *Ontario*, **172**-4
on the left of /an ðə lɛft ʌv/ *a la izquierda*, **13**-8
on the right of /an ðə raɪt ʌv/ *a la derecha*, **13**-9
on top of /an tap ʌv/ *en la parte superior de*, **13**-1
open /ˈoʊpən/
    ...a present /ə ˈprɛzənt/ *abrir un regalo, abrir un obsequio*, **229**-32
    ...mail /meɪl/ *abrir la correspondencia*, **150**-5
    ...your book /yər bʊk/ *abra su libro*, **20**-10
open /ˈoʊpən/ *abierto(a)*, **15**-37
opens /ˈoʊpənz/ *abre*, **198**-11
opera /ˈaprə/ *ópera*, **205**-25
operate /ˈapəˌreɪt/ *opera*, **165**-15
operating room /ˈapəˌreɪtɪŋ rum/ *sala de operaciones*, **138**-5
operating table /ˈapəˌreɪtɪŋ ˈteɪbəl/ *mesa de operaciones*, **138**-8
operation /ˌapəˈreɪʃən/ *operación*, **139**-11
operator /ˈapəˌreɪtər/ *operador, operadora*, **16**-17
opossum /əˈpasəm/ *zarigüeya*, **190**-7
opposites /ˈapəzɪts/ *opuestos*, **14-15**
optometrist /apˈtamətrɪst/ *un optometrista, una optometrista*, **141**-23
orange /ˈɔrɪnʤ/ *naranja, anaranjado*, **10**-19, **83**-3
orange juice /ˈɔrɪnʤ ʤus/ *jugo de naranja*, **88**-27
    carton of... /ˈkartn ʌv/ *cartón de jugo de naranjas*, **97**-10
orangutan /əˈræŋəˌtæŋ/ *orangután*, **182**-13
orbit /ˈɔrbɪt/ *órbita*, **176**-6
orca /ˈɔrkə/ *orca*, **189**-7
orchard /ˈɔrtʃərd/ *huerto*, **152**-1
orchestra /ˈɔrkəstrə/ *orquesta*, **204**-8

saucepan /ˈsɔsˌpæn/ cacerola, 94–10
saucer /ˈsɔsər/ plato pequeño, 101–19
Saudi Arabian /ˈsɔdi əˈreɪbiən/ Arabia Saudita, 44–19
sauna /ˈsɔnə/ sauna, 159–20
sausages /ˈsɔsɪʤez/ salchichas, 87–6
sauté /sɔˈteɪ/ salteé, sofría, 93–19
savings account passbook /ˈseɪvɪŋz əˈkaʊnt ˈpæsˌbʊk/ libreta de cuenta de ahorros, 51–14
saw /sɔ/ serra, aserra, cortar, 165–10
saw /sɔ/
  circular... /ˈsɜrkyələr/ sierra circular, 161–31
saxophone /ˈsæksəˌfoʊn/ saxofón, 207–11
scale /skeɪl/ báscula, 99–7
  postal... /ˈpoʊstəl/ báscula postal, 52–15
scales /skeɪlz/ escamas, 189–6
scallions /ˈskælyənz/ cebollines, 85–27
scallops /ˈskæləps/ vieiras, 87–19
scan /skæn/ escanear, 24–34
scanner /skænər/ escáner, 25–14
scar /skar/ cicatriz, 33–7
scarecrow /ˈskɛrˌkroʊ/ espantapájaros, 152–12
scared /skɛrd/ asustado(a), 39–19
scarf /skarf/ bufanda, 104–18
schedule /ˈskɛʤul/ horario, 128–22
  student... /ˈstudnt/ estudiante, 23–25
SCHOOL /skul/ ESCUELA, 18–25
school /skul/ escuela, 47–6
  start... /start/ empezar la escuela, 31–3
  take your child to... /teɪk yər ʧaɪld tə/ llevar a su hijo a la escuela, llevar a su hija a la escuela, 34–10
school bus /skul bʌs/ autobús escolar, 23–12, 118–12
school library /skul ˈlaɪˌbrɛri/ biblioteca escolar, 23–7
school nurse /skul nɜrs/ enfermero / enfermera escolar, 23–8
SCHOOL SUBJECTS /skul ˈsʌbʤɪkts/ MATERIAS ESCOLARES, 192–201
school zone /skul zoʊn/ zona escolar, 118–8
science /ˈsaɪəns/ ciencia, 194–195
science fiction /ˈsaɪəns ˈfɪkʃən/ ciencia ficción, 208–6
scientist /ˈsaɪəntɪst/ científico(a), 148–16
scissors /ˈsɪzərz/
  pair of... /pɛr ʌv/ tijeras, 117–23
score /skɔr/ resultado, 223–19
scoreboard /ˈskɔrˌbɔrd/ tablero de resultados, 223–18
scorpion /ˈskɔrpiən/ escorpión, 181–23
scouring pad /skaʊrɪŋ pæd/ fibra limpiadora, 80–14
scramble /ˈskræmbəl/ revuelva, 92–7
scraper /skreɪpər/ espátula, 163–11
screen /skrin/ pantalla, 25–20
screw /skru/ tornillo con punta, 163–22
screwdriver /ˈskruˌdraɪvər/ desarmador, destornillador, 160–18
scroll bar /skroʊl bar/ barra de desplazamiento, 25–10
scrub /skrʌb/ restregar, 79–11
scrub brush /skrʌb brʌʃ/ cepillo para restregar, 80–20
scuba diver /ˈskubə ˈdaɪvər/ buzo, 189–13
sculptor /ˈskʌlptər/ escultor, escultora, 203–17
sculpture /ˈskʌlpʧər/ escultura, 203–16
sea /si/ mar, 188–189
sea anemone /si əˈnɛməni/ anémona de mar, 189–25
seafood /ˈsiˌfud/ mariscos, 86–87
seagull /ˈsiˌgʌl/ gaviota, 189–1
sea horse /si hɔrs/ caballo de mar, 189–14
seal /sil/ foca, 187–12
seam /sim/ costura, 117–25
seashell /ˈsiˌʃɛl/ concha marina, 211–22
season /ˈsizən/ estación, 92–14
seasons /ˈsizənz/ estaciones, 7
seat /sit/ silla, asiento, 19–26, 125–27, 205–20
  find your... /faɪnd yər/ encontrar su asiento, 126–9
seat belt /sit bɛlt/ cinturón de seguridad, 121–12, 125–28

fasten... /ˈfæsən/ abrochar el cinturón de seguridad, 126–12
  unfasten your... /ʌnˈfæsən yər/ desabrochar el cinturón de seguridad, 126–22
sea urchin /si ˈɜrʧɪn/ erizo de mar, 189–22
seaweed /ˈsiˌwid/ alga marina, 189–9
second /ˈsɛkənd/ segundo, 3, 4
second-hand store /ˈsɛkənd-hænd stɔr/ tienda de artículos de segunda mano, 48–14
secretary /ˈsɛkrəˌtɛri/ secretario, 155–19
security /səˈkyurəti/
  go through... /goʊ θru/ pasar por seguridad, 126–5
security checkpoint /səˈkyurəti ˈʧɛkˌpɔɪnt/ punto de control, punto de revisión de seguridad, 125–10
security deposit /səˈkyurəti dɪˈpɑsɪt/
  pay a... /peɪ ə/ pagar un depósito, 64–7
security guard /səˈkyurəti gard/ guardia de seguridad, 51–2, 148–8
sedan /səˈdæn/ sedán, 118–19
see /si/ ver, 64–4
seed /sid/ semilla, 179–24
seesaw /ˈsiˌsɔ/ sube y baja, 214–7
select /səˈlɛkt/ seleccionar, 24–32
sell /sɛl/ vender, 150–14
semi /sɛmi/ semi, 118–25
semicolon /ˈsɛmiˌkoʊlən/ punto y coma, 196–18
Senate /ˈsɛnɪt/ Senado, 201
senator /ˈsɛnətər/ senador, senadora, 200–10
send /sɛnd/ enviar, 53–24
senior (citizen) /ˈsinyər (ˈsɪtəzən)/ persona de la tercera edad, 31
sentence /ˈsɛntns/ enunciado, 196–3
  copy the... /ˈkɑpi ðə/ copie el enunciado, 20–4
September /sɛpˈtɛmbər/ septiembre, 7–24
serve /sɜrv/
  ...a meal /ə mil/ servir una comida, 102–16
  ...in the military /ɪn ðə ˈmɪləˌtɛri/ pertenecer al ejército, 201–18
  ...on a jury /ɑn ə ˈʤuri/ ser miembro del jurado, 201–17
server /ˈsɜrvər/ mesera, camarero(a), 101–4, 101–6, 148–18
  signal the... /ˈsɪgnəl ðə/ llamar al mesero mesera, hacer una seña al mesero/mesera, 102–18
  thank the... /θæŋk ðə/ agradecerle, darle las gracias al mesero, 102–21
set /sɛt/ poner, 102–5
set /sɛt/ foro, 205–19
set of knives /sɛt ʌv naɪvz/ juego de cuchillos, 94–2
seven /ˈsɛvən/ siete, 2
seventeen /ˌsɛvənˈtin/ diecisiete, 2
seventeenth /ˌsɛvənˈtinθ/ decimoséptimo, 3
seventh /ˈsɛvənθ/ séptimo, 3
seventy /ˈsɛvənti/ setenta, 2
sewing /ˈsoʊɪŋ/ costura, 117
sewing machine /ˈsoʊɪŋ məˈʃin/ máquina de coser, 117–20
sew on /ˈsoʊ ɑn/ coser, 115–22
sex /sɛks/ sexo, 43–5
shade /ʃeɪd/
  window... /ˈwɪndoʊ/ cortinilla, 74–8
shake hands /ʃeɪk hændz/ estrechar las manos, 40–4
shake out /ʃeɪk aʊt/ sacudir, 79–14
shampoo /ʃæmˈpu/ shampú, 144–2
shapes /ʃeɪps/ figuras, 193
share /ʃɛr/
  ...a book /ə bʊk/ comparta un libro, 21–21
  ...a dessert /ə dɪˈzɜrt/ compartir un postre, 102–19
shark /ʃark/ tiburón, 189–12
shave /ʃeɪv/ rasurarse, 34–6
shaving cream /ˈʃeɪvɪŋ krim/ crema para afeitar, 144–16
shawl /ʃɔl/ chal, 104–23
sheep /ʃip/ carnero, oveja, 152–23

stepfather /ˈstɛpˌfɑðər/ padrastro, 27-8
stepladder /ˈstɛpˌlædər/ escalera de tijera, escalera de mano, 80-23
stepmother /ˈstɛpˌmʌðər/ madrastra, 27-5
steps /stɛps/ escalones, 69-15
stepsister /ˈstɛpˌsɪstər/ hermanastra, 27-12
stereo (system) /ˈstɛriˌoʊ (ˈsɪstəm)/ sistema estéreo, 226-15
sterile pad /ˈstɛrəl pæd/ almohadilla estéril, 143-25
sterile tape /ˈstɛrəl teɪp/ cinta estéril, 143-26
stethoscope /ˈstɛθəˌskoʊp/ estetoscopio, 141-1
sticky notes /ˈstɪki noʊts/ notas autoadhesivas, 155-26
still life /stɪl laɪf/ naturaleza muerta, 203-2
sting /stɪŋ/
    bee... /bi/ picadura de abeja, 135-28
stingray /ˈstɪŋreɪ/ raya, 189-20
stir /stɜr/ revuelva, 93-20
stir-fried vegetables /stɜr-fraɪd ˈvɛʤtəbəlz/ verduras salteadas, verduras sofritas, 91-20
stitches /ˈstɪʧɛz/ puntadas, 139-28
stockbroker /ˈstɑkˌbroʊkər/ corredor(a) de bolsa, 148-13
stockings /ˈstɑkɪŋz/ calcetas, medias calcetín, 107-6
stomach /ˈstʌmək/ estómago, 133-29
stomachache /ˈstʌməkˌeɪk/ dolor de estómago, 135-12
stool /stul/ banco, 70-21
stop /stɑp/ pararse, detenerse, detener, 123-10, 227-30
stop /stɑp/ alto, 118-2
stopper /ˈstɑpər/ tapón, 194-22
storage space /ˈstɔrɪʤ speɪs/ espacio para almacenamiento, espacio para guardar cosas, 67-1
stores /stɔrz/ tiendas, 48-49
storm /stɔrm/ tormenta, 166-14
stove /stoʊv/ estufa, 70-6
    camping... /ˈkæmpɪŋ/ estufa de excursión, 213-15
stow /stoʊ/ guardar, 126-10
straight /streɪt/ derecho, 130-1
    ...skirt /skɜrt/ falda recta, 111-18
straight hair /streɪt hɛr/ pelo lacio, cabello lacio, 33-17
straight leg /streɪt lɛg/
    ...jeans /ʤinz/ jeans rectos, pantalones de mezclilla rectos, 111-11
straight line /streɪt laɪn/ línea recta, 193-7
strainer /ˈstreɪnər/ coladera, 94-18
strap /stræp/ tirante, 128-15
straw /strɔ/ popote, pajilla, 90-13
strawberries /ˈstrɔˌbɛriz/ fresas, 83-25
    box of... /bɑks ʌv/ canastilla de fresas, 97-20
stream /strim/ arroyo, 169-6
street /strit/ calle, 47-27
street address /strit əˈdrɛs/ domicilio, 43-11
streetlight /ˈstritˌlaɪt/ arbotante, poste de luz, 58-4
street musician /strit myuˈzɪʃən/ músico ambulante, 59-22
street vendor /strit ˈvɛndər/ vendedor ambulante, 58-12, 214-28
stretch /strɛʧ/ estirar, estirarse, 126-19
stretcher /ˈstrɛʧər/ camilla, 139-27
string /strɪŋ/ cuerda, 207
string beans /strɪŋ binz/ ejotes, 85-28
striped /straɪpt/ a rayas, 113-20
stroller /ˈstroʊlər/ carriola, 57-11
strong /strɔŋ/ fuerte, 14-3
student /ˈstudnt/ estudiante, 19-25
student ID /ˈstudnt aɪ di/ identificación de estudiante, 43-19
student schedule /ˈstudnt ˈskɛʤul/ horario de estudiante, 23-25
studio (apartment) /ˈstudioʊ (əˈpɑrtmənt)/ apartamento estudio, 67-9
study for a test /ˈstʌdi/ estudiar para un examen, 19-33
subtraction /səbˈtrækʃən/ substracción, resta, 193-27
suburbs /ˈsʌbˌɜrbz/ suburbios, 63-21
subway (train) /ˈsʌbˌweɪ (treɪn)/ metro, 128-18
subway line /ˈsʌbˌweɪ laɪn/ ruta, línea del metro, 128-16
suede /sweɪd/ ante, 113-8

sugar /ˈʃʊgər/
    sift... /sɪft/ cierna..., 93-28
sugar bowl /ˈʃʊgər ˈboʊl/ azucarera, 101-10
suit /sut/
    business... /ˈbɪznɪs/ traje, 104-29
suite /swit/ suite, 159-5
summer /ˈsʌmər/ verano, 7-13
sun /sʌn/ sol, 166-9, 176-18
sunbather /ˈsʌnˌbeɪðər/ persona que toma el sol, 211-19
sunburn /ˈsʌnˌbɜrn/ quemadura de sol, 135-27
Sunday /ˈsʌnˌdeɪ/ domingo, 6-11
sunflowers /ˈsʌnˌflaʊərz/ girasoles, 179-29
sunglasses /ˈsʌnˌglæsɪz/ lentes de sol, 109-14
sunny /ˈsʌni/ soleado, hace sol, 167-25
sunrise /ˈsʌnˌraɪz/ salida del sol, amanecer, 5
sunscreen /ˈsʌnˌskrin/ protector solar, 144-22, 211-24
sunset /ˈsʌnˌsɛt/ puesta del sol, obscurecer, 5
sunshine /ˈsʌnˌʃaɪn/ luz, rayos del sol, 166-13
super /ˈsupər/ super, 67-3
superintendent /ˌsupərɪnˈtɛndənt/ un intendente, una intendente, 67-3
supermarket /ˈsupərˌmɑrkət/ supermercado, 48-27, 98-99
supervisor /ˈsupərˌvaɪzər/ supervisor, supervisora, 156-9
supplies /səˈplaɪz/ utencilios, 162-163
supply cabinet /səˈplaɪ ˈkæbənɪt/ gabinete, cómoda, 155-22
Supreme Court /suˈprim kɔrt/ Suprema Corte, 200-8
surf /sɜrf/ hacer surf, 210-30
surfboard /ˈsɜrfˌbɔrd/ tabla de surf, 211-16
surfer /ˈsɜrfər/ surfista, 211-15
surgeon /ˈsɜrʤən/ cirujano, cirujana, 139-10
surgical mask /ˈsɜrʤɪkəl mæsk/ mascarilla quirúrgica, 139-13
surname /ˈsɜrneɪm/ apellido, 43-2
surprised /sərˈpraɪzəd/ sorprendido(a), 39-22
sushi /ˈsuʃi/ sushi, 91-23
suspenders /səˈspɛndərz/ tirantes, 109-5
suspense /səˈspɛns/ suspenso, 208-7
SUV /ɛs yu vi/ camioneta, 118-22
swallow /ˈswɑloʊ/ ingerir, 136-10
sweater /ˈswɛtər/ suéter, 104-20
    cardigan... /ˈkɑrdiˌgən/ suéter abierto, 111-15
    crew neck... /kru nɛk/ suéter de cuello redondo, 111-14
    turtleneck... /ˈtɜrtlˌnɛk/ suéter de cuello de tortuga, 111-16
    V-neck... /vi-nɛk/ suéter con cuello V, 111-13
sweatpants /ˈswɛtpænts/ pants, pantalones deportivos, 104-4
sweatshirt /ˈswɛtʃɜrt/ sudadera, 104-3
sweep /swip/ barrer, 79-4
sweet potato /swit pəˈteɪtoʊ/ camote, 84-22
swim /swɪm/ nadar, 210-32
swimmer /ˈswɪmər/ nadador, nadadora, 211-8
swimming pool /ˈswɪmɪŋ pul/ alberca, 159-21, 218-34
swimming trunks /ˈswɪmɪŋ trʌŋks/ traje de baño, shorts de baño, 107-9
swimsuit /ˈswɪmˌsut/ traje de baño, 107-7
swimwear /ˈswɪmˌwɛr/ ropa para nadar, 106-107
swing /swɪŋ/ columpiarse, 183-26
swings /swɪŋz/ columpios, 214-2
Swiss cheese /swɪs ʧiz/ queso suizo, 88-24
switch /swɪʧ/
    light... /laɪt/ interruptor de luz, 72-24
swollen ankle /ˈswoʊlən ˈæŋkəl/ tobillo inflamado, 135-11
swordfish /ˈsɔrdˌfɪʃ/ pez espada, dorado, 87-23, 189-3
symptoms /ˈsɪmptəmz/ síntomas, 134-135
synagogue /ˈsɪnəˌgɑg/ sinagoga, 47-7
syrup /ˈsɪrəp/ jarabe, 88-13
table /ˈteɪbəl/ mesa, 19-17, 70-32
    bus the... /bʌs ðə/ levantar la mesa, 102-25
    clear the ... /klɪr ðə/ levantar la mesa, 102-25
    set the... /sɛt ðə/ poner la mesa, 102-5
    wipe the... /waɪp ðə/ limpiar la mesa, 102-22
tablecloth /ˈteɪbəlˌklɔθ/ mantel, 101-11

Index

269

cargar una camioneta o camión, *load a van or truck*, **64**–10
cargar una camioneta, *load a truck*, **64**–10, *load a van*, **64**–10
cargar, *carry*, **29**–6, *load*, **150**–6
caricatura, *cartoon*, **209**–14
caries, *cavity*, **141**–32
carnaval, *carnival*, **216**–19
carne asada, *barbecue*, **69**–6, *barbeque*, **228**–9
carne de res molida, *ground beef*, **87**–8
carne de res, *beef*, **86**
carne, *meat*, **86–87**
carnero, *sheep*, **152**–23
carnes frías, *cold cuts*, **88**–21
carnes, *meats*, **99**–2
carnicera, *butcher*, **146**–20
carnicero, *butcher*, **146**–20
caro, *expensive*, **14**–15
carpeta, *file folder*, **155**–20, *folder*, **25**–5, **155**–20
carpintera, *carpenter*, **147**–26
carpintero, *carpenter*, **147**–26
carretilla, *dolly, hand truck*, **157**–19, *wheelbarrow*, **69**–26
carriola, *stroller*, **57**–11
carrito para compras, *shopping cart*, **99**–17
carro compacto, *compact car*, **118**–30
carro de alquiler, *taxi*, **128**–4
carro de servicio de una ama de llaves, *housekeeping cart*, **159**–2
carro deportivo, *sports car*, **118**–24
carro para equipaje, *luggage cart*, **159**–16
carrusel, *carousel*, **214**–14, *merry-go-round*, **214**–14
carta de naturalización, *Certificate of Naturalization*, **43**–26
carta, *letter*, **52**–2, **196**–1
cartel, *poster*, **19**–23
cartera, *wallet*, **109**–15
cartón de huevos, *carton of eggs*, **97**–23
cartón de jugo de naranja, *carton of orange juice*, **97**–10
cartón de naranjas, *carton of orange juice*, **97**–10
Casa Blanca, *White House*, **200**–7
casa de campo, *cottage*, **63**–3
casa de granja, *farmhouse*, **63**–8, **152**–15
casa duplex, *duplex*, **63**–6, *two-family house*, **63**–6
casa adosada, *townhouse*, **63**–12
casa flotante, *houseboat*, **63**–13
casa móvil, *mobile home*, **63**–7
casa remolque, *RV* **118**–16,
casa, *home / house*, **63**–1, **68–69**
casada, *married*, **26**–27
casarse, *get married*, **31**–12
cascada, *waterfall*, **169**–9
casco de fútbol americano, *football helmet*, **220**–25
casco, *hard hat*, **156**–8
casilla para votar, *voting booth*, **200**–3
casillero, *cubby*, **57**–12
casimir, *cashmere*, **113**–9
cassette de video, *video(cassette)*, **226**–22
cassette, *cassette*, **226**–16
castillo de arena, *sand castle*, **211**–25
castillo, *castle*, **63**–19
castor, *beaver*, **190**–15
catálogo computarizado, *computerized catalog*, **55**–6
catálogo electrónico, *online catalog*, **55**–6
catálogo, *catalog*, **52**–14
catarro, *cold (illness)*, **135**–5
catcher, *catcher*, **220**–8
catorce, *fourteen*, **2**
catsup, *ketchup*, **90**–16
cavar una zanja, *dig a trench*, **165**–22
cavar, *dig*, **165**–22
CD, *CD*, **226**–13
CD-ROM, *CD-ROM*, **25**–1
cebolla, *onion*, **84**–15
cebollines, *green onions*, **85**–27, *scallions*, **85**–27

cebra, *zebra*, **185**–12
ceda el paso, *yield*, **118**–10
ceja, *eyebrow*, **133**–34
celebraciones, *celebrations*, **228–229**
celebrar un cumpleaños, *celebrate a birthday*, **31**–20
celebrar, *celebrate*, **31**–20
Celsius, *Celsius*, **166**–1
cenar, *eat dinner*, **34**–19, *have dinner*, **34**–19
centavo, *one cent*, **8**–1
centímetro, *centimeter*, **163**–2
central de consultas, *reference desk*, **55**–5
central de enfermeras, *nurses' station*, **138**–1
central de taxis, *taxi stand*, **128**–1
centro comercial, *mall*, **47**–3
centro de copiado, *copy shop*, **48**–15
centro de negocios, *business center*, **159**–7
centro médico, *medical center*, **140–141**
cepillar el pelo, *brush hair*, **144**–10
cepillar madera, *brush wood*, **165**–23, *plane wood*, **165**–23
cepillar, *brush*, **34**–3
cepillo de baño, *toilet brush*, **75**–30
cepillo de dientes, *toothbrush*, **34**–3, **144**–15
cepillo para pelo, *hairbrush*, **144**–10
cepillo para restregar, *scrub brush*, **80**–20
cerámica, *pottery*, **203**–18
ceramista, *potter*, **203**–19
cerca, *fence*, **69**–24
cerca, *near*, **13**–15
cerebro, *brain*, **133**–24
cerezas, *cherries*, **83**–21
cerillo, *bagger*, **99**–18
cerillos, *matches*, **213**–23
cero, *zero*, **2**
cerrada, *closed*, **15**–38
cerrado, *closed*, **15**–38
cerradura está trabada, *lock is jammed*, **77**–11
cerradura, *lock*, **67**–28
cerrajero, *locksmith*, **77**–22, **148**–7
cerrar, *close*, **20**–9, *shut*, **15**–38
certificado de escuela secundaria, *high school diploma*, **43**–28
cesarse, *be married*, **26**–27
césped, *grass*, **69**–8, *lawn*, **69**–8
cesto de basura, *wastebasket*, **75**–31
chabacano, *apricot*, **83**–16
chal, *shawl*, **104**–23
chaleco de seguridad, *safety vest*, **157**–27
chaleco salvavidas, *life jacket*, **211**–14
chaleco, *vest*, **104**–26
chalet, *chalet*, **63**–5
chamarra gruesa, *heavy jacket*, **111**–2
chamarra ligera, *light jacket*, **111**–1
chamarra, *jacket*, **104**–16
champiñón, *mushroom*, **85**–32
chapa de seguridad, *dead-bolt lock*, **67**–28
charola de galletas, *tray of pastries*, **97**–11
charola de pastitas, *tray of pastries*, **97**–11
charola para hielo, *ice tray*, **88**–4
charola para horno, *cookie sheet*, **95**–21
charola para pintura, *paint tray*, **163**–15
charola, *tray*, **101**–29
chef, *chef*, **101**–1
chelo, *cello*, **207**–20
cheque de viajero, *traveler's check*, **9**–24
cheque personal, *personal check*, **9**–25
cheque, *check*, **51**–13, **101**–31
chequeo médico, *checkup*, **141**–18, *physical (exam)*, **141**–18
chequera, *checkbook*, **51**–12
cheques de viajero, *traveler's check*, **9**–24
chícharos, *peas*, **85**–30
chícharos, *split peas*, **93**–20
chilena, *Chilean*, **44**–8

chileno, *Chilean*, **44**-8

chimenea, *chimney*, **69**-1, *fireplace*, **72**-27

chimpancé, *chimpanzee*, **182**-3

china, *Chinese*, **44**-23

chino, *Chinese*, **44**-23

chocolates, *chocolates*, **228**-5

chofer de camión, *truck driver*, **148**-26

chofer de taxi, *cab driver*, **128**-5, *taxi driver*, **128**-5, **148**-17

chongo, *bun*, **33**-22

chuletas de puerco, *pork chops*, **87**-3

chuletas de cerdo, *pork chops*, **87**-3

chuletas de cordero, *lamb chops*, **87**-1

chuletas de ternera, *veal cutlets*, **87**-13

chupón, *pacifier*, **57**-25

cicatriz, *scar*, **33**-7

ciclista, *cyclist*, **214**-25

ciclopista, *bicycle path*, **216**-17

ciega, *blind*, **135**-18

ciego, *blind*, **135**-18

cielo, *sky*, **166**-10

cien dólares, *one hundred dollars*, **8**-11

cien mil, *one hundred thousand*, **2**

cien, *one hundred*, **2**

ciencia ficción, *science fiction*, **208**-6

ciencia, *science*, **194-195**

científica, *scientist*, **148**-16

científico, *scientist*, **148**-16

cierna azucar, *sift sugar*, **93**-28

cierna, *sift cinnamon*, **93**-28

cierna, *sift*, **93**-28

cierre, *zipper*, **117**-24

cierren su libro, *close your book*, **20**-9

cilindro, *cylinder*, **193**-25

cima, *peak*, **169**-1

címbalos, *cymbals*, **207**-2

cinche, *thumbtack*, **155**-23

cinco centavos, *five cents*, **8**-2

cinco dólares, *five dollars*, **8**-7

cinco para las siete, *five of seven*, **5**, *five to seven*, **5**

cinco y media, *half past six*, **5**

cinco, *five*, **2**

cincuenta centavos, *fifty cents*, **8**-5

cincuenta dólares, *fifty dollars*, **8**-10

cincuenta, *fifty*, **2**

cinta adhesiva, *tape*, **155**-9, **226**-16,

cinta aislante, *electrical tape*, **160**-19

cinta de audio, *tape*, **155**-9, **226**-16

cinta de medir, *tape measure*, **117**-28, **163**-3

cinta estéril, *sterile tape*, **143**-26

cinta métrica, *tape measure*, **117**-28, **163**-3

cinta para conductos, *duct tape*, **163**-31

cinta transportadora, *conveyor belt*, **156**-6

cinta, *masking tape*, **163**-13

cintura, *waist*, **133**-11

cinturón de seguridad, *seat belt*, **121**-12, **125**-28

cinturón para herramientas, *tool belt*, **160**-12

cinturón, *belt*, **109**-6

circo, *circus*, **216**-15

circuito interruptor, *circuit breaker*, **77**-13

Círculo Antártico, *Antarctic Circle*, **174**-4

Círculo Ártico, *Arctic Circle*, **174**-2

círculo, *circle*, **193**-16

circunferencia, *circumference*, **193**-13

ciruela, *plum*, **83**-15

cirujana, *surgeon*, **139**-10

cirujano, *surgeon*, **139**-10

cita, *appointment book*, **155**-14

cítara, *sitar*, **207**-18

ciudad, *city*, **43**-12, **63**-20

ciudadana, *citizen*, **200**-4

ciudadanía, *citizenship*, **200-201**

ciudadano, *citizen*, **200**-4

clarín, *bugle*, **207**-10

clarinete, *clarinet*, **207**-14

clase turista, *coach (class)*, **125**-23, *economy (class)*, **125**-23

clásica, *classical*, **209**-28

clásico, *classical*, **209**-28

clavadista, *diver*, **189**-13, **218**-33

clavar un clavo, *hammer a nail*, **165**-9

clavar, *hammer*, **165**-9

clavija, *plug*, **226**-6

clavo, *nail*, **163**-20

claxon, *honk*, **123**-14, *horn*, **121**-21, **185**-23

cliente, *customer*, **51**-7, **101**-7, *diner*, **101**-7

clima, *weather*, **166-167**

clip, *paper clip*, **155**-29

closet, *closet*, **74**-1

club de golf, *golf club*, **220**-13

club de teatro, *drama club*, **23**-23

club español, *Spanish club*, **23**-22

clutch, *clutch*, **121**-25

cobertor, *comforter*, **74**-16

cobija, *blanket*, **74**-2

coche compacto, *compact car*, **118**-30

coche de alquiler, *taxi*, **128**-4

coche deportivo, *sports car*, **118**-24

cochera, *garage*, **69**-16

cocina, *kitchen*, **70-71**

cocinando, *cooking*, **92-93**

cocinar, *cook*, **79**-22, **93**-24, **150**-1

cocinar, *do the cooking*, **79**-22

cocinera, *cook*, **146**-4

cocinero, *cook*, **146**-4

coco, *coconut*, **83**-13

cocodrilo, *crocodile*, **182**-19

código de área, *area code*, **16**-22

código de barras, *bar code*, **9**-21

código postal, *zip code*, **43**-14, **52**-7

codo, *elbow*, **133**-9

cofre, *hood*, **121**-30

cohete, *rocket*, **176**-4

cojín eléctrico, *heating pad*, **142**-21

cojín, *cushion*, **72**-2, *throw pillow*, **72**-9

col, *cabbage*, **84**-8

cola de caballo, *ponytail*, **33**-24

coladera, *strainer*, **94**-18

colador, *colander*, **95**-27

colcha, *bedspread*, **74**-17

colchón de aire, *air mattres*, **213**-26

colchón, *mattress*, **74**-13

colchoneta, *rest mat*, **57**-5

coletas, *pigtails*, **33**-26

colgar el teléfono, *hang up the phone*, **17**-29

colgar, *hang (up)*, **115**-24

colgarse, *hang*, **183**-28

colibrí, *hummingbird*, **182**-10

coliflor, *cauliflower*, **84**-16

colina, *hill*, **169**-22

collar, *collar*, **117**-12, *necklace*, **109**-8

colmillo, *tusk*, **185**-24, **187**-17

colocar ladrillos, *lay bricks*, **165**-5

colombiana, *Colombian*, **44**-5

colombiano, *Colombian*, **44**-5

colores primarios, *primary colors*, **10**

colores, *colors*, **10-11**

Columbia Británica, *British Columbia*, **172**-2

columpiarse, *swing*, **183**-26

columpio para bebé, *baby swing*, **57**-6

columpios, *swings*, **214**-2

coma, *comma*, **196**-11

comedia, *comedy*, **208**-2

comején, *termites*, **76**-26

giro postal, *bill,* **52**–1, **101**–31, *money order,* **51**–19

gis, *chalk,* **19**–3

glaciar, *glacier,* **169**–4

globo terráqueo, *globe,* **19**–9

globo, *balloon,* **229**–24

glúteos, *buttocks,* **133**–47

gobierna, *rules,* **198**–7

gobierno de Estados Unidos, *U.S. government,* **200**–**201**

golf, *golf,* **220**–12

golfista, *golfer,* **220**–14

golfito, *miniature golf,* **216**–16

goma, *glue,* **155**–25

gorda, *fat,* **15**–25

gordo, *fat,* **15**–25

gorila, *gorilla,* **182**–7

gorra de béisbol, *baseball cap,* **109**–27, *baseball hat,* **109**–27

gorrión, *sparrow,* **185**–18

gorro tejido, *knit hat,* **109**–26

gota de lluvia, *raindrop,* **166**–23

gotas para los ojos, *eyedrops,* **142**–13

gotea, *drips,* **77**–5

gotea, *faucet drips,* **77**–5, *leaks,* **77**–3

goteo intravenoso, *intravenous drip,* **138**–4, *IV,* **138**–4

gotero, *dropper,* **194**–21

grabadora de video, *camcorder,* **226**–4

grabadora, *boom box,* **226**–17, *cassette player,* **19**–24, *tape recorder,* **19**–24

graderías, *bleachers,* **23**–5

grado universitario, *college degree,* **43**–27

graduación, *graduation,* **23**–19

graduada, *graduated,* **194**–20

graduado, *graduated,* **194**–20

graduarse de preparatoria, *graduate from high school,* **31**–5

gráfica, *graphic artist,* **146**–7

gráfico, *graphic artist,* **146**–7

grafito, *graffiti,* **61**–8

gramo, *gram,* **96**

granada, *pomegranate,* **83**–4

grande, *big,* **14**–2, *large,* **14**–2

granero, *barn,* **152**–3

granizo, *hail,* **166**–18

granja, *farm,* **152**–**153**

granjero, *farmer,* **152**–14

grapas, *staples,* **155**–27

griega, *Greek,* **44**–15

griego, *Greek,* **44**–15

grillo, *cricket,* **181**–22

gripa, *flu,* **135**–14

gripe, *flu,* **135**–14

gris oscuro, *taupe,* **10**–18

gris, *gray,* **10**–23

grúa, *tow truck,* **118**–13

guacal de melones, *crate of melons,* **97**–30

guacal, *crate,* **97**–30

guajolote, *turkey,* **152**–27

guante de boxeo, *boxing glove,* **218**–18

guantera, *glove compartment,* **121**–18

guantes de hule, *rubber gloves,* **80**–18

guantes de látex, *latex gloves,* **139**–12

guantes, *gloves,* **109**–1

guardar los platos, *put away the dishes,* **79**–24

guardar, *put away,* **79**–24, *stow,* **26**–10

guardería, *daycare center,* **56**–**57**

guardia de seguridad, *security guard,* **51**–2, **148**–8

guepardo, *cheetah,* **185**–13

guía de recorridos turísticos, *tour guid,* **148**–22

guía telefónica, *telephone book,* **16**–8

guiar, *lead,* **37**–18

guijarro, *pebble,* **181**–17

guión, *hyphen,* **196**–19

guitarrista, *guitarist,* **205**–15

guitarrra, *guitar,* **207**–22

gusano, *worm,* **190**–18

habas, *lima beans,* **84**–21

hablar, *speak,* **150**–3, *talk,* **21**–20

hable en un grupo, *talk with a group,* **21**–20

hace sol, *sunny,* **167**–25

hacen la rueda, *produce the wheel,* **198**–2

hacer ejercicio, *exercise,* **34**–16, *work out,* **34**–16

hacer el oficio, *do housework,* **34**–21

hacer el pago de la casa, *make the house payment,* **65**–26

hacer el pago, *make the payment,* **65**–26

hacer la tarea, *do homework,* **34**–17

hacer las conexiones de una casa, *wire a house,* **165**–8

hacer preguntas, *ask questions,* **64**–5

hacer surf, *surf,* **210**–30

hacer trampa en un examen, *cheat on a test,* **18**–31

hacer un cumplido, *compliment,* **40**–10, **102**–13

hacer un depósito, *make a deposit,* **51**–27

hacer un examen, *take a test,* **19**–34

hacer una cita, *date,* **31**–9

hacer una cita, *make an appointment,* **137**–21, **64**–2

hacer una oferta, *make an offer,* **65**–19

hacer una reservación, *make a reservation,* **102**–1, **159**–24

hacer una reverencia, *bow,* **204**–27

hacer una seña al mesero, *signal the server,* **102**–18

hacerse a un lado, *pull over,* **123**–20

hacha, *ax,* **160**–5

hacia fuera, *off,* **13**–7

hacia, *toward,* **130**–7

halcón, *falcon,* **187**–19, *hawk,* **181**–1

halibut, *halibut,* **189**–30

halloween, *Halloween,* **228**–13

hamaca, *hammock,* **69**–7

hambre, *hungry,* **38**–10

hambruna, *famine,* **171**–4

hamburguesa, *hamburger,* **90**–4

hay niebla, *foggy,* **167**–29

helado, *freezing,* **166**–7, *ice cream,* **88**–3

helecho, *fern,* **182**–16

helicóptero, *helicopter,* **125**–12

Hemisferio Norte, *Northern Hemisphere,* **174**–6

Hemisferio Sur, *Southern Hemisphere,* **174**–7

hemorragia nasal, *bloody nose,* **135**–29

heno, *hay,* **152**–13

hermana, *sister,* **27**–15

hermanastra, *stepsister,* **27**–12

hermano, *brother,* **27**–17

hermosa, *beautiful,* **14**–14

hermoso, *beautiful,* **14**–14

herramienta, *tool,* **160**–12

herramientas manuales, *hand tools,* **160**

herramientas para electricidad, *power tools,* **161**

herramientas, *tools,* **160**–**161**

hidrante, *fire hydrant,* **58**–11

hiedra, *ivy,* **179**–27

hielera, *cooler,* **211**–18

hielo, *ice,* **166**–24

hiena, *hyena,* **185**–5

hígado, *liver,* **87**–12, **133**–28

higienista dental, *dental hygienist,* **141**–25

higos, *figs,* **83**–22

hija, *child,* **30**, *daughter,* **27**–22

hijo, *child,* **30**, *son,* **27**–21

hilo dental, *dental floss,* **144**–13

hilo para bordar, *embroidery thread,* **224**–23

hilo, *thread,* **117**–27

hip hop, *hip hop,* **209**–27

hipopótamo, *hippopotamus,* **185**–7

hockey sobre hielo, *ice hockey,* **223**–17

hockey, *jockey player,* **223**–22

hoja, *leaf,* **179**–13

mostrador, *countertop*, **70**–5
motel, *motel*, **47**–4
motocicleta, *motorcycle*, **118**–32
motor, *engine*, **121**–32, *motor*, **121**–32
mozo, *handyman*, **77**–17
mudarse, *move in*, **65**–25, *move*, **31**–17
mueblería, *furniture store*, **48**–8
muebles, *furniture*, **64**–12, **79**–9
muerta, *dead*, **14**–12
muerto, *dead*, **14**–12
muestre su identificación, *show your ID*, **126**–2
mujer de negocios, *businesswoman*, **146**–23
mujer embarazada, *pregnant woman*, **141**–11
mujer, *woman* , **15**–40
muleta, *crutch*, **141**–14
multicontacto, *power strip*, **25**–12
multiplicación, *multiplication*, **193**–28
multiplicado por, *multiplied by*, **193**–5
mundo, *World*, **174**–**175**
muñeca torcida, *sprained wrist*, **135**–10
muñeca, *doll*, **224**–19, *wrist*, **133**–7
mural, *mural*, **203**–15
murciélago, *bat*, **182**–4, **220**–7
muro de tablarroca, *drywall*, **163**–4
muro prefabricado, *drywall*, **163**–4
músculo, *muscle*, **133**–2
museo, *museum*, **59**–24, **216**–20
musgo, *moss*, **187**–6
música, *music*, **209**
música, *musician*, **148**–24
músico ambulante, *street musician*, **59**–22
músico, *musician*, **148**–24
muslo, *thigh*, **133**–13
muslos, *thighs*, **87**–27, *legs*, **87**–33
nabo, *turnip*, **84**–17
nacer, *be born*, **31**–1
nacionalidades, *nationalities*, **44**–**45**
nadador, *swimmer*, **211**–8
nadadora, *swimmer*, **211**–8
nadar, *swim*, **210**–32
nalgas, *buttocks*, **133**–47
naranja, *orange*, **10**–19, **83**–3
narcisos, *daffodils*, **179**–22
nariz, *nose*, **133**–37
naturaleza muerta, *still life*, **203**–2
navaja de bolsillo, *pocket knife*, **213**–21
navegar, *sail*, **198**–4
Navidad, *Christmas*, **229**–19
negociar el precio, *negotiate the price*, **65**–20
negro, *black*, **10**–22
neptuno, *Neptune*, **176**–21
nerviosa, *nervous*, **38**–6
nervioso, *nervous*, **38**–6
nevando, *snowing*, **167**–28
nido, *nest*, **190**–3
niebla, *fog*, **166**–16
nietos, *grandchildren*, **27**–23
nieve, *snow*, **166**–19
nigeriano, *Nigerian*, **44**–20
nigeriano, *Nigerian*, **44**–20
niña preescolar, *preschooler*, **56**–34
niña pequeña, *toddler*, **56**–33
niña, *child*, **30**
niña, *girl*, **57**–13
niñera, *babysitter*, **147**–30, *childcare worker*, **57**–17
niñero, *childcare worker*, **57**–17
niño preescolar, *preschooler*, **56**–34
niño pequeño, *toddler*, **56**–33
niño, *boy*, **57**–14, *child*, **30**, *infant*, **30**, **56**–32
níque, *nickel*, **8**–2
nivel, *level*, **160**–16

no entrar, *do not enter*, **118**–5
no hay corriente, *power is out*, **77**–1
noche, *night*, **5**
nombre, *first name*, **43**–3, *name*, **43**–1
norte, *north*, **130**–19
Norteamérica, *North America*, **174**–8
nostálgica, *homesick*, **39**–16
nostálgico, *homesick*, **39**–16
nota de venta, *receipt*, **9**–14
notas autoadhesivas, *sticky notes*, **155**–26
noticias, *news*, **209**–12
novecientos once, *911*, **16**–5
novela, *novel*, **55**–20
noveno, *ninth*, **3**
noventa, *ninety*, **2**
noviembre, *November*, **7**–26
nube, *cloud*, **166**–12
nublado, *cloudy*, **167**–26
nueces de nogal, *walnuts*, **83**–34
nueces de pecana, *pecans*, **83**–30
nueces, *nuts*, **82**–**83**
Nueva Inglaterra, *New England*, **172**–11
nueva, *new*, **5**–31
nueve, *nine*, **2**
nuevo, *new*, **5**–31
número de cuenta bancaria, *checking account number*, **51**–11
número de teléfono, *phone number*, **16**–23, *telephone number*, **16**–23, **43**–9
número de Seguro Social, *Social Security card*, **43**–8, **43**–21
número telefónico, *phone number*, **16**–23
números, *numbers*, **2**–**3**
nutria, *otter*, **187**–7
nylon, *nylon*, **113**–10
oasis, *oasis*, **181**–15
obedecer la ley, *obey the law*, **201**–15
obedecer, *obey*, **201**–15
oboe, *oboe*, **207**–13
obra de teatro, *play*, **205**–17
obscurecer, *dusk*, **5**, *sunset*, **5**
obscurezca, *darken*, **21**–29
obsequio, *gift*, **228**–11, *present*, **228**–11
observatorio, *observatory*, **176**–8
obstetra, *obstetrician*, **141**–10
obstruido, *clogged*, **77**–2
océano, *ocean*, **169**–24, **211**–5
ochenta, *eighty*, **2**
ocho, *eight*, **2**
octavo, *eighth*, **3**
octubre, *October*, **7**–25
oeste, *west*, **130**–22, *western*, **208**–7
oferta, *sale*, **9**–12
oficial de policía, *police officer*, **61**–20, **148**–11
oficial de tránsito, *traffic cop*, **58**–6
oficina de correo, *post office*, **52**–**53**
oficina principal, *front office*, **156**–2
oficina, *office*, **154**–**155**
ofrecer una bolsa para sobras, *offer a doggie bag*, **102**–20
ofrecer, *offer*, **102**–20
oídos perforados, *pierced ears*, **33**–20
ojal, *buttonhole*, **117**–14
ojo, *eye*, **133**–39
ola, *wave*, **211**–9
olla, *pot*, **94**–5
olmo, *elmtree*, **179**–6
once, *eleven*, **2**
Ontario, *Ontario*, **172**–4
onza, *ounce*, **96**, **97**–3
ópera, *opera*, **205**–25
opera, *operate*, **165**–15
operación, *operation*, **139**–11
operador, *machine operator*, *operator*, **157**–14, **16**–17

pintor de casas, *house painter*, **148**–14
pintor, *painter*, **203**–9
pintora de casas, *house painter*, **148**–14
pintora, *painter*, **203**–9
pintura, *paint tray*, **163**–15, *paint*, **163**–14, **203**–10, *painting*, **203**–7
pinza para colgar ropa, *clothespin*, **107**–2
pinzas eléctricas, *curling iron*, **144**–5
pinzas, *pliers*, **160**–15
pinzas, *tweezers*, **143**–31
piojos, *lice*, **135**–4
pique ajo, *dice garlic*, **92**–2
pique zanahorias, *chop carrots*, **93**–23
pique, *chop*, **93**–23, *dice*, **92**–2
pirámide, *pyramid*, **193**–21
piropear, *compliment*, **40**–10, **102**–13
piso, *floor*, **72**–14
pista de boliche, *bowling alley*, **216**–5
pista de hielo, *ice (skating) rink*, **223**–20
pista de patinaje, *skating rink*, **223**–20
pista, *runway*, **125**–13, *track*, **128**–14, **220**–16, **220**–18
pistaches, *pistachios*, **83**–32
pistachos, *pistachios*, **83**–32
pistola de silicón, *caulking gun*, **160**–8
pizarrón, *blackboard*, **19**–6, *white board*, **19**–14
pizza, *pizza*, **90**–1
placa, *license plate*, **121**–8
plancha, *iron*, **116**–2
planchar, *iron*, **115**–23, *press*, **115**–23
planear, *plan*, **150**–16
planetario, *planetarium*, **216**–3
planetas, *planets*, **176**
planta de interiores, *house plant*, **72**–29
plantar, *plant*, **153**–29
plata, *silver*, **10**–24
plataforma de embarque, *loading dock*, **157**–18
plátano, *banana*, **83**–29
platillos, *cymbals*, **207**–2
plato pequeño, *saucer*, **101**–19
plato principal, *main course*, **101**–27
plato, *plate*, **70**–23, **101**–23
platón, *bowl*, **101**–14
platos, *dishes*, **70**–3
playa, *beach*, **169**–23, **210**–211
playera tipo polo, *polo shirt*, **111**–7
plaza, *city square*, **58**–59
plomería, *plumbing*, **161**
plomero, *plumber*, **77**–15, **148**–15
pluma, *feather*, **187**–23, *pen*, **19**–19
plumero, *feather duster*, **80**–1
plutón, *Pluto*, **176**–20
pobre, *poor*, **15**–28
podadora de pasto, *lawn mower*, **69**–9
poder ejecutivo, *Executive branch*, **201**
Poder Judicial, *Judicial branch*, **201**
Poder Legislativo, *Legislative branch*, **201**
polilla, *moth*, **181**–21
pollo con salsa teriyaki, *chicken teriyaki*, **91**–21
pollo, *chicken*, **87**–31, **152**–28
Polo Norte, *North Pole*, **174**–1
Polo Sur, *South Pole*, **174**–5
polvo facial, *face powder*, **144**–26
poncharse una llanta, *have a flan tire*, **123**–21
poncho, *poncho*, **104**–11
poner aire a las llantas, *put air in the tires*, **123**–18
poner conexiones, *wire*, **65**–8
poner gasolina, *get gas*, **123**–15, *get gas*, **23**–15
poner la mesa, *set the table*, **102**–5
poner un muro, *put up drywall*, **165**–1
poner un sello a, *put a stamp on*, **53**–23
poner un timbre postal en, *put a stamp on*, **53**–23
poner una estampilla en, *put a stamp on*, **53**–23

poner una inyección, *give a shot*, **137**–25
poner, *put up*, **165**–1
ponerle una inyección, *give him a shot*, **137**–25
ponerse en cuclillas, *squat*, **37**–23
ponerse sus audífonos, *put on your headphones*, **126**–16
ponerse, *put on*, **114**–8
póngase de pie, *stand up*, **21**–19, **37**–15
pop, *pop*, **209**–22
popote, *straw*, **90**–13
por ciento, *percent*, **193**–4
por, *along*, **130**–18, *times*, **193**–5
porche, *porch*, **69**–14
porrista, *cheerleader*, **220**–26
portafolios, *briefcase*, **109**–16
portaobjeto, *slide*, **194**–28, **214**–5
portarse bien, *behave*, **29**–24
portarse mal, *misbehave*, **29**–25
portería, *goal*, **223**–21, *goalpost*, **220**–24
portero, *concierge*, **159**–13, *doorman*, **67**–25
poste de luz, *streetlight*, **58**–4
postre, *dessert*, **101**–28
precio de oferta, *sale price*, **9**–23
precio normal, *full price*, **9**–22, *regular price*, **9**–22
precio, *price*, **9**–18
preguntar, *ask*, **64**–5
premiar, *praise*, **29**–17
prendedor, *pin*, **109**–12, **117**–21
prender, *light*, **102**–3
prensa de tornillo, *vise*, **160**–13
preocupada, *worried*, **39**–15
preocupado, *worried*, **39**–15
preparar la cena, *make dinner*, **34**–18
prescripción, *prescription*, **142**–15
presenta, *introduces*, **198**–17
presentar un examen, *take a test*, **19**–34
presentar, *introduce*, **40**–15
presidente, *president*, **200**–11
préstamo, *loan*, **65**–22
pretzels, *pretzels*, **99**–26
prima, *cousin*, **27**–11
primavera, *spring*, **7**–12
primera clase, *first class*, **125**–22
primero, *first*, **3**
primo, *cousin*, **27**–11
prisión, *jail*, **61**–26, *prison*, **61**–26
prisionera, *prisoner*, **61**–27
prisionero, *prisoner*, **61**–27
prisma, *prism*, **194**–7
probador, *dressing room*, **114**–3
probarse, *try on*, **114**–4
probeta graduada, *graduated cylinder*, **194**–20
problemas caseros, *household problems*, **76**–77
procesador de alimentos, *food processor*, **94**–8
producir, *produce*, **198**–2
productos agrícolas, *produce*, **99**–1
productos congelados, *frozen foods*, **99**–4
productos de papel, *paper products*, **99**–8
productos enlatados, *canned goods*, **99**–12
productos lácteos, *dairy products*, **99**–3
profundidad, *depth*, **193**
programa de entrevistas, *talk show*, **209**–17
programa de juegos, *game show*, **209**–15
programa para computadora, *computer program*, **25**–25, *software*, **25**–25
programa para niños, *children's program*, **209**–19
programa sobre la naturaleza, *nature program*, **209**–18
programa, *program*, **2**, **5**–23
programas de televisión, *TV programs*, **209**
programas de TV, *TV programs*, **209**
prohibida la vuelta en U, *no U-turn*, **118**–11
prohibida vuelta a la izquierda, *no left turn*, **118**–6

tarjetas, *cards*, **224**–1
tarjetero, *business card file*, **155**–15
tarro, *mug*, **70**–30
tartán, escocés, *plaid*, **113**–19
taxi, cab, *taxi* **128**–4
taxista, *cab driver*, **128**–5, *taxi driver*, **128**–5, **148**–17
taza de café, *cup of coffe*, **97**–13
taza, *cup*, **96**, **97**–2, **101**–18
tazas medidoras, *measuring cups*, **95**–23
tazón, *bowl*, **70**–24, *mixing bowl*, **94**–12
té helado, *iced tea*, **88**–9
té, *tea*, **90**–12
teatro de títeres, *puppet show*, **214**–10
teatro, *theater*, **47**–11
techo gotea, *roof leaks*, **77**–3
techo tiene una gotera, *roof leaks*, **77**–3
techo, *ceiling*, **72**–17, *roof*, **69**–4
tecla, *key*, **25**–18, **67**–31
teclado eléctrico, *electric keyboard*, **207**–25
teclado, *keyboard*, **25**–21, **207**
teclee su número de identificación personal, *enter your PIN*, **51**–25
técnica en computación, *computer technician*, **146**–10
técnica laboratorista, *lab technician*, **139**–15
técnico en computación, *computer technician*, **146**–10
técnico laboratorista, *lab technician*, **139**–15
tejer con agujas, *knit*, **224**–25
tejer con gancho, *crochet*, **224**–26
tela para hacer jeans, *denim*, **113**–6
telas, *fabrics*, **112**–113
Telecomedia (de situación), *sitcom*, **209**–13
teléfono celular, *cell phone*, **16**–20, *mobile phone*, **16**–20
teléfono inalámbrico, *cordless phone*, **16**–19
teléfono público, *pay phone*, **16**–1
teléfono, *telephone*, **16**–17, **155**–12
telenovela, *soap opera*, **209**–16
telescopio, *telescope*, **176**–9
telesilla, *chairlift*, **222**–8
televisión, *television*, **226**–19
temperatura, *temperature*, **135**–15
tendedero, *clothesline*, **107**–1
tender la cama, *make the bed*, **79**–1
tenedor, *fork*, **101**–21
tener náusea, *nauseous*, **135**–19
tener un accidente, *have an accident*, **123**–19
tener un ataque cardíaco, *have a heart attack*, **136**–13
tener un bebé, *have a baby*, **31**–15
tener un dolor, *be in pain*, **136**–1
tener un electrochoque, *get a shock*, **136**–14, *get an electric shock*, **136**–14
tener una conversación, *have a conversation*, **17**–28, **40**–6
tener una reacción alérgica, *have an allergic reaction*, **136**–12
tenis, athletic *shoe*, **109**–23, *sneaker*, **109**–22, *tennis*, **220**–1
tercero, *third*, **3**
terciopelo, *velvet*, **113**–3
termina, *ends*, **198**–14
terminal de taxis, *taxi stand*, **128**–1
terminal, *terminal*, **124**–1
termitas, *termites*, **76**–26
termómetro para carnes, *meat thermometer*, **94**–17
termómetro, *thermometer*, **143**–30, **166**–8
termostato, *thermostat*, **72**–25
terraza, *deck*, **69**–5
terremoto, *earthquake*, **171**–5
testigo, *witness*, **61**–17
tetera, *kettle*, **70**–7
tetera, *tea kettle*, **70**–7, *teapot*, **70**–29
tía, *aunt*, **27**–3
tianguis, *flea market*, **48**–30
tibio, *warm*, **166**–4
tiburón, *shark*, **189**–12

tiempo, *time*, **4**–**5**
tienda de artículos de segunda mano, *second-hand store*, **48**–14, *thrift shop*, **48**–14
tienda de artículos deportivos, sporting *goods store*, **48**–6
tienda de campaña, *tent*, **63**–2, **213**–24
tienda de departamentos, *department store*, **48**–25
tienda de electrónica, *electronics store*, **48**–1
tienda de mascotas, *pet store*, **48**–21
tienda de música, *music store*, **48**–10
tienda de regalos, *gift shop*, **159**–22, *gift shop*, **48**–4, **159**–22
tienda de ropa, *clothing store*, **48**–2
tienda de video, *video store*, **48**–18
tiendas, *shops*, **48**–**49**, *stores*, **48**–**49**
TIERRA Y ESPACIO, *EARTH AND SPACE*, **166**–**177**
Tierra, *Earth*, **176**–26
tierra, *soil*, **152**–10
tierras polares, *polar lands*, **186**–**187**
tigre, *tiger*, **182**–9
tijeras de podar, *hedge clippers*, **69**–25
tijeras, *pair of scissors*, **117**–23
tilandés, *Thai*, **44**–26
timbre postal, *stamp*, **52**–5
timbre, *call button*, **139**–21, *doorbell*, **69**–13
tina de baño, *bathtub*, **75**–22
tintorería, *dry cleaner*, **48**–17
tío, *uncle*, **27**–4
tipos de casas, *types of homes*, **62**–**63**
tira de contactos, *power strip*, **25**–12
tirante, *strap*, **128**–15
tirantes, *suspenders*, **109**–5
titular, *headline*, **55**–18
título, *title*, **55**–19, **196**–8
toalla de manos, *washcloth*, **75**–29
toalla, *towel*, **75**–26
toallas de papel, *paper towels*, **80**–7
toallitas húmedas para bebé, *baby wipes*, **57**–24
tobillo inflamado, *swollen ankle*, **135**–11
tobillo, *ankle*, **133**–15
tobogán, *toboggan*, **222**–7
tocador, *dresser*, **74**–6
tocar el claxon, *honk the horn*, **123**–14
tocar, *touch*, **40**–5
tocino, *bacon*, **88**–20
toma la presión sanguínea, *check blood pressure*, **137**–23
tomar el teléfono, *pick up the phone*, **17**–24
tomar la autopista, *get on the highway*, **123**–12
tomar su presión arterial, *check his blood pressure*,**137**–23
tomar un baño, *take a bath*, **34**–22, *bathe*, **29**–7
tomar un descanso, *take a break*, **20**–14, *take a coffee break*, **34**–12
tomar un mensaje, *take a message*, **150**–12
tomar un paseo, *take a walk*, **34**–20
tomar un receso, *take a break*, **20**–14, *take a coffee break*, **34**–12
tomar un vuelo, *taking a flight*, **126**–**127**
tomar una decisión, *make a decision*, **65**–18, **151**–26
tomar una ducha, *take a shower*, **34**–4
tomar una foto, *take a photograph*, **203**–26
tomar una orden, *take an order*, **102**–11
tomar una pastilla, *take a pill*, **137**–27
tomar una píldora, *take a pill*, **137**–27
tomar una siesta, *take a nap*, **34**–15
tomar vacaciones, *take a vacation*, **31**–19
tomarse la temperatura, *take your temperature*, **137**–19
tome un receso, *take a break*, **20**–14
topo, *mole*, **33**–27, **190**–16
tórax, *chest*, **133**–46
tormenta, *storm*, **166**–14
tornado, *tornado*, **171**–11
tornillo con punta, *screw*, **163**–22
tornillo sin punta, *bolt*, **163**–21

vender, *sell*, **150**–14
venezolana, *Venezuelan*, **44**–4
venezolano, *Venezuelan*, **44**–4
venta de cochera, *garage sale*, **216**–9
venta de garaje, *garage sale*, **216**–9
ventana está rota, *window is broken*, **77**–10
ventana, *window*, **25**–3, **69**–10
ventanilla de cajero, *teller window*, **51**–5
ventanilla de servicio a automovilistas, *drive-up window*, **51**–21
ventilador de techo, *ceiling fan*, **72**–16
ventilador, *vent*, **72**–23
ventisca, *blizzard*, **171**–2
Venus, *Venus*, **176**–27
ver casas, *look at houses*, **65**–17
ver el apartamento, *see the apartment*, **64**–4
ver el menú, *look at the menu*, **102**–7
ver la televisión, *watch televisión*, **34**–25
ver un mapa, *look at a map*, **123**–11
ver, *see*, **64**–4
ver, *watch*, **34**–25, **109**–11
verano, *summer*, **7**–13
verde limón, *lime green*, **10**–7
verde olivo, *olive green*, **10**–6
verde, *green*, **10**–5
verdeazul, *teal*, **10**–8
verduras congeladas, *frozen vegetables*, **88**–1
verduras salteadas, *stir-fried vegetables*, **91**–20
verduras sofritas, *stir-fried vegetables*, **91**–20
verduras, *vegetables*, **84**–**85**
verificar el aceite, *check the oil*, **123**–16
verificar los monitores, *check the monitors*, **126**–6
verificar su equipaje, *check your baggage*, **126**–3
verificar, *check*, **21**–24
vestíbulo, *lobby*, **67**–22, **159**–9
vestido de maternidad, *maternity dress*, **104**–24
vestido largo, *gown*, **104**–5
vestido, *dress*, **104**–1
vestidor, *locker room*, **218**–35
vestir ropa casual, *dress casual clothes*, **111**–25
vestirlo, *dress*, **29**–11
vestirse, *get dressed*, **34**–8
veterinaria, *vet*, **148**–28, *veterinarian*, **148**–28
veterinario, *vet*, **148**–28, *veterinarian*, **148**–28
vía, *track*, **128**–14, **220**–16, **220**–18
viajar, *travel*, **31**–23
viaje por carretera, *road trip*, **122**–**123**
vicepresidenta, *vice president*, **200**–12
víctima, *victim*, **61**–16
videograbadora, *VCR*, **226**–21, *videocassette recorder*, **226**–21
vieiras, *scallops*, **87**–19
vieja, *old*, **14**–21, **15**–32
viejo, *old*, **14**–21, **15**–32
viento, *wind*, **166**–17, **171**–24
viernes, *Friday*, **6**–9
vietnamita, *Vietnamese*, **44**–27

vigésimo primero, *twenty-first*, **3**
vigésimo, *twentieth*, **3**
vikingos navegan, *Vikings sail*, **198**–4
villa, *villa*, **63**–11
viña, *vineyard*, **152**–8
viñedo, *vineyard*, **152**–8
violeta, *violet*, **10**–15
violetas, *violets*, **179**–23
violín, *violin*, **207**–21
violonchelo, *cello*, **207**–20
visa, *visa*, **43**–23
visitante, *visitor*, **139**–17
visitar, *visit*, **40**–3
visor, *diving mask*, **211**–26
vitaminas, *vitamins*, **142**–20
viva, *alive*, **14**–11
víveres y artículos comprados, *groceries*, **99**–22
vivero, *nursery*, **216**–4
VIVIENDA, *HOUSING*, **62**–**81**
vivo, *alive*, **14**–11
volante, *steering wheel*, **121**–24
volar, *fly*, **181**–20, *fly*, **37**–1, **198**–13
volcán, *volcano*, **169**–3
voleibol, *volleyball*, **220**–10, *volleyball*, **220**–9
volquete, *dump truck*, **118**–21
volver a llenar el vaso, *refill the glass*, **102**–14
volver a servir agua, *refill*, **102**–14
volverse a casar, *be remarried*, **27**–30
vomitar, *throw up*, **137**–18, *vomit*, **137**–18
votación, *ballot*, **200**–2
votar, *vote*, **201**–14
vuelan, *fly*, **37**–1, **198**–13
vuelta a casar, *be remarried*, **27**–30, *remarried*, **27**–30
vuelto a casar, *be remarried*, **27**–30, *remarried*, **27**–30
wafles congelados, *frozen waffles*, **88**–2
Web, *Web*, **25**–29
windsurfista, *sailboarder*, **211**–13
wok, *wok*, **95**–28
World Wide Web, *World Wide Web*, **25**–29
yeso, *cast*, **141**–15
yoga, *yoga*, **218**–2
yogurt, *yogurt*, **88**–12
zanahoria, *carrot*, **84**–19
zapatería, *shoe store*, **48**–3
zapatilla, *pump*, **109**–18, *sneaker*, **109**–22
zapatos, *shoes*, **108**–**109**
zarigüeya, *opossum*, **190**–7
zarpa, *paw*, **185**–27
zona escolar, *school zone*, **118**–8
zoológico, *zoo*, **216**–2
zorrillo, *skunk*, **190**–22
zorra, *fox*, **187**–11
zorro, *fox*, **187**–11
zueco, *clog*, **109**–20
zurcir, *mend*, **115**–21

Credits

Illustrators

Denny Bond: pp. 38–39, 48–51, 90–91, 106–107, 130–131, 190–191, 202–203, 214–215 (©Denny Bond)

Higgins Bond: pp. 184–185, 212–213 (©Higgins Bond/Anita Grien)

James Edwards: pp. 9, 18–19, 34–37, 64–65, 116–117, 122–123 (©James Edwards/The Beranbaum Group)

Mike Gardner: pp. 32–33, 110–111, 145 (32–37), 146–151, 200–201, 228–229 (©Mike Gardner)

Patrick Gnan: pp. 68–69, 168–169, 178–179 (©Patrick Gnan/IllustrationOnLine.com)

Gershom Griffith: pp. 20–21, 26–27, 100–101, 104–105, 126–127, 196 (20–25), 220–221 (©Gershom Griffith/Craven Design)

Lane Gregory: pp. 114–115 (©Lane Gregory/Gwen Walters Artist Representative)

Sharon and Joel Harris: pp. 132–133, 182–183 (©Sharon and Joel Harris/IllustrationOnLine.com)

Phil Howe: pp. 3, 58–59, 70–71, 92–95 (©Phil Howe/IllustrationOnLine.com)

Ken Joudrey: pp. 52–53 (©Ken Joudrey/Munro Campagna)

Bob Kayganich: pp. 5, 12–13, 14 (21, 22, 31, 32), 15 (17, 18, 27, 28, 29, 30), 16 (4–6, 9–11), 17 (12–19, 24–29), 24–25, 54–55, 76–77, 96–97, 176–177, 180–181, 194 (1, 10, 11, 12), 195 (3, 5, 17, 19) (©Bob Kayganich/IllustrationOnLine.com)

Alan King: pp. 10–11, 46–47, 120–121, 142–143, 154–155, 210–211 (©Alan King/IllustrationOnLine.com)

Barbara Kiwak: pp. 28–29, 60–61, 102–103, 108–109, 204–205 (©Barbara Kiwak/Gwen Walters Artist Representative)

Greg LaFever: pp. 152–153, 222–224 (©Greg LaFever/Scott Hull Associates)

Mapping Specialists: pp. 44–45, 172–175 (©Mapping Specialists)

Precision Graphics: pp. 22 (24, 25), 23 (26, 27), 30–31, 42–43, 50 (10–13), 51 (14, 19), 52 (1, 2, 3, 8), 78–79, 118–119, 124–125, 134–137, 140–141, 158–159, 162 (1, 2), 164–167, 186–189, 201 (5–13), 218–219, 227 (26–31) (©Precision Graphics)

John Schreiner: pp. 80–81, 86–87 (©John Schreiner/IllustrationOnLine.com)

Dave Schweitzer: pp. 208–209 (©Dave Schweitzer/Munro Campagna)

Beryl Simon: pp. 170–171 (©Beryl Simon)

Carol Stutz: pp. 198–199, 216–217 (©Carol Stutz)

Gerad Taylor: pp. 6–7, 66–67, 72–75, 88–89, 98–99, 128–129, 192–193 (©Gerad Taylor/IllustrationOnLine)

Gary Torrisi: pp. 22–23, 138–139, 156–157 (©Gary Torrisi/Gwen Walters Artist Representative)

Meryl Treatner: pp. 56–57, 112–113 (©Meryl Treatner/Chris Tugeau)

Photos

All photographs not otherwise credited are owned by ©Thomson/ELT.

Unit One UNIT ICON CREDIT: ©Tom Grill/CORBIS; 2 all: ©Hemera Photo-Objects; 3 center: ©Hemera Photo-Objects; 4 center: ©Hemera Photo-Objects; 4 bottom: ©Royalty-Free/CORBIS; 5 all: ©Hemera Photo-Objects; 6 bottom: ©F.SCHLUSSER.PHOTOLINK/Getty; 8 bottom: ©C Squared Studios/Getty; 14 most: ©Hemera Photo-Objects; 14 (12): ©Thinkstock LLC/Index Stock Imagery, Inc.; 14 (14): ©Louis K. Meisel Gallery/CORBIS; 14 (33): ©Paul Sonders/CORBIS; 14 (34): ©Tom Brakefield/CORBIS; 15 (3): ©Dmitri Iundt/CORBIS; 15 (4): ©Randy Faris/CORBIS; 15 (5, 6, 27): ©John Coletti; 15 (15, 16): ©C Squared Studios/Getty; 15 (25): ©Melissa Goodrum; 15 (26): ©Catherine Ledner/Stone/Getty; 15 (35, 36): ©Jacque Denzier Parker/Index Stock Imagery; 15 (37, 38, 39, 40): ©Hemera Photo-Objects; 16 left: ©Scott Baxter/Getty; 16 center: ©David Buffington/Photodisc Green/Getty; 17 bottom left: ©COMSTOCK Images

Unit Two UNIT ICON CREDIT: ©Royalty-Free/CORBIS; 24 top right: ©Hemera Photo-Objects; 24 bottom left: ©David Shopper/Index Stock Imagery, Inc.

Unit Three UNIT ICON CREDIT: ©Thinkstock/Getty; 27: ©Royalty-Free/CORBIS; 29 top left: ©SW Productions/Photodisc Green/Getty; 29 top right: ©Royalty-Free/CORBIS; 29 center left: ©Jerry Koontz/Index Stock Imagery, Inc.; 29 center right: ©Zefa Visual Media-Germany/Index Stock Imagery, Inc.; 29 bottom left (small): ©Chris Carroll/CORBIS; 29 bottom left (big): ©Hemera Photo-Objects; 29 bottom right (small): ©Ariel Skelley/CORBIS; 29 bottom right (big): ©Royalty-Free/CORBIS

Unit Four UNIT ICON CREDIT: ©Jose Luis Pelaez, Inc./CORBIS; 40 (1): ©Ghislain & Marie David de Lossy/The Image Bank/Getty; 40 (7): ©Stewart Cohen/Index Stock Imagery, Inc.; 40 (8, 16, 18, 20): ©Hemera Photo-Objects; 40 (9): ©Michael Newman/PhotoEdit; 40 (10): ©Jerry Tobias/CORBIS; 40 (15): ©David Young-Wolff/PhotoEdit; 40 (17): ©Patrik Giardino/CORBIS; 40 (19): ©Don Romero/Index Stock Imagery, Inc.; 41 (3): ©Francisco Cruz/SuperStock; 41 (4, 11, 22): ©Hemera Photo-Objects; 41 (5): ©GeoStock/Photodisc Green/Getty; 41 (12): ©Royalty-Free/CORBIS; 41 (13): ©SW Productions/Index Stock Imagery, Inc.; 41 (14): ©SuperStock; 41 (21): ©Morocco Flowers/Index Stock Imagery, Inc.; 41 (23): ©Steve Prezant/CORBIS; 41 (24): ©Myrleen Ferguson Cate/PhotoEdit; 42 top: ©Shuji Kobayashi/Stone/Getty; 42 center: ©Image Source/SuperStock; 42 bottom: ©Michael Newman/PhotoEdit; 44 top left: ©Hemera Photo-Objects; 44 top right: ©Springfield Photography/Alamy; 44 bottom left: ©Peter Guttman/CORBIS; 44 bottom right: ©Hemera Photo-Objects; 45 all: ©Hemera Photo-Objects

Unit Five UNIT ICON CREDIT: ©Photodisc Collection/Getty; 54: ©Mitchell Gerber/CORBIS; 56 top right: ©Hemera Photo-Objects; 56 center left: ©Willie Holdman/Index Stock Imagery Inc.; 56 center right: ©Stewart Cohen/Taxi/Getty; 56 bottom left: ©Chris Carroll/CORBIS; 56 bottom right: ©Hemera Photo-Objects

Unit Six UNIT ICON CREDIT: ©Cydney Conger/CORBIS; 62 (1): ©Cydney Conger/CORBIS; 62 (2): ©Dean Conger/CORBIS; 62 (3): ©Bob Krist/CORBIS; 62 (4): ©Vince Streano/CORBIS; 62 (5): ©Elfi Kluck/Index Stock Imagery Inc.; 62 (6): ©Craig Lovell/CORBIS; 62 (7): ©Michael Newman/PhotoEdit; 62 (8): ©RO-MA Stock/Index Stock Imagery Inc.; 62 (9, 10): ©Hemera Photo-Objects; 62 (11): ©Massimo Listri/CORBIS; 62 (12): ©Joseph Sohm; Visions of America/CORBIS; 62 (13): ©Reinhard Eisele/CORBIS; 62 (15): ©Yvette Cardozo/Index Stock Imagery Inc.; 62 (16): ©Philip Coblentz/Brand X Pictures; 62 (17): ©Phil Cantor/SuperStock; 63 (14): ©Pawel Libera/CORBIS; 63 (18): ©Rene Sheret/Stone/Getty; 63 (19): ©Mitch Diamond/Index Stock Imagery Inc.; 63 (20): ©Anselm Spring/Image Bank/Getty; 63 (21): ©Royalty-Free/CORBIS; 63 (22): ©Joseph Sohm; ChromoSohm Inc./CORBIS; 63 (23): ©Michael S. Yamashita/CORBIS; 67: ©Hemera Photo-Objects

Unit Seven UNIT ICON CREDIT: ©Burke-Triolo Pruductions/Getty; 82–85 most: ©Hemera Photo-Objects; 82 (5): ©Photodisc Collection/Getty; 82 (11): ©Seide Preis/Getty; 82 (17): ©Royalty-Free/CORBIS; 82 (24): ©Picture Arts/CORBIS; 82 (27): ©Keith Seaman/FoodPix; 82 (33): ©Maximilian Stock, LTD/FoodPix; 83 (7): ©Photodisc Inc./Getty; 83 (28): ©Paul Poplis/FoodPix; 84 (2): ©Judd Pilosoff/FoodPix; 84 (9, 18): ©Royalty-Free/CORBIS; 84 (10): ©John Coletti; 84 (20): ©Picture Arts/CORBIS; 84 (21): ©Evan Sklar/Food Pix; 84 (22): ©Cindy Jones/FoodPix; 84 (30): ©Craig Orsini/Index Stock Imagery Inc.; 85 (25): ©Picture Arts/CORBIS

Unit Eight UNIT ICON CREDIT: ©C Squared Studios/Getty; 97 bottom right: ©Hemera Photo-Objects; 112 (1, 10): ©Veer Incorporated; 112 (2): ©Royalty-Free Division/Masterfile; 112 (3): ©Nick Koudis/Getty; 112 (4): ©Barry David Marcus/SuperStock; 112 (6): ©Jules Frazier/Getty; 112 (7): ©D. Boone/CORBIS; 112 (11): ©Stacy Gold/National Geographic/Getty; 113 (5): ©Royalty-Free/CORBIS; 113 (8): ©Veer Incorporated; 113 (9): ©Reuters/CORBIS; 113 (12): ©Francisco Rojo Alvarez/Getty

Unit Nine UNIT ICON CREDIT: ©Wes Thompson/CORBIS

Unit Ten UNIT ICON CREDIT: ©Herrmann/Starke/CORBIS; 140 top center: ©Hemera Photo-Objects; 142 all: ©Hemera Photo-Objects; 144 (1): ©Amy Etra/PhotoEdit; 144 (2, 3, 12, 14, 15): ©Photodisc Collection/Getty; 144 (4, 7, 13): ©John Coletti; 144 (5, 8, 10, 11): ©Hemera Photo-Objects; 144 (6): ©Siede Preis/Photodisc Green/Getty; 144 (9): ©Joe Atlas/Brand X Pictures; 145 top left: ©Stockbyte/Ablestock; 145 (16): ©Michael Newman/PhotoEdit; 145 (17, 20, 23, 26, 28): ©John Coletti; 145 (18): ©COMSTOCK Images; 145 (19, 21, 24, 25, 27): ©Hemera Photo-Objects; 145 (22): ©C Squared Studios/Photodisc Green/Getty; 145 (29, 30, 31): ©Joe Atlas/Brand X Pictures

Unit Eleven UNIT ICON CREDIT: ©PictureNet/CORBIS; 160–163 most: ©Hemera Photo-Objects; 160 (1, 4, 7, 18): ©COMSTOCK Images; 160 (3): ©C Squared Studios/Photodisc Green/Getty; 160 (9): ©Seide Preis/Photodisc Green/Getty; 160 (12): ©Photodisc Green/Getty; 161 (24, 30): ©C Squared Studios/Photodisc Green/Getty; 161 (26): ©Royalty-Free/CORBIS; 161 (32): ©Stockbyte; 162 (3): ©Seide Preis/Photodisc Green/Getty; 162 (4, 5, 28): ©John Coletti; 162 (6): ©Patrick Olear/Photo Edit; 162 (7, 14, 17): ©C Squared Studios/Photodisc Green/Getty; 162 (8): ©Jules Frazier/Getty; 162 (12): ©COMSTOCK Images; 163 (18): ©Royalty-Free/CORBIS; 163 (19, 29): ©John Coletti; 163 (20, 22, 24): ©Seide Preis/Photodisc Green/Getty; 163 (30): ©Widstock/Alamy

Unit Twelve UNIT ICON CREDIT: ©L. Clarke/CORBIS; 174: ©Digital Vision

Unit Thirteen UNIT ICON CREDIT: ©Digital Vision/Getty; 183 (25): ©Hemera Photo-Objects; 184 (1): ©Hemera Photo-Objects; 186 (7): ©Photodisc Collection/Getty; 191 (29): ©Jules Frazier/Getty

Unit Fourteen UNIT ICON CREDIT: ©Don Farrall/Getty; 194 (8, 14): ©Hemera Photo-Objects; 194 (9): ©Dennis MacDonald/PhotoEdit; 194 (7): ©Thinkstock LLC/Index Stock Imagery, Inc.; 194 (13): ©Seide Preis/Photodisc Green/Getty; 195 (18, 20, 21, 22, 27): ©Hemera Photo-Objects; 195 (15): ©Widstock/Alamy; 195 (23, 24, 25, 26): ©Seide Preis/Photodisc Green/Getty; 195 (28, 30): ©COMSTOCK Images; 195 (29): ©TRBfoto/Photodisc Green/Getty

Unit Fifteen UNIT ICON CREDIT: ©Don Farrall/Getty; 203: ©Hemera Photo-Objects; 206–207 most: ©Hemera Photo-Objects; 206 (1, 6, 22): ©Photodisc Collection/Getty; 206 (8, 18, 19): ©C Squared Studios/Photodisc Green/Getty; 207 (3, 13, 15, 16, 17, 26, 28): ©Photodisc Collection/Getty; 207 (2): ©Spencer Grant/PhotoEdit; 207 (27): ©Photodisc Green/Getty

Unit Sixteen UNIT ICON CREDIT: ©Digital Vision/Getty; 212 (1): ©Hemera Photo-Objects; 223 (25): ©Hemera Photo-Objects; 224–226 most: ©Hemera Photo-Objects; 224 (1): ©Royalty-Free/CORBIS; 224 (22): ©John Coletti; 225 (15): ©C Squared Studios/Getty; 225 (16): ©ACE STOCK LTD/Alamy; 225 (19): ©Erin Garvey/Index Stock Imagery, Inc.; 226 (1): ©C Squared Studios/Getty; 226 (3): ©COMSTOCK Images; 226 (7): ©F.Schlusser/PhotoLink/Getty; 227 most: ©COMSTOCK Images; 227 (9): ©Mediacolor's/Alamy; 227 (14, 15, 19, 21, 23): ©Hemera Photo-Objects; 227 (20): ©Judith Collins/Alamy; 227 (24, 25): ©John Coletti